Income Distribution, Inflation, and Growth

Income Distribution, Inflation, and Growth

Lectures on Structuralist Macroeconomic Theory

Lance Taylor

The MIT Press
Cambridge, Massachusetts
London, England

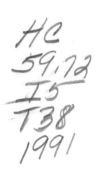

This book was set in Palatino by Asco Trade Typesetting Ltd., Hong Kong, and was printed and bound in the United States of America.

Library of Congress Cataloging-in-Publication Data

Taylor, Lance.
  Income distribution, inflation, and growth: lectures on structuralist macroeconomic theory / Lance Taylor.
    p.   cm.
  Includes bibliographical references and index.
  ISBN 0-262-20079-1
    1. Income distribution—Developing countries.   2. Inflation (Finance)—Developing countries.   3. Developing countries—Economic policy.   4. Economic development.
  5. Macroeconomics.   I. Title.
  HC59.72.I5T38   1991
  339.5'09172'4—dc20   91-10654
                                                                              CIP

Contents

List of Tables

List of Figures

Foreword

In this book Lance Taylor enlarges upon his earlier WIDER study of the economies of developing countries—*Varieties of Stabilization Experience: Towards Sensible Macroeconomics in the Third World* (Oxford: Clarendon Press, 1988)—in which, through a review of stabilization experiences of 18 developing countries, he showed clearly that the economies of these countries differ in their institutional relationships and structural linkages. In the present book he makes a major contribution to the development of analytical tools that enhance the understanding of the functioning of such economies and the complex problems they face. Taylor adopts an analytical approach that goes well beyond the assumptions of mainstream economics in that it considers postulates derived from the stylized facts of the contemporary Third World economic situation.

The crucial question Taylor seeks to answer at the outset is the one posed by Amartya Sen in his 1963 article "Neo-classical and Neo-Keynesian Theories of Distribution" (*Economic Record* 39: 54–64): How can the macroeconomic system adjust to satisfy a number of plausible restrictions that might be imposed upon it? Taylor illustrates the various possiblities through the use of a simple model, and by juggling equations and variables, he systematically shows how different causal schemes can be derived. He follows this by discussion of different types of short-run adjustments and corresponding models of growth. Among the other methodological questions Taylor explores here are income distribution effects on growth and output, equilibria under capacity constraints, and the implications of turning to mainstream macro models to resolve Third World economic problems.

An important feature of the book is Taylor's comprehensive study of structuralist inflation theories. The structuralists claim that the causes of inflation are nonmonetary in nature. Following this tradition, Taylor reviews the causes and behavior of inflation under different circumstances and illustrates this with models. He discusses in depth the implications of worker-capitalist conflicts, stagflation, the effectiveness of orthodox stabilization programs, as well as some recent policy initiatives to combat inflation. Taylor's intuition into the causes and cures of inflation will certainly benefit the ongoing debate on this issue.

Finally, Taylor treats at length several aspects of growth and approaches to modeling growth. The models incorporate institutional and production relationships under constraints of foreign exchange and gaps in domestic resources, as well as underutilized capacity. Taylor develops models that apply to both historical and present-day interactions between North and South in the world economic system. The usefulness of these models can be highlighted by citing two examples from the book. A two-sector growth model demonstrates the implications of redirecting investment in an "agriculture-first" strategy for India in terms of increased income and slower population growth in that sector. Another model applies different assumptions of financial flows to show how growth and terms of trade interact between the North and South in the short and medium runs. This book will be of immense interest to both the scholar and the practitioner.

Lal Jayawardena
World Institute for Development
Economics Research
Helsinki

Acknowledgments

Many people helped at various stages of this book, not the least students at MIT, Delhi University, the University of Pavia (in a visit generously organized by Gianni Vaggi), and in numerous seminars elsewhere. I am also grateful to Emily Gallagher for keeping my act together at MIT, and to the World Institute for Development Economics Research (WIDER) and its director, Lal Jayawardena, for unstinting support this past lustrum. Specific comments on various points in the manuscript came from Mohammed al-Sabah, Edward Amadeo, Robert Blecker, François Boye, Sandy Darity, Amitava Dutt, Jose Maria Fanelli, Mohan Rao, Jørn Rattsø, Juliet Schor, and Sweder van Wijnbergen. I did my best to respond to them all.

My family plus feathered and furry friends were as usual of wonderful support. Comments of the geese, in particular Luke Skywalker and Megæra, were instrumental in helping me unravel the complexities of neoclassical optimal growth.

Income Distribution, Inflation, and Growth

1

Methodology, Money, and Growth

Economics is, or ought to be, a historical science. Its events unfold in chronological and not logical time, irreversibly and affected by chance and contingencies that occur only once. An "experiment" rerunning economic history (if such a notion makes sense) would not give data series perturbed from the originals by random shocks. Rather, contingencies would switch the economy onto another set of rails, running through country perhaps broadly similar or perhaps radically different from that traversed before.

Looking backward, historically, we could map the two journeys and even explain why they took the courses they did. We might try to forecast the scenery to be expected along a third trip, but the predictions would be subject to all the errors inherent in inductive inference based upon unique past events. Among others, one can list inaccurate observation, faulty generalization, even the possibility that the economy's time flow could catastrophically bifurcate, in the mathematicians' tongue. The bottom line is that economic analysis cannot rely on idealized, reproducible experiments to delimit its content; irreducible history is built into all its data points.

This perspective—which draws heavily on Joan Robinson (1974) and is admirably displayed in the context of the geological sciences by Gould (1987)—has strong implications for economic theory. Theory necessarily must take the form of generalizations about broadly similar experiences in the past; "first principles" of the physicists' sort cannot lie at its base. This book is about such generalizations at the economywide level with the focus on developing (especially semi-industrialized) countries. This chapter sets out initial observations about the task at hand.

We begin in the following two sections with the methodological setting, discussing the nature of history-based theory, and then the stylized facts and the sorts of assumptions that underlie the models we deploy. Section 1.3 draws contrasts between this "structuralist" approach and current "mainstream" macro models based on stylized optimization problems that microeconomic "agents" are supposed to solve in choosing their behavior. Sections 1.4 and 1.5 review theories about economic growth and the role of financial assets (especially money) that have appeared over the past century or three. The history of economic thought provides a much broader perspective on these issues than does the mainstream, and several ideas are appropriated for later use in our discussions of income distribution, inflation, and growth. Finally, section 1.6 outlines the contents of the chapters to come.

1.1   Structuralist Methodology

Algebra is the chosen vehicle for discussing macroeconomics in this book, but not all historically based hypotheses are easily expressed in the idiom of Greek letters and graphs. Regardless of whether they can be formalized, it is not certain how well generalizations from history will describe new experience.

Hyperinflations exemplify the sorts of events that can be quantified—to a degree. During the dozen or so episodes in this century, money velocity V has tended to rise; the microeconomic rationale is that people keep less money as accelerating prices make it increasingly costly to hold. One can write the equations $MV = PX$, $\hat{P} = (dP/dt)/P$, and $V = V(\hat{P})$ using a convenient functional form for the latter, and feel fairly certain that they will fit the data from new hyperinflations now or next year. But in Nicaragua in the mid-1980s the equations applied *after* a two-year period during which the money supply M ballooned to pay for defense spending, output X stagnated, and V surprisingly fell. The price level P only began to spiral when the *contra* invasion was three years old. In Nicaragua's particular circumstances, did patriotism plus price controls stave off the hyperinflation, perhaps ultimately making it worse? What is clear *is* that simple extrapolation of a fairly well-established theory to a new empirical case did not give precise results (Taylor, Ocampo, et al. 1989).

For other sorts of generalizations, mathematical formulations are not useful at all. In financial discussions (as we will see below) both Banking School/structuralist radicals and conservatives basing themselves upon the Coase (1937) theorem argue that if the needs of trade demand it, an appropriate financial vehicle will appear. Kindleberger (1984) shows from history that sometimes a Coaseian solution emerges; sometimes not. Unquantifiable contingencies (why wasn't the financial wizard to launch the junk bonds of the era born?) and institutions underlie the observed event. The same is surely true of major historical changes such as the emergence of the factory system. Neither Landes (1969), who stresses technological reasons for the rise of centralized production with strong controls over workers, nor Marglin (1974), who argues that the causes inhered in social class, can be shoehorned into equation form.

These examples suggest that theory has to take the form of parables or stories designed to explain the past, some formalizable and some not. Available "facts" may fit two or more homilies tolerably well. Ideally, one could prove Landes or Marglin (or both) wrong by putting together enough counterexamples, or find detailed reasons why the Coase theorem in a particular circumstance did or did not apply. But again, scholarship alone may not suffice. The choice among possible theories often must be made on metatheoretical grounds: the aesthetics that underlie one's own version of Occam's razor (simplicity is in the eye of the beholder), informed personal views about how enterprises and their employees interact, ideas about what limits financial innovation in particular cases (what was the regulatory climate in a broad sense?), even the present political implications of the line of analysis that one adopts. Criteria of this nature entered into the selection of the models presented in this book.

Multiplicity of theories goes hand in hand with a hierarchy of explanations—one can tell different stories at different levels of the economic system. The conventional distinction is between micro (household and firm behavior) and macro (nationally or globally aggregated models), but intermediate stages are of interest in specific contexts: Interactions between sectors producing traded and nontraded goods and between the agricultural sector and the rest of a developing economy are obvious examples. What sorts of stories does one want to tell at different levels of the hierarchy, and how well do they hang together?

Mainstream economists have a clear answer to this question. It can usefully be stated now in initial form, pending further discussion in section 1.3. The dominant view is that macro models *can* be derived from first principles; they *should* be justified by stylized optimization exercises that micro firms and households supposedly undertake. Besides denigrating the historical nature of their science, economists ape overly speculative physicists and legalistic mathematicians lost in proofs in assuming this stance, but it has been the consensus at least around the North Atlantic since Paul Samuelson's (1947) methodological revolution achieved full force a generation ago. Since then, graduate students have learned far more optimization mathematics and far less about history and institutions than is intellectually safe.

Blanchard and Fischer (1989) give a clear presentation of popular macro-economic theories. One is their model of growth, a refinement of the Mill-Marshall-Ramsey-Solow tradition in growth theory described below. The economy stays at full employment with its growth rate set by aggregate saving, said to be the outcome of the solution by each household of a calculus of variations problem incorporating the family's discounted preferences for consumption now and in the (possibly endless) future as well as its perfectly foreseen (up to a random shock) prospects for making money from work or asset returns. In another example, money demand is determined by firms' and households' minimizing costs of going to the bank to get enough currency to satisfy "cash in advance" constraints of the form $M_i \geq P_i X_i / V_i$ for each agent i: Something like the quantity theory's equation of exchange $MV = PX$ follows from aggregating the extremal solutions.

Such optimization parables can be entertaining—the "Keynes-Ramsey rule" by which the optimally saving household equates the marginal consumption utility loss from extra saving to the discounted marginal productivity gain that its investment creates is undeniably neat. However, apart from other difficulties pointed out below, the mainstream's faith in optimization often blinds its adherents to obvious historical and institutional facts. An applied saving/consumption problem in Kuwait gives an example.

If it could all be pumped and sold, the value of Kuwait's oil in the ground is immense—at least $10 million per Kuwaiti family at 1990 prices. An optimal saving model with "plausible" parameters applied to a Kuwaiti household would suggest a lifelong party—interest income could support an endless princely life. Unfortunately, OPEC politics and a finite market limit annual oil sales to about $50,000 per household, and the population grows at over 3 percent per year. High income is on hand for Kuwaitis in 1990, but unless the oil price or politically feasible production dramatically soar, their expanding numbers will erode the good life in a couple of decades. Crucial saving and investment decisions confront the economy now; its living standard will slip steadily downward unless the party is postponed.

This view of Kuwait's medium-term prospects seems obvious. But blinded by the preconceptions of their theory, world-class neoclassical economists missed it by a mile. Wielding their favored optimal saving tools, they ignored local circumstances and institutional barriers and in the late 1980s came up with recommendations that Kuwaitis step up their consumption. Analagous oversights of institutional realities by orthodox scholars fixated on the latest optimizing tricks are easy to find all around the world.[1]

1.2 Stylized Macroeconomic Relationships and Facts

The moral of the Kuwait example is that realistic macroeconomics has to be based upon what Kaldor (1961) called "stylized facts," or empirical generalizations drawn hierarchically at the macro, sectoral, and micro levels about the economy at hand; Kaldor's view naturally extends to hypotheses about how the system functions as well. As will become evident to the reader, the models herein are based on an eclectic mix of "old" structuralist development theory, ideas borrowed from Cambridge (England) and Marxist economists, and even some ripples from the mainstream. The stylized representations of institutions and production relationships built into the algebra are characteristic of developing countries, but to a large extent carry over to industrialized economies as well. There is no reason to believe that neoclassical theory applies "better" to rich economies than poor ones—the author's personal experience and predilections dictate this particular book's emphasis on the Third World. The facts and macroeconomic linkages that are built into the models include the following:[2]

1. Economically powerful actors—institutions such as the state or corporations, interest groups such as landlords or rentiers, and even traditional classes such as the peasantry or unorganized labor—are not always price-takers. They can influence price and/or quantity changes in certain markets. The seats of power differ from economy to economy, and change with local institutional arrangements and history. Identifying centers of power and specifying the price and quantity inflexibilities they create is indispensable to model design.

2. Macroeconomic causality is influenced by microeconomic detail, but on the whole it flows from investment, exports, and fiscal demand as predetermined variables (or demand "injections") to income, import, and output flows which generate savings supplies (or "leakages"). Shifting income and wealth distributions play essential roles in macro adjustment to historical processes such as capital accumulation and technical progress and to exogenous shocks. There is no reason to believe that macroeconomic equilibrium will involve full employment of either labor or installed capacity economywide.

3. The money supply is often endogenous or "passive," adjusting to the level of activity and rate of inflation. However, this general view does not deny the possibility that a sufficiently determined Central Bank governor (backed by political authorities willing to cut the fiscal deficit) can at times dramatically reduce money supply growth in an austerity program.

4. The inflation rate may even at times slow down in response to tight money. But a more characteristic structuralist view is that in many sectors, production as opposed to the price level falls in response to cuts in demand, while the roots of inflation lie in unresolved distributional conflicts and propagation mechanisms such as the indexation of contracts.

5. Forms of financial intermediation that have developed over time strongly influence the macro system. Feedbacks between the real and financial sides of the economy can be mediated by large portfolio shifts (e.g., capital flight) as well as changes in asset rates of return. In developing economies financial fragility can lead rapidly to macroeconomic collapse.

6. In part due to the process of import-substituting industrialization, imported intermediate and capital goods are required to support local production and capital formation, respectively; foreign exchange to buy these imports can be a binding constraint.

7. Development is not a balanced or harmonious process. Technical change tied to new investment on the part of independently acting firms is an important contributor to growth. Private capital formation is as likely to be "crowded in" by public investment through complementarities as "crowded out" by rising interest rates charged by banks. For some sectors, production techniques with economies of scale or decreasing costs may only become profitable in small economies when the income distribution adjusts to switch demand in their direction; alternatively, several sectors might have to expand simultaneously in a "big push" (Rosenstein-Rodan 1961).

How are these views about the economy incorporated into formal models? Structuralists' practice has five key features. First, they begin their analysis by singling out economically relevant sets of people and institutions and specifying how they fit into available data on income and wealth distributions. In Adelman and Robinson's (1989) phrase, they work with an "extended functional distribution" based on the institutional structure of the economy at hand. Each set of economic actors typically is related to a functional category of the income distribution (wages, corporate profits, receipts of unincorporated enterprise) or a production sector; it has different behavior patterns and partial controls over the system. In practice, a group, class, or institution may be labeled by specific income flows rather than membership in an identifiable cluster of firms or individuals, but that is a shortcut. The justification for taking it is the belief that actions both of legal persons such as the state or corporate sector and of real households reflect their positions in the economic system as revealed by their principal income source. They interact according to behavioral rules the modeler specifies, with consequent repercussions on macroeconomic equilibrium.

In this book all the models incorporate extended functional distributions characteristic of the Third World, across which savings propensities, consumption and investment behavior, portfolio choices, and power over price formation differ. Typical entries in the distributional matrix include nonagricultural firms that gather profit income from markup pricing and undertake investment projects costing more than their own savings flows; rentiers who receive distributed profits, interest, and other financial incomes, suffer capital losses and gains on their (often considerable) assets, and save more than they invest; workers who get income from wages nominally fixed in the short run, don't save very much, and battle with firms about how wage increases will respond to unemployment and price inflation; agriculturalists whose saving rates are often high but whose income fluctuates sharply, following flexible price movements; and urban and rural "marginals" who pick up residual income flows, suffer from deprivation of basic needs, and save at low, often negative rates. The state in its fiscal, public investment, and central banking roles, the commercial banks, and foreigners also enter as interdependent but powerful actors. The room for maneuver available to any actor depends on the institutions and history of the economy at hand; incorporating them in convincing fashion is part of the model-building art.

A second distinctive feature of structuralist models is that they are *not* set up in "real" terms (i.e., with only relative prices). Rather, they explicitly include prices and income flows in nominal or money terms, which are what actual firms, people, and ministers of finance face. Examples abound: Workers may be concerned about their "real" purchasing power (e.g., a wage index divided by a price index), but in practice they struggle or negotiate with management over a money wage. Rapidly rising money wage rates in turn can trigger price inflations that affect everybody's economic decisions. The Central Bank may be concerned with a "real" exchange rate (e.g., the ratio of indexes of prices of traded and nontraded goods), but it manipulates the nominal peso to yen conversion factor—real or relative prices of traded goods may or may not respond. The finance minister worries about meeting payment obligations from a nominally fixed budget—if she underestimates inflation, money will have to be printed or the government's real spending will fall.

Third, these examples suggest that prices are under varying degrees of control by different groups in the economy. A focus on nominal magnitudes permits realistic treatments of financial markets and economic power. As already noted, the models herein postulate that power plays a role in price formation. For example, econometric studies almost always show that firms (especially in manufacturing) mark up variable production costs by a fixed margin to set prices. The markup rate is usually interpreted as the outcome of an oligopoly position on the output side and perhaps efficiency wage considerations for inputs. Other markets may have more flexibly varying prices, reflecting competitive behavior on the part of actors on both sides. The state may be able to intervene directly to control markups or public enterprise prices (e.g., the sale prices of gasoline and diesel fuel from refineries it controls) but finds controlling flex-prices costly in terms of holding stocks, importing, and "making" markets. Nominal price accounting provides the flexibility to include these and similar considerations in applied models.

Working with money income accounts also makes it easy to link the goods-producing and financial sectors of the economy through flows of funds. Each economic class or actor (e.g., wage-earners, the government, or the rest of the world) has a "financial surplus" defined as the excess of its saving over its investment. The sum of nominal surpluses across the economy must be zero, though each one separately may be positive or negative. For example, rentiers and (perhaps) farmers usually save more than they invest and industrial firms do the opposite. Among households, wage-earners typically have lower saving rates than farmers or rentiers. The overall public sector may save substantially or dissave, but after it pays for public investment, its financial surplus is usually negative.

Shifts in surpluses depend on nominal price movements. Further price and quantity financial adjustments (at times involving asset and liability stocks which are the cumulations of flows) in response to changed positions can be built into macro models. The feedbacks to commodity prices and quantities are often important. Effects of interest rate movements on investment demand are a classic example. Others involve portfolio movements and changes in wealth. For example, if rentiers hold assets abroad in the wake of capital flight, nominal currency devaluation will make them richer in local currency terms. A consequent reduction in their saving rate could have important macroeconomic implications, either for output changes or inflation.

Fourth, there is the question of how much of the mainstream approach to borrow, namely, what degree of microeconomic rationality and price-mediated substitution should be included in a model specification? As a matter of convenience and common sense, the models with more than one sector presented here incorporate consumer response to relative price shifts. If the staple food becomes more expensive, people will consume more or less of it, depending on income and substitution effects in complete systems of demand equations which are easy to write down. More important, dearer food may lead purchases of other goods to fall if its own demand is income inelastic. When there is a large agricultural sector, the macroeconomic implications of such Engel effects on the level of industrial output and agriculture's terms of trade can be profound.

Elsewhere in the system, asset-holders usually try to shift their portfolios to keep up with changing rates of return. Price-induced substitution among production inputs may be considered, if it seems practically relevant. Econometric evidence rarely supports strong firm-level changes in labor demand as real wages vary, but there may be price-induced shifts among similar inputs such as copper and aluminum, citizen- and guest-workers, or gas and oil. Such responses are efficiently modeled by neoclassical production theory. On the output side the total volume of agricultural production is not very price responsive, but acreages devoted to specific crops are. Export volumes and investment are at times sensitive to prices and asset returns, depending on the economy at hand.

The moral from these examples is that price responsiveness may or may not be empirically important, or central to the questions the model is supposed to address. If not, it can usefully be suppressed to focus attention on issues that are more relevant to the task at hand.

The fifth point about models is that their behavior depends crucially upon their description of causal linkages in the macroeconomic system. As discussed in the following chapters, there are many ways in which the economy can adjust when it is perturbed—output levels or the income distribution across classes may change, interest rates may vary, positions of wealth may expand or erode. A model-builder has to select *which* of these adjustment mechanisms to build into his or her equations—the character of the solutions will depend upon the choice. In the jargon, a model's "closure" has to be chosen and justified on the basis of empirical and institutional analysis of the economy at hand. Setting closure is impossible unless class structures and economic power relationships have already been defined. Searching for sites of power and macro causal links is the key to the structuralist approach.

1.3   The Mainstream Alternative

With such economywide relationships constraining growth and income distribution, how does micro behavior fit in? The viewpoint adopted here is that macroeconomics matters at its own level in the hierarchy of theories, and that the regularities one builds into macro models require justification much more from historical and institutional analysis (some microeconomic) than from optimization games that idealized firms or households are supposed to play. Indeed, optimization is likely to be misleading not only in practical matters like policy analysis in Nicaragua or Kuwait but intellectually as well. There are several reasons why the mainstream approach leads into a dead end.

To begin, micro behavior is conditioned by macro constraints. Hart (1986) illustrates the issues neatly in terms of agricultural labor markets, but her insight extends to other arenas as well. She shows how national political and economic realities partly determine the form and content of local contracts. Sharecropping replaced more communal forms of land control (which did not favor landlords) in Java after the Indonesian military *coup* of 1966 destroyed Communist party activity in the countryside. In a longer perspective Geertz (1963) argues that sharecropping itself spread as an aspect of agricultural "involution" forced upon Java by extraction of ever-growing surpluses by the Dutch during the colonial period.

For present purposes the key generalization from Hart and Geertz is that one must draw on macro level information to delimit boundaries within which peasants, landless, and landlords, or industrial workers and employers interact. They may well behave sensibly or with rational intent within their particular bottles—or bottlenecks—of feasible choice, but the first thing to get clear is just how much freedom they deploy.

Neoclassical economics sidesteps such questions by postulating a particular form of "rationality," which in practice boils down to optimization of a simple objective function (maximization of utility or profits, minimization of costs) subject to one or a few easily specified algebraic limitations of an essentially local nature. Households select their consumption basket subject to a budget ceiling, but neoclassicals rarely ask how this restriction is likely to move after labor market rules are revised in the wake of the slaughter of local Communist cadres. Following a tendency well exemplified by Stiglitz (1988), the neoclassical focus is always on demonic optimizations by "agents" subject to given constraints, rather than historical analysis of how the constraints affect macro equilibrium subject to plausible closure assumptions, as they themselves change over time.

Not only are economywide restrictions underspecified in neoclassical models, but their definition of rationality goes too far. Common sense plus a host of theories of the mind suggest that maximizing something does not fully describe social or personal behavior, even in the narrow economic sphere. Everyone knows examples of states, enterprises, and people who have acted in distinctly nonrational fashion (in both the economists' and more common usages of the word). Moreover optimized actions subject to simple constraints are unwise behavior precisely because they represent extremal results. If the rules of the game shift, an optimized system can rapidly become extinct.[3] In the economics jargon, a change in constraints can turn a "first-best" course of action rapidly into a second- (or nth-) best mess. As a practical matter, perceptions of binding limitations constantly change. Since the 1960s there have been two energy crises per decade, with corresponding hue and cry and reallocation of resources. Nonoptimal, flexible response is appropriate to the changing nature of the problems of the day.

Despite the fact that they rarely assume extremal positions, economic actors at times move in the directions that optimizations suggest—as we have already noted, predictions from the models are useful as metaphors but not exact descriptions of how firms or people act. For example, the notion that a monopolist raises prices to maximize profits can be taken as a rough explanation for everyday empirical facts. The model helps rationalize why airfares in the United States in the late 1980s tended to higher into cities dominated by a single carrier as its "hub." Even if it handled only 80 percent of the local traffic, the dominant airline could still jack up its tariffs, although it surely left first- and second-order conditions for complete maximization (taking into account the other carriers' reactions) unsatisfied.

The current mainstream recipe for constructing macroeconomic models errs in taking optimization not as a metaphor but as an exact description of how economic actors behave—first their individually extremal decisions are derived in exacting detail and then heroic simplifying assumptions are made so that they can be aggregated to give the macro view. For these models to be mathematically tractable, incredible hypotheses about people's ability to process information and even such minutiae as their mortality patterns are required.

For example, in the two favored macroeconomic growth models, either optimally saving families live forever and maximize utility with perfect foresight about all future events or else mortals in their "overlapping generations" die at a rate independent of their ages (Blanchard and Fischer 1989, chs. 2 and 3). The aggregated extremal solutions coming from such assumptions give saddlepoint (un)stable growth paths, akin in consumption/capital space to a pendulum balanced at the peak of its swing. As a description of reality, saddlepath growth is difficult to swallow—were the international debtor countries of the late 1980s on unique borrowing paths maximizing their discounted social welfare when they took tens of billions of dollars of bank credits a scant decade before?

In a sensible view of the world, people, firms, and nations save and invest, and borrow and spend, with economic motivation but without the benefits of eternal optimization or perfect foresight (how many imperfectly foreseen depressions, revolutions, and wars radically altering the economic environment have occurred in the twentieth century; how many North American gay men in the 1970s glimpsed the shadow of AIDS?), while some governments maintain fiscal balance without clear visions of their infinite, intertemporal budget constraints. Historically based generalizations about how groups of people, the state, and foreigners behave are a more appropriate basis for macro analysis than optimizations requiring information beyond feasible computation or belief. Unresolved social tensions in borrowing countries and both borrowers' and lenders' misperceptions of the willingness of the latter to continue to supply funds led to the 1980s debt debacle, just as imperfect knowledge, corruption and cupidity, and political constraints provoked similar crises over the preceding 150 years (Darity and Horn 1988).

The key issue is how best to utilize knowledge of history and institutions along with common sense to describe how people make economic decisions under fundamental uncertainty (we don't have enough knowledge to put complete probability distributions on future events), with insecure rationality (we still live in the century of Freud), and subject to social and political driving forces beyond personal control. Metaphors such as satisficing, animal spirits, externalities, and class consciousness will be adopted to describe micro behavioral patterns here—their epistemological basis is close to what Dennett (1987) calls an "intentional stance."

The sources of useful generalizations can be very diverse. Ultimately they derive from reasoned integration of firsthand, journalistic, or scholarly observation of how people and institutions have behaved in the past. An optimizing rationale for any particular generalization can always be provided after it has been made: like the amoeba, neoclassical economics is good at incorporating any new bit of intellectual nourishment that comes its way. The fact that the new economic ideas more often than not come from structuralists—the preface in Pasinetti (1981) contains an illuminating list—suggests that the mainstream amoeba has a difficult time maintaining an intellectually fruitful environment in which to thrive.

1.4 Theories of Economic Growth

Since this book is mostly about macroeconomics, an immediate question posed by the foregoing reflections is how do micro (and "meso") level actions influence the macro scene? The answers depend on the institutional structure built into a macro theory and its internal causal links. This and the following section set out the contents that economists have suggested for models of output growth and the financial system, several of which are incorporated into our formal models.[4]

Chakravarty (1980) distinguishes what he calls the Mill-Marshall and Marx-Schumpeter traditions in the theory of economic growth—the first author in each pair representing a watershed from the classical models of Smith and Ricardo. To these strands, we can add an underconsumptionist or stagnationist tradition which extends naturally to deal with issues such as foreign exchange restrictions on growth and the agricultural/nonagricultural terms of trade, and finally the models proposed in Cambridge, England, after World War II which built on the ideas of Kalecki and Keynes to deal with issues of distribution and growth.

Neither Mill nor Marshall fits with complete comfort into Chakravarty's box (Mill was well aware of class and gender conflict, while Marshall had much to say on the importance of historical processes and economies of scale as well as anticipating many of Keynes's insights into the trade cycle); nonetheless their approach to growth theory leads ultimately to the optimal saving exercises that we have already discussed. According to his writings gathered by Whitaker (1975), the young Marshall followed Mill in setting out a growth model stressing the steady accumulation of physical capital and dropping the classical population theory via which demand for labor (from the wage fund) controls supply via Malthusian checks. Both Englishmen largely ignored the macroeconomic implications of increasing returns, the potential contradiction between technical change and the real wage or employment brought out by Ricardo in his famous chapter "On Machinery" (which greatly influenced Marx), and indeed all macro aspects of class conflict and cumulative processes besides the productive use of saving. The gist of their model can be summarized in the form of three hypotheses:

1. There is an aggregate production function incorporating substitution between capital and labor. Production takes place under constant returns to scale.

2. The labor force grows in "natural" units, but per worker "efficiency" in production also rises due to technical progress and greater skills (the latter in part resulting from more education).

3. Saving comes from desires for deferred consumption and to ensure inheritance; both motivations underlie thrifty "waiting." Output not consumed is hitchlessly transformed into new capital formation, and as the stock of capital goes up the rate of interest (or profit) falls.

In a few words, growth results from saving generated by forces of productivity and thrift, plus exogenous technical change.

As Solow (1956) and subsequent neoclassical work based on Ramsey's (1928) optimal saving and Diamond's (1965) overlapping generations models have shown, these hypotheses support an analytical engine of considerable power (even if recent versions rely on saddlepath growth). Nonetheless, it is a generalization based upon the English capitalism of thrifty family firms that was ceasing to prevail even in Victorian times. Factors the model omits include the following:

1. The links between growth of money and credit institutions and industrialization—one thinks of Gerschenkron's (1962) emphasis on the role of commercial banks in guiding German industrial expansion last century.

2. There are different rates of technical change (not to mention wage and profit rates) across sectors, suggesting that noncompetitive market structures endure.

3. Risk pooling and reduction advanced greatly in Marshall's day due to growth of financial intermediation and the corporate business form.

4. The state intervened at many levels to speed economic growth, creating labor skills by education, imposing labor discipline, and pursuing an activist commercial policy in sharp disagreement with the tenets of the nineteenth- (and twentieth-) century neoclassical theory of trade.

5. Investment projects undertaken by firms were essential both to create

aggregate demand and to embody new techniques. In both developing and now industrialized economies, public investment played an essential complementary role.

6. Investment and saving can also get out of gear, creating inflationary or contractionary tendencies depending on which is potentially greater. The question about how investment injections are made equal to saving leakages is simply not addressed by the neoclassical model. We give it prominence in the chapters that follow.

7. As opposed to the utility maximization that dominates Ramsey-style optimal saving models, consumer choice in Marshall's time and now appears to be rather passive. Households happily dissave to switch to innovative products as entrepreneurs make them appear—how many staples of 1990 advanced economy consumption baskets (VCR's, FAX machines, shopping center sushi bars) even existed ten years before? As Pasinetti (1981) emphasizes, the genius of capitalism resides in forestalling an unemployment crisis by inventing new products to replace old ones as demand for them subsides.

No existing theory of growth deals adequately with all these issues, although some of the models sketched in the following chapters go part way. In so doing, they utilize insights into the growth process that one can glean from Schumpeter and Marx.

To summarize Marx's views on growth (or anything else, for that matter) in a way acceptable to all his readers is impossible. Following Chakravarty, all we can do here is set out a number of points that he raised, which can be inserted into simple, formal models that fall well short of capturing the complexity and internal contradictions of his perceptions of growth under capitalism and other modes of production:

1. Indeed, the first thing to note is that Marx emphasized that economies change in irreversible historical time in an overall institutional framework such as "capitalism," "feudalism," or "oriental despotism." Any such mode of production can be characterized by specific social devices for appropriation of surplus product over necessary consumption. This classical insistence on the primacy of processes determining the income distribution is adopted by most structuralist authors.

2. Marx concentrated on the capitalist mode, in which growth results from both accumulation and endogenous technical change. Producers adopt new methods to edge out competitors or because rising labor power can wipe out surplus value, thereby wiping out capitalists as well.

3. Competition among capitalists tends to equalize profit rates across sectors. However, sectoral demand and supply levels may not mesh, giving rise to a "disproportionality crisis." Similarly, aggregate demand may not equal supply. Money provides a vehicle for hoarding purchasing power, which can lead to a "realization crisis" or slump.

4. Both kinds of crises interact in a cyclical theory of growth, well described by Sylos-Labini (1984). At the bottom of a cycle the real wage is held down by a large "reserve army" of unemployed workers, and capitalists can accumulate freely. However, as output expands the reserve army is depleted and the real wage may rise. Capitalists search for new labor-saving technologies and also invest to build up the stock of capital and reduce employment via input substitution. Excessive funds tied up in machinery, sectoral imbalances, and lack of purchasing power on the part of capitalists to sustain investment (or of workers to absorb the output that new investment produces) can all underlie a cyclical collapse. Lewis (1954) translated Marx's story of cyclical upswing into a long-run theory of economic growth, with "surplus labor" replacing the reserve army. More recent, explicitly Marxist authors (discussed in chapter 11) stress the fall in investment that may occur in response to a profit squeeze as labor gains in bargaining power over a sequence of cycles.

5. Accumulation and growth may occur as these processes unfold, perhaps accompanied by a falling rate of profit, increased immiserization of the working class, or both. Both Marx and some recent authors see cyclical profit squeezes culminating in a steadily declining rate of profit over time.

Schumpeter took over much of Marx's supply-side vision and combined it with a provocative analysis of how the economy responds to technical innovation in forging his own defense of capitalism: He called his teacher Eugen von Böhm-Bawerk a "bourgeois Marx" but could have applied the label equally to himself. His *Theory of Economic Development* (German version 1912; American edition 1934) resembles Marx in emphasizing technical advance under a given set of institutions but also is very Keynesian (or Wicksellian) in building the growth process around the supply of credit and macro adjustments to changes in investment demand. Following Taylor and Arida (1988), a sketch of the theory goes as follows:

The starting point is rather like Mill-Marshall-Solow steady growth, which Schumpeter calls "circular flow." An economy in circular flow may be expanding, but it is not "developing" in his terminology. Development occurs only when an entrepreneur makes an innovation—a new technique, product, or way of organizing things—and shifts production coefficients or the rules of the game. He gains a monopoly profit until other people catch on and imitate, and the economy moves to a new configuration of circular flow.

The invention or insight underlying the innovation need not be the entrepreneur's—Schumpeter's "new man" simply seizes it, puts it in action, makes his money, and (more likely than not) passes into the aristocracy as he retires. Ultimately, his innovation and fortune will be supplanted by others in the process of "creative destruction" that makes capitalist economies progress.

The key analytical question about this process refers to both the financial and real sides of the economy—how does the entrepreneur obtain resources to innovate? An endogenous money supply and redistribution of real income flows are required to support his efforts.

To get his project going, the entrepreneur must invest—an extra demand imposed upon an economy already using its resources fully in circular flow. To finance investment, he obtains loans from the banks; new credit and thereby money are created in the process. The bank loans are used to purchase goods in momentarily fixed supply. Their prices are driven up, so real incomes of other economic actors decline. The most common examples are workers receiving temporarily fixed nominal wages or the cash flows of noninnovating firms. There is "forced saving" as workers' lower real incomes force them to consume less; groups that receive windfall income gains are assumed to have higher saving propensities so that overall aggregate demand declines. Meanwhile, routine investment projects may be cut back.

The transition between states of circular flow is demand-driven from the investment side (though, of course, the innovation may involve production of new goods or increases in productivity) and short-run macro adjustment takes place through income redistribution via forced saving with an endogenously varying money supply. In a longer run there can be a cyclical depression due to "autodeflation" as bank loans are repaid; workers can regain real income via falling costs. In later versions of the model Schumpeter emphasized that bankruptcy of outdated firms can also release resources for innovators, but the essentials are the same.

Finally, it is clear that Schumpeter is describing a "punctuated" growth process (Eldredge 1985), as firms and their innovations rise and fall in creative destruction—the analogy to stasis suddenly interrupted by disappearances and arrivals of species as described by Eldredge and Gould is clear. Schumpeter's methodological perspective is identical to that of Marx and the paleontologists: Both economic and biological growth can only be analyzed in chronological, not logical time. Formal models of these processes must permit the existence of multiple equilibria or diverse "basins" and "attractors" for the trajectories of the differential equations describing the evolution of the economy over time. Switching attractors is a mathematical metaphor for transforming the nature of circular flow.

Like other theorists of his "post-Wicksellian" generation,[5] Schumpeter characteristically assumed that resources are fully employed: Under such circumstances forced saving is an excellent mode of macroeconomic adjustment. However, if output can vary to equate saving with investment, one arrives at a class of "stagnationist" growth models which underlie much discussion of the economic development process, such as by Lustig (1980) and Chakravarty (1987). In rich countries Kalecki (1971) by far is the most distinguished exponent of this tradition.

To understand the issues, it is useful to begin with possible stagnation as a result of regressive income redistribution in a model with one sector, and then bring in multisectoral complications. Suppose that investment responds to increased capacity utilization as in an accelerator (but not so strongly as to give rise to Harrodian stability problems of the type discussed below). Then a distributional shift against high-consuming wage-earners can lead to lower investment and growth: A higher profit share or lower real wage reduces consumption demand and capacity utilization, and capital formation may slow down. With reduced enterprise cash flows, the profit rate (the product of the profit share and the output/capital ratio) may also decline along with the real wage. Chapter 3 provides the details of how all this works out.

Now suppose that instead of modifying the economywide marginal propensity to save, income redistribution alters only the pattern of consumer purchases by sector while leaving aggregate demand unchanged (i.e., all sectors have identical wage and profit shares and workers and capitalists have the same marginal propensities to consume). The wealthy may prefer to buy more services and sophisticated manufactures at the margin, for example, and the poor simple industrial products and food. If redistribution occurs and sectoral demand patterns change, and if investment demand by sector responds, the economy may switch to another configuration of circular flow. The results may not be heartening for proponents of progressive redistribution, as shown in chapter 10. A change in sectoral demand composition may create jobs but slow overall growth if investment in the favored sector is not strongly stimulated by its own output increases. Bringing aggregate demand movements back into the story can further complicate its plot, especially if differences in saving rates between classes interact with sectorally differing profit shares as demand patterns change.

Stagnationist logic lies behind many redistribution proposals that have appeared over the years. The French-Swiss reformer Sismondi (1815) recommended progressive redistribution in the wake of the Napoleonic Wars to stimulate French industrialization—more prosperous workers would demand clothing and textiles and propel investment in those sectors. The same theme appeared in the writings of last century's Populists in Russia and is debated in India today. Causality was reversed by Latin American structuralists like Furtado (1972) and Tavares (1972). If industrialization beyond production of simple goods like food and textiles is to occur, they said, then under present social conditions income concentration is necessary to sustain demand for more sophisticated commodities since their production is likely to be subject to minimum cost-effective size requirements due to economies of scale. Finally, wage-led or "fair" growth in the United States may well be on the political agenda in the 1990s after the regressive income and wealth redistributions of the two preceding decades.

These ideas are illustrated below in several ways, with the main theme being that demand changes can stimulate processes that cumulate over time to alter the nature of supply. In chapter 10 we ask whether redistribution and/or state intervention can raise demand enough to make profitable production processes with fixed overheads that have constant marginal but decreasing average costs. Alternatively, intervention may be required to guide "make or buy" choices in an economy that has potential economies of scale but also is imperfectly open to trade in the sense that import and export prices are not equal. Under appropriate circumstances progressive income shifts or public policy can bring economies of scale into play that can have profound economywide effects of the sort invoked by Young (1928) and his student Rosenstein-Rodan with his Big Push. In contrast, chapter 11 provides another formalization. Investment may be subject to scale economies, but it can respond to consumer demand for "luxuries" and lead to creation of a middle class which in turn buys more luxuries and stimulates further investment growth. In all these stories there is a movement between growth equilibria, or configurations of circular flow.

These last examples also suggest that stagnationist analysis can overlap with distributional changes like those underlying forced saving. Scenarios involving multiple commodities or sectors lie close at hand. Two are particularly relevant in the Third World: limitations on growth imposed by shortages of foreign exchange, and interactions between sectors adjusting to excess demand respectively via changes in output and a flexible price.

The ever-present danger of "external strangulation" in developing economies is an old theme in structuralist thought, dating to the work of the Economic Commission for Latin America in Santiago in the 1950s at least. The notion was formalized by Chenery and Bruno (1962) in the two-gap model incorporating separate foreign exchange and saving restrictions on growth.

The saving constraint follows naturally from Harrod-Domar algebra of the sort discussed below: Investment has to be financed by either national saving or capital inflows from abroad. But the inflows also cover the trade deficit. Industrialization via import substitution (the only way to build up local production capacity that has been discovered so far) means that the economy becomes dependent on imports of intermediate goods—without them, local factories cannot work. At the same time import substitution rarely extends to capital goods, so up to half of investment spending takes the form of purchases from abroad. There is a sharp trade-off between current production and capital formation, which only additional foreign exchange can relieve. If domestic output is limited by scarcity of convertible dollars or yen, inflationary forced saving macroeconomic adjustment often occurs.

The saving and foreign gaps have been extended in recent work (Bacha 1990; Taylor 1990c) to take into account two important fiscal effects. First, after the debt crisis, many governments nationalized foreign obligations— the state is liable for external payments on debt. Second, as noted above, econometric work in the 1980s typically showed that there is a strong "crowding-in" effect of public on private capital formation (contrary to the crowding-out of private by public spending through rising interest rates in financial markets that is frequently presumed). The consequence is a "fiscal gap" limiting growth because public (and therefore total) capital formation is cut back. Attempts to relieve fiscal burdens by relying on forced saving or the inflation tax (discussed below) became ever more frequent in the 1980s. The multiple, interacting problems posed by saving, foreign exchange, fiscal, and inflation gaps are a source of much current policy concern.

Turning to models with two broad commodities domestically supplied, a frequently used specification is based upon one sector where supply is limited by available capacity and the price adjusts to clear the market, plus a second sector in which production meets demand. This two-sector specification blends forced saving, Engel demand effects, and output adjustment in an illuminating fashion. It can be applied in various contexts, for instance, to analyze the agricultural terms of trade, to discuss "Dutch disease" problems when a traded goods sector has its price fixed from the world market and a nontraded sector has an adjusting price, and to do global macroeconomics between a "North" exporting industrial goods and a "South" selling primary products. We take up all three versions in chapter 9, but the nature of the model can be illustrated with the first interpretation here.

Models focusing on the relative price of food (or agriculture's terms of trade) date at least from the controversy between Ricardo and Malthus about whether England's Corn Laws limiting grain imports should or should not be repealed. To address this question, we assume that "industry" has prices fixed by a markup over prime costs and its output is determined by demand, while "agriculture" has fixed supply and a market-clearing price in the short run.

To see how the model works, we can ask how the two markets interact. Suppose that the terms of trade shift toward agriculture, say due to a reduction of food imports. Industrial output can either rise or fall. It will be pushed up by increased demand from higher agricultural income but also held down by reduced real nonagricultural spending power (real wages drop due to forced saving from dearer food). The latter effect will be stronger insofar as Engel's law makes food demand income inelastic, so the loss in workers' spending power primarily forces down their demand for industrial goods. Under such circumstances letting more imports into the economy will doubly benefit the industrial sector—food prices fall and output expands. Although he used a different model to argue his case, this outcome is consistent with Ricardo's advocacy of repeal of the Corn Laws.

The alternative view was espoused by Malthus in his *Principles of Political Economy*, where the argument can be interpreted in terms of distributional effects on aggregate demand. Agriculture is reponsible for a big proportion of income and consumer spending. Farmers (or landlords for Malthus) hit by adverse terms of trade will cut their purchases, reducing economic activity overall. Whether a Ricardian or Malthusian distributional configuration applies in developing countries today is highly relevant for policy—the answer according to applied computable general equilibrium models (Taylor 1990b) seems to go either way.

Besides import policy, other state interventions can affect the terms of trade. Fiscal expansion or increased investment, for example, will bid up the flexible price to generate forced saving to help meet the increased injection of demand. Ellman (1975) argues that food price-induced forced saving supported the Soviet industrialization push of the 1930s, in contrast to Preobrazhenski's (1965) suggestion that the terms of trade be shifted *against* agriculture by a monopsonistic state to extract an investable surplus.

Two final questions about fix-price/flex-price models[6] are how to use them to describe inflation and growth. Determination of the growth rate depends crucially on how causality in the macroeconomic system runs. If saving-investment balance in the North, for example, regulates expansion of the world economy, then the primary export terms of trade and capital formation in the South will tag along as adjusting variables. Contrariwise, slow growth in a dominant fixed-supply sector can determine behavior of the whole system. Specific models are discussed in chapter 9.[7]

With regard to inflation, we can begin by observing that structuralist theory typically attributes steadily rising prices to conflicting income claims. In the capitalist/worker story—a favorite of theorists but not necessarily the most relevant to developing economies—suppose that prices are set as a markup over wages and costs of imported intermediate goods. If the markup rate or import cost rises, prices follow and the real wage declines. Workers counter by pushing up money wages—the instrument over which they have a degree of control. But then prices go up further through the markup, wages follow, and so on. In Joan Robinson's (1962) phrase, there is an "inflation barrier" below which the real wage cannot fall before a money wage inflation is set off. It will run more rapidly insofar as the distributional conflict is sharp and "propagation mechanisms" such a contract indexation work fast.

The conflict can be over the price of food—this is where flex-prices enter the inflation process in a model popular in Latin America that was first proposed by Noyola (1956) and Sunkel (1960) after Kalecki (1976) sketched an inflationary terms of trade model in lectures in Mexico City in 1953. These structuralist authors suggested land reform as a solution. It would shift out the agricultural supply function, and thereby alleviate wage pressure resulting from a limited supply of food. The surprisingly complex implications of such an "agriculture-first" strategy are sketched in chapter 9.

Cambridge growth theory—our final topic in this section—took off from Keynes, Kalecki, and Sraffa (1960) in several directions. Despite coming from Oxford, Harrod (1939) produced the first model in the tradition. It demonstrated potential macroeconomic instability from two contradictions inherent in a stagnationist interpretation of Keynes. The first was between the "natural" (population increase plus labor efficiency gain) and the "warranted" (investment equals saving) rates of growth. As we will see in chapter 2, Solow (1956) bypassed the possibility that the rates might not equalize by postulating full employment and letting saving determine investment along Mill-Marshall lines to make the warranted and natural rates the same.

Harrod's second contradiction (which Solow implied he resolved but really just swept under the rug by having saving drive capital formation) hinged on a stronger response of investment than saving to higher output. If the accelerator is very strong, a small positive output shock along the warranted "knife-edge" growth path would make injections increase more than leakages, so that output would rise further, and so on. For demand-determined real GDP in a stagnationist model, this sort of instability is unlikely on empirical grounds, but as we will see in chapters 3 and 4, it can underlie a plausible model of hyperinflation when supply limitations bind.

After World War II Kaldor (1957), Pasinetti (1962), and Robinson (1962) followed Marx, Schumpeter, and the stagnationists in setting up models emphasizing interactions between income distribution and growth, in historical time. Kaldor's and Pasinetti's growth analysis used forced saving as the macroeconomic adjustment mechanism under an assumption of full employment; the latter's explicitly class-based model gives rise to interesting possibilities for multiple equilibria (discussed in chapter 11).

Cambridge economists—Robinson and Kaldor especially—also criticized facile neoclassical distribution theories based on marginal productivity. Kaldor's doubts are reviewed in the next chapter. Harcourt (1972) ably summarizes the reswitching controversy which Sraffa and Robinson (1953–54) effectively launched. Their Cambridge defeated the one in Massachusetts in the debate about reswitching, but the victory had no effect on subsequent mainstream practice. As we have seen, well-behaved aggregate production functions continue to rule the neoclassical growth roost.

Finally, Kaldor like other dissident economists emphasized the importance of economies of scale and the endogeneity of technical change. His "technical progress function" which tied increases in labor productivity to capital accumulation was the initial influential attempt to deal with endogenous technical advance. As discussed in chapter 2, very recent neoclassical models that link productivity levels to available stocks of physical or human capital (Romer 1986; Lucas 1988) are a belated reinvention of a well-oiled Kaldorian wheel. Great originality rarely characterizes mainstream model design.

1.5   Money and Credit

How does money affect macroeconomic equilibrium? This question has been hotly debated among both economists and noneconomists for the past 300 years. It can be posed from at least three angles:

1. Does money largely control, or just respond to developments elsewhere in the economy, namely, is it "active" (exogenous and determined prior to other variables) or "passive" (endogenous) most of the time?

2. Do changes in the money supply mostly affect the volume of activity, or the price level? What are the channels via which money has its impacts on quantities and prices?

3. Should we concentrate analysis on changes in "money" (banking system liabilities) or "credit" (banking system assets)?

Over the long sweep of economic analysis, one can find eminent partisans of all eight analytical positions implicit in this three-way classification. Table 1.1 presents an outline. We will go through the entries to sketch informally the theoretical views underlying each position, roughly in chronological order. Lessons for subsequent models will also be drawn.

The earliest participants in the table are two political parties—the "Hats" and the "Caps"—which appear in the active/quantities/credit and active/prices/credit slots. They flourished in a parliamentary democracy for a few decades between Divine Right despots in Sweden in the mideighteenth century. As their names suggest, the parties represented the big and small merchant bourgeoisie, respectively. These rather obscure histor-

Table 1.1
Positions of different monetary analysts

Causal status of money/credit	Main effects of money/credit			
	On prices		On quantities	
	Via money	Via credit	Via money	Via credit
Passive	Hume	Thornton Wicksell Schumpeter	Malthus Banking School	Marx Kaldor Real Business Cycle School
Active	Ricardo Currency School Mill Monetarists	"Caps"	Keynes	"Hats" Law Minsky

ical groupings are of interest because the Hats and Caps were, respectively, among the first proponents of distinctively "structuralist" and "monetarist" positions in financial theory (Kindleberger 1985).

The Hats were policy activists, urging credit creation to spur the Baltic trade. The Caps countered with arguments that excessive spending could lead to inflation, payments deficits, and related ills. The Hats took power after a period of slow Cap growth and (as often happens with expansionist parties), pushed too hard—they lost power in an inflation and foreign exchange crisis in 1765. Despite their respective policy failures, the intellectual points raised by the politically warring Swedes carry down through the years.

Both parties were fundamentally mercantilist. Their basic macro model can be summarized by the equations

$$J = I + B = J(\text{credit}),$$

$$S = S(\text{population, unemployment, real wage}),$$

$$J - S = 0,$$

where J stands for demand injections (investment I and the trade surplus B) and S represents saving leakages. Various policy instruments and social processes were assumed to regulate the variables in the equations, *viz* Malthusian checks for population, the poorhouse for unemployment, forced saving for the real wage (not much discussed), and tariffs and export subsidies for trade balance.

Investment could also be spurred by credit creation, a point stressed by John Law, a Scotsman who sought to stimulate French growth early in the eighteenth century by setting up development banks. That his scheme led to the Mississippi Bubble—one the earliest speculative booms—has echoes in the financial instability theories of Hyman Minsky (1975, 1986), a contemporary economist who also emphasizes that banks actively create credit that can have a strong influence on output via "Keynesian" channels. Indeed, as we will see in chapters 5 and 6, Minskyian feedbacks between real output and expansionary finance can be so strong as to lead to macro instability. John Law's fortunes might have fared better, had he been able to listen to the future and hear what his distant analytical descendent Minsky had to say.

Caps, Hats, and Law all argued as if money and credit could be controlled by the relevant authorities. Part of the intellectual reaction against mercantilism took the form of making money (or "specie") as well as the trade surplus endogenous in the short run. David Hume (1752, 1969), a first-rate philosopher turning into a best-selling historian, is usually credited with this advance in economic analysis, although his contemporary Richard Cantillon and Thomas Mun more than a century earlier also set out the mechanics of price/specie-flow balance of payments adjustment.

Hume's location in the passive/prices/money slot follows from a model that might be written as

$$D = D(M)$$

$$X = X(\text{employment})$$

$$MV = PX$$

$$\dot{M} = X - D\left(\frac{PX}{V}\right) = B(P_w - P)$$

Aggregate demand D depends on the money stock M while (assuming full employment) output X is predetermined. The expansion in the money supply $\dot{M}$ ($=dM/dt$) is given by specie inflow resulting from the trade surplus $B = X - D$; in this sense money is passive or endogenous. Since money drives the price level P via the equation of exchange $MV = PX$, money expansion $\dot{M}$ is an inverse function of P. The last expression for $\dot{M}$ normalizes this response around a "world" price P_w.

The story is simple, and well-known. A big money stock means that there is a high domestic price level and excess demand. The trade surplus becomes negative when D is high, meaning that specie flows out of the country and prices fall. Aggregate demand ceases to draw in imports and "our" exports sell better—the trade deficit declines toward equilibrium. Policymakers' attempts to stimulate output by monetary expansion (e.g., by raising the banking system's money/specie multiplier) will backfire in this model; their attempt will just drive up prices and worsen the trade deficit. Although they reasoned on different grounds and far less cogently, the Caps would have heartily approved of this conclusion.

The next major players in the table are Malthus and Ricardo, who sit opposed in the northeast and southwest corners. We have already seen that the former argued along proto-Keynesian lines that food prices should be kept high by import restrictions so that landlords (notoriously low savers) would spend on luxuries to support industrial demand. A precursor of the structuralist Banking School, Malthus thought that the money supply and/or velocity adjusted endogenously to meet demand, or the "needs of trade."

Ricardo, a superb monetary theorist, differed from Malthus in accepting supply-side determination of output, or Say's law (not necessarily a bad approximation in a period in which agriculture still was the dominant producing sector). He naturally followed the monetarist trail, most notably in 1810 when he attacked "excessive" British note issue to finance the war against Napoleon. His evidence included a premium on gold in terms of notes within Britain, and a fall of the exchange value of sterling in Hamburg and Amsterdam. His logic was based on the quantity theory and purchasing power parity—standard components of all subsequent monetarist theory.

Ricardo's main policy recommendation was a Friedmanite rule called the "currency principle," recommending that the outstanding money stock should be strictly tied to gold reserves. Money could not be created for frivolous purposes such as war finance, and its supply would only fluctuate in response to movements of gold. In effect Ricardo sought to steer monetary policy along the trail blazed by Hume.

The Currency School, which took the monetarist side in British financial debates well into the nineteenth century, was founded on the basis of Ricardo's principle. Its greatest victory was Peel's Charter Act of 1844 for the Bank of England, which put a limit on the issue of notes against securities. Above the limit, notes had to be backed by gold. This triumph of principle in practice was short-lived, since there was a run against English banks in 1847. The Bank of England acted (correctly) as what Bagehot (1873, 1962) later called a "lender of last resort," pumping resources into commercial banks in danger of collapse. To this end, the Charter Act had to be suspended.[8]

As the Currency School flourished, John Stuart Mill was putting together his own economic synthesis. Although he had some sympathy for the Banking School (see below), Mill is placed in the active/prices/money slot because he codified the doctrine of "loanable funds" which underlies much subsequent mainstream thought (including the latest twists on the Ramsey optimal growth model, as we will see in appendix 2.A). Following Henry Thornton, a contemporary of Ricardo, Mill let the interest rate adjust to erase any difference between aggregate saving and investment, thereby clearing the market for loanable funds. In effect this theory *postulates* the full employment of the Mill-Marshall growth model and relies upon changes in the interest rate to attain macroeconomic balance.

Loanable funds is a nonmonetary theory of the rate of interest, of the sort later criticized by Keynes (discussed in chapter 2). It incorporates Patinkin's (1965) "dichotomy" in that money can affect only the price (and presumably wage) level, without any influence on the volume of production. This is the ultimate monetarist position, with echos in both Irving Fisher's suggestion that monetary policy should be actively deployed to control prices and Milton Friedman's argument against active policy because its effects on output only are visible with "long and variable lags" while money rules the price level best in the long run.

The final entries in the broadly monetarist left columns of table 1.1 are Thornton, Wicksell, and Schumpeter (with respect to his short-run macro adjustment scenario, at least) in the passive/prices/credit niche. We concentrate on Knut Wicksell (1935) as the key player, even though much of his analysis was anticipated by Thornton almost one hundred years before. It also bears note in passing that the Keynes of the *Treatise on Money* (1930) was a stalwart post-Wicksellian along with Schumpeter. Only his revised views in *The General Theory* (1936) place him in the active/quantities/money cell.

Wicksell extended loanable funds theory by proposing that inflation is a "cumulative process" based on the discrepancy between new credit demanded by investors and new deposit supply from desired saving (corresponding to a zero rate of inflation) at a rate of interest fixed by the banks. Suppose that the rate is set too low. Then an excess of new credits over new deposits leads to money creation; via the equation of exchange at presumed full employment, the consequence is rising prices. Inflation is the outcome of endogenous monetary emission, driven by credit creation.

The key analytical question is how saving and investment are brought together to secure macroeconomic equilibrium ex post. Forced saving provides part of the adjustment, if wages are incompletely indexed to price increases. The rest comes from the "inflation tax," a dynamic version of the well-known "real balance effect," which states that people increase their saving to restore the real value of their money stock M/P which is squeezed when P rises. If output X and velocity V are assumed constant in the equation of exchange $MV = PX$, then the inflation tax interpretation rests on the equations

$$\frac{\dot{M}}{PX} = \frac{\dot{P}(M/P)}{PX} = \hat{P}/V,$$

which follow from the growth rate version of the equation of exchange, $\hat{M} = \hat{P}$. After the first equality, $\dot{P}(M/P)$ is the instantaneous loss in real balances from price increases $\dot{P}$, which wealth-holders are supposed to make good by extra saving so that the "tax" effectively cuts aggregate demand. The expression after the second equality shows that the tax base erodes as V rises when inflation speeds up (the monetarists' favorite stylized fact).[9]

Wicksell thought that after a time, bankers would raise the interest rate to its "natural" level to bring the cumulative inflation to a halt, but for present purposes this ending is not essential to his story. The key point is that through both the inflation tax and forced saving, a rising price level liquidates ex ante excess aggregate demand. Models illustrating this inflation theory appear in chapter 4. It is the monetarist alternative to the structuralist inflation model sketched at the end of section 1.4.

Now we should turn our attention to the remaining entries in table 1.1, beginning with the passive/quantities/money Banking School, the main rival of the Currency School in last century's British debate. The group is famous (or notorious, depending on one's perspective) for espousing the doctrine of "real bills" stating that banks should discount all solid, non-speculative commercial paper, that is, true or real bills. How in practice a banker should identify paper tied firmly to the needs of trade was not spelled out; indeed Adam Smith (an early proponent of the doctrine) thought that banks should concentrate on real trade to avoid ratifying currency speculation. Extreme members of the Banking School finessed Smithian fears with a "law of reflux" through which excessive lending would drive up activity and/or prices and lead the private sector to pay off loans and buy gold: There would be an automatic contraction of the money supply in response to too aggressive attempts to expand it! Hume's shade reappears in structuralist guise, although without his specie flow considerations.

Real bills ideas have downside implications as well. If credit needs are *not* satisfied by banks, then new, nonbank financial instruments are likely to be invented to meet the needs of trade. We have already observed that such a Coaseian outcome sometimes happens, sometimes not, but it is implicit in Banking School views. Among structuralists, reflux notions show up in the 1959 report on the British monetary system by the Radcliffe Committee and in Kaldor (1982). The latter is worth quoting:

> If ... more money comes into existence than the public, at the given or expected level of incomes or expenditures, wishes to hold, the excess will be automatically *extinguished*—either through debt repayment or its conversion into interest-bearing assets ...

One notes a certain affinity in structuralist positions across 150 years.

The final entries in the table are the Real Business Cycle School and Marx, perhaps demonstrating that economic perceptions can unite strange political bedfellows. The former group is of recent origin, at the mainstream's neoclassical verge extreme. Its members argue that business cycles in advanced economies are due to strong substitution responses (labor vs. leisure choices, and so on) to supply-side shocks to the macro system. They deem money unimportant because it is endogenous, subject to "reverse causality" (Blanchard and Fischer 1989, ch. 7). They are joined by Kaldor and the post-Keynesians Davidson and Weintraub (1973) in their view that typical Central Bank responsiveness to trade plus the presence of inside money render monetary aggregates endogenous: Their leads and lags with output depend on institutions and contingencies beyond the analytical reach of Granger-Sims causality tests and similar econometric probes.

Marx, as always, is more complex. The existence of money was central to his view of capitalism, incarnated in the famous $M - C - M'$ sequence, in which exploitation arises as money M is thrown into circulation or capital C, which yields a money return M': surplus value is $M' - M$. *Access* to M gives capitalists a leg up in the economy, making their extraction of surplus possible.

At a more applied level of abstraction, Marx roughly adhered to Banking School ideas, at times arguing that velocity varies to satisfy the equation of exchange. This view is consistent with endogeneity of inside money, such as financial obligations created and destroyed by transactions among firms. Building on the reproduction schemes in volume 2 of *Capital*, Foley (1986a) has extended this approach to set up real/financial "circuit of capital" models in which endogenous fluctuations can occur. Some flavor of his work appears in the financial crisis models of chapter 6.

1.6   Chapter Outlines

The rest of this book develops formal models built around the ideas just set out about stylized facts (especially regarding income distribution), growth, and linkages between the financial and real sides of the economy. In summary, the chapter contents go as follows:

Chapter 2 takes up the question already raised several times of how to specify "closure," or define the causal structure of macro models. Sen (1963) put the issue in the following fashion: How can the macroeconomic system adjust to satisfy a number of plausible restrictions that might be imposed upon it, such as an investment function independent of saving, an exogenously fixed level of employment or capacity utilization, or a predetermined real wage?

The possibilities are illustrated with a simple seven-equation model of the quantity/price side of the economy (initially ignoring money) in two variants—with the price level determined by a markup, or by a neoclassical cost function in conjunction with the usual marginal productivity conditions. If all plausible restrictions are imposed, both variants of the model are overdetermined (Sen's basic point). By juggling equations and variables, a taxonomy of different causal schemes or closures can be derived. The ones that have been most widely discussed are

Output adjustment à la Keynes (*General Theory*) and Kalecki, with an independent investment demand function and variable employment.

Forced saving (presupposing differences in savings propensities across classes), with an independent investment function but output determined by full employment of labor, full capacity use, or available foreign exchange. One implication is the "paradox of thrift," with implications for political economy taken up in chapter 3.

Determination of investment by saving under full employment, in the Mill-Marshall tradition. As we have seen, an adjustment mechanism sometimes invoked involves flows of loanable funds, whereby the interest rate adjusts to bring investment demand into line with flow saving supply.

An alternative neoclassical/monetarist adjustment story relies on significant real balance effects, via which price increases reduce the real value of the money stock. Money-holders increase their saving to reconstitute their wealth. Demand falls in parallel with forced saving, but due to redistribution of wealth instead of income. The inflation tax is a dynamic version of this story.

A neo-Marxian model, with the real wage determined from class struggle, and saving-driven investment.

The chapter closes with diagrams illustrating the different causal schemes and a discussion of how different forms of short-run adjustment extend naturally into corresponding models of growth. Investment determination by savings leads into neoclassical and neo-Marxian growth analysis, and forced saving under full employment into Kaldor-style models (which also feature endogenous technical progress). Stagnationist models can be based on an independent investment function, and either adjusting output or else forced saving and the inflation tax when output is fixed by the available capital stock or foreign exchange. In both cases convergence of dynamic income distribution processes to equilibrium defines a steady state.

Finally, two appendixes are devoted to mainstream formulations. The first demonstrates that the version of the Ramsey optimal saving model favored during the 1980s boils down to equilibration of saving and investment by the interest rate in the market for loanable funds. The second shows how distributional effects put the overlapping generations growth model into grave peril of dynamic instability.

Chapter 3 continues the theme of its predecessor, asking how income redistribution (measured by changes in the real wage) influences growth and output, in Keynes-Kalecki and mainstream/monetarist model closures.

The first question is whether progressive redistribution will stimulate aggregate demand. The answer in a Kaleckian growth model, as we have seen, depends, inter alia, on differential saving patterns from wage and profit income, and the relative strength of profitability and accelerator effects in investment demand. Regimes in which real wage increases raise and lower demand are identified; following recent jargon, they can be called "wage-led," "consumption-led," or "stagnationist" (an alternative use of a word we have already applied to investment-driven growth models in general) and "profit-led," "investment-led," or "exhilarationist," respectively.

The next question is how the macro system reaches equilibrium when, for instance, output cannot change due to a capacity constraint. Forced saving is introduced as a stable adjustment mechanism when there is a positive demand shock in the wage-led case—rising prices reduce the real wage and consumer spending. When a real wage reduction increases demand, however, a rising price level propagates into a hyperinflation analagous to Harrod's instability in growth models. In the stable case the paradox of thrift is discussed (attempts at progressive redistribution fail when capacity limits bind), and the real balance effect is shown to complement forced saving in leading to equilibrium. Both mechanisms produce a downward sloping-aggregate demand curve, but the real balance effect has come to dominate mainstream thought, since it also provides a rationale for money wage reductions as a tool to stimulate the level of economic activity.

To see how, we introduce a marginal productivity labor demand schedule, following Keynes in the *General Theory*. Money wage cuts are shown not to affect the level of output under the Keynes-Kalecki principle of effective demand. However, if real balance effects are strong, dichotomy between prices and quantities ceases to apply, along with Keynes's argument about the ineffectiveness of wage cutting. Mainstream macro models go a step further, replacing effective demand with the equation of exchange, as a simplified representation of the real balance effect. Money wage adjustment now leads to full employment (or at least stable inflation) in steady state. Indeed, in the real business cycle view, only productivity shocks prevent the economy from lodging in long-run equilibrium.

In closing, the chapter's models are used in an appendix to reinterpret and extend the so-called "disequilibrium" but still quite neoclassical macroeconomics popularized by Malinvaud (1977) and applied by many others.

Chapter 4 asks how income redistribution interacts with inflation. We begin with a review of cost-based, "conflicting claims" inflation theories, incorporating worker-capitalist conflict and rules for wage indexation. "Inertial" inflation in which last period's overall inflation rate is an unbiased predictor of all of this period's price increases is pointed out as an interesting (although in practice not very robust) special case.

A simplified conflicting claims model is then put together with a Wicksellian cumulative process inflation, but with the real wage instead of the interest rate as the key variable. The equation of exchange is assumed to hold with constant velocity (if velocity is an increasing function of the inflation rate, we get saddlepoint instability à la the mainstream). The implication is that monetary expansion leads automatically to inflation, with the inflation tax serving as the main macroeconomic adjustment mechanism. The rhetoric of orthodox inflation stabilization in such a framework stresses restriction of monetary emission, but in fact tight money is usually ratified by reducing worker bargaining power and cutting the real wage so that the inflation tax is complemented by forced saving.

In practice, the austerity associated with orthodox stabilization programs typically reduces output, while inflation goes on because of conflicting social claims and indexation mechanisms as emphasized by structuralists. Price freezes and de-indexation (a "heterodox shock") are a recent policy response to this problem, based on inertial inflation theory. By eliminating the inflation tax, the shock stimulates demand. If the real wage rises with output, as is likely, then in a wage-led system demand will rise further still. This positive feedback loop can drive the economy back toward forced saving inflationary adjustment at full capacity (at least for some sectors), a switch in direction that has run recent Latin American stabilization efforts off the rails.

Two appendixes illustrate saddlepath dynamics when velocity depends on the inflation rate, and sketch Wicksell's original model in which the interest rate adjusts to choke off the cumulative process, at least in part.

An investment-driven, non-full employment (i.e., stagnationist) growth model in chapter 5 draws on ideas from chapters 3 and 4 to discuss how different sorts of macro policies affect short-run adjustment and growth prospects over time. On the financial side, the model brings the interest rate and a money demand function together with a money supply process based on government borrowing, while growth is determined by saving and investment functions subject to an evolving real wage.

In the short run, diagrams similar to the IS/LM presentation are used to illustrate possible "crowding-in" and "crowding-out" effects of greater output on capital formation (via interest rate decreases and increases, respectively) as well as inflationary cost-push effects of higher interest charges on loans for working capital. Many long-run results (including the potential instability of heterodox shocks) carry over from chapters 3 and 4 into this new framework, which includes velocity as a stable state variable—a plausible interpretation of its famous relative constancy over time. The model is also used to illustrate financial instability of the type discussed by Minsky, which depends on strong reactions of investors' confidence to crowding-in along a negatively sloped LM schedule. The outcomes can include divergence from macroeconomic equilibrium, limit cycles, or even mathematically chaotic dynamics of real and financial macro variables.

These possibilities are explored further in chapter 6. It describes recent work by several economists who, inspired by Minsky, have developed models of financial fragility, leading to cyclical adjustment or collapse. Their analysis has basically followed two lines, with instability arising due to shifts in a "confidence variable" such as expected future profitability of firms or the expected return to a speculative asset, or else because of changes in firms' balance sheets as they run up debt for investment and other, more speculative purposes (basically an endogenous inside money story).

Instabilities of both sorts are illustrated in the context of financial speculation following in the wake of regressive income redistribution and/or repressed aggregate demand. Portfolios are assumed to comprise money, loans, and a speculative asset called "gold." Redistribution away from wages or tight money causing stagnationist output contraction leads to low investment plus a shift in asset preferences toward gold.

Dynamics in the models hinge around private wealth-holders speculating on increasing gold prices, or firms borrowing more from banks on the basis of their appreciated gold holdings. In either case the resulting increase in the spot gold price can feed back into a speculative boom, possibly accompanied by output stagnation. The boom either continues until the model ceases to apply, chaos ensues, or there is cyclical convergence to a new equilibrium in which increasing financial disintermediation leads to desired portfolio shifts away from gold.

Chapter 7 turns to the problems posed by economic openness in a stylized semi-industrialized country, starting with international trade. Traded
goods take the form of exports and intermediate imports (but no "competitive" imports as in mainstream trade models). Income distribution now
becomes an issue among three parties—domestic wage and profit recipients,
and the rest of the world.

A first result is that currency devaluation is inflationary from the side
of costs, reducing the real wage. By processes similar to forced saving,
output contraction can easily follow if exports are not strongly elastic to
exchange rate increases (or real wage cuts).

It is easy to show from the model that if devaluation is contractionary,
then money wage increases are expansionary—the nominal exchange rate
and wage enter the system symmetrically except for the signs of their
effects. These responses can underlie a stop-go export cycle if the volume
of foreign sales responds to the real exchange rate (the nominal rate
divided by the price level) with a lag. Nominal depreciation then leads
output to decline, meaning that with a Phillips curve the money wage (and
therefore the price level) falls, leading to more depreciation still. The lagged
export reponse may finally restore the activity level, but then wage increases and appreciation can follow, making exports decline. Such fluctuations are by no means unknown in the developing world.

The expansionary money wage increase also means that a tight monetary policy which succeeds in driving down prices and wages to satisfy
the equation of exchange will reduce output and improve the trade account. The contraction could be offset by fiscal expansion, but in an
orthodox stabilization that would be an unusual move. Indeed, with contractionary devaluation one can show that a policy package to improve the
trade balance while holding the activity level constant should combine
depreciation with more fiscal dissaving. In practice, the IMF would contem-
plate such a package with great reserve.

We next bring in capital market considerations—in particular, portfolio
choice by the private sector between assets held domestically and abroad.
The foreign assets can play a role like chapter 7's "gold" in providing a
vehicle for destabilizing speculation. An example is provided by the "orthodox shock" anti-inflation programs which had unhappy results in South
America's "Southern Cone" countries of Argentina, Chile, and Uruguay
during the late 1970s.

Under ongoing inflation the programs were based on slowing a "crawling peg" exchange depreciation scheme to brake inflation via expectational
shifts and the invocation of trade theory's "law of one price" which states

that the domestic price of a traded good should be its world price times the exchange rate. Reducing the speed of depreciation initially makes foreign assets less attractive, leading to capital repatriation and monetary expansion via increased bank reserves. If inflation doesn't slow (as it didn't in the inertial Southern Cone), exchange appreciation also makes output expand. The problem is that the trade deficit gradually widens, making assets abroad look appealing again. Capital flight soon signals speculation against a maxi-devaluation; the resultant further loss in reserves brings it forward in time. When the maxi happens the speculators are rewarded, but the effects on the real side of the economy can be severe. They become so much worse as domestic economic chaos makes renewed capital repatriation an unfavorable investment option indeed.

Chapter 8 continues with these open economy themes, by showing how macro adjustment takes place subject to gap constraints of the sort discussed in section 1.4. The first two restrictions are the mainstream's internal and external balance relations, or the saving and foreign exchange gaps in development economists' jargon. Next comes an investment function building in the crowding-in effect via complementarities of public on private capital formation discussed in section 1.2. Finally, there is a potential contradiction between the inflation rate necessary to achieve macro balance through forced saving and the inflation tax, and structural inflation from the side of costs.

Diagrams are used to illustrate how the economy can adjust via both endogenous variable changes and policy moves to satisfy the saving, foreign resource, and investment gaps, first taken pairwise and then as a set. The inflation gap is brought into the discussion to emphasize the open economy complications of heterodox anti-inflation shocks.

Finally, the methodology of growth projections is considered. The first topic is the potential trade-off in terms of the growth rate between cutting public investment and running a faster inflation to meet foreign resource limits—inflation turns out to be the less costly option. The chapter ends with analysis of the conditions under which ratios of internal and external public debt to the capital stock will not become unbounded. The requirements for boundedness (and thereby avoidance of potential "debt traps") are not likely to be satisfied in many developing countries today.

Chapter 9 is about the fix-price/flex-price model discussed in section 1.4. As we have already observed, there are several cases to which the model applies: the debate between Ricardo and Malthus about the possible effects of repealing the Corn Laws, the Soviet industrialization debate of the 1920s, a model that Kalecki outlined in his Mexico City lectures which emphasizes the role of changing prices of nontraded goods in reaching macro equilibrium (this interpretation anticipated later stories about "Dutch disease" in economies that receive windfall gains in trade), and interactions between the "North" and "South" in the world macroeconomic system.

Simple analytical and graphical tools are set up to analyze the agricultural, traded/nontraded, and North–South examples. The nature of temporary equilibrium in each model is first discussed, followed by exploration of their financial and/or dynamic extensions. For example, will redirecting investment programs in an "agriculture first" strategy of the sort that Chakravarty (1987) suggests for India lead to increased income and slower population growth in the sector (by speeding the demographic transition) or harm peasants by reducing their terms of trade? A two-sector growth model helps illustrate the issues involved.

Next, a model with traded and nontraded sectors is used to illustrate macroeconomic implications of favorable and unfavorable external shocks: In both cases inflation can result. The model also demonstrates how the stagflationary effects of devaluation discussed in chapter 7 carry over when quotas on imports generate "rents" via flexible internal prices charged for the foreign goods by parties holding the quota rights. If the rights become a financial asset, further contractionary channels may open

To close the chapter, a third growth model is deployed to show how Northern and Southern growth and terms of trade interact in the short and medium runs, first without consideration of international finance and then in a version containing interest-sensitive international debt and capital flows.

An appendix is devoted to reinterpretation of the two-gap model in fix-price/flex-price terms. Under strong assumptions the foreign gap is transformed into a market-clearing equation for home goods, with the implication that a "correct" real exchange rate would obviate the disequilibria stressed in chapter 8. Practical reasons why gap problems cannot simply be traced to exchange rate misalignment are pointed out. The role of exchange rate adjustment in equilibrating traded and nontraded goods markets is also considered. When the foreign gap binds, real appreciation results from economic expansion but worsens the external position, reversing the causality of the models in chapter 7.

Fix-price/flex-price models already show how intersectoral linkages can complicate macroeconomic analysis. Chapter 10 discusses four more cases of policy relevance. In these exercises we assume that a sector's capital stock is fixed once it is installed there, while sectoral investment functions respond to profitability signals. Under appropriate stability conditions the system will settle down to a steady state, with all sectors' capital stocks expanding at the same rate.

The first model has only one sector, but two possible production technologies—without and with economies of scale. At an initial equilibrium, the increasing returns to scale (IRS) technique may generate a lower potential profit rate than its constant returns (CRS) alternative—hence it will not be adopted. The CRS equilibrium is locally stable, and a nonmarginal change is required to push the economy into IRS circular flow: Such a possibility of multiple equilibria is characteristic of increasing returns. In the chapter 10 example, progressive income redistribution or a public sector push can provoke a transition, but other possibilities could be modeled as well.

In practice, increasing returns are hard to distinguish from induced technical advance, the focus of the second model. The distinction between stagnationist and exhilarationist aggregate demand responses is important here, since it determines whether faster labor productivity increases raise or lower the capital stock growth rate in steady states. Export-led growth à la South Korea is an exhilarationist outcome, while stagnation may occur in other historical circumstances.

In the third model with two sectors, we ask in temporary equilibrium whether income redistribution toward workers will strongly raise the labor income share, after sectoral outputs adjust in a demand-driven system set up to emphasize compositional effects (markups are assumed equal in both sectors and savings rates of the two classes are the same, but their consumption baskets differ). A tax–transfer program will have distributional leakages if it creates many jobs (a result reminiscent of the paradox of thrift in chapters 2 and 3) but at the same time increase the steady state rate of growth. The moral is that income redistribution and changes in demand composition more generally can have complex effects, a conclusion that would only be strengthened in the presence of economies of scale or induced technical change.

The last model deals with trade policy: In particular, will "equal incentives" or "level playing fields" as advocated by mainstream economists lead to maximization of output growth? A three-sector setup including home goods, an industry substituting intermediate imports, and an export product is used to explore this question. The answer is that there is no particular growth benefit to be expected from noninterventionist trade policy. In other words, industrial strategies aimed at stimulating potential "leading sectors" may make a substantial amount of sense.

Chapter 11 deals with interactions between class conflict and growth, in three complementary models. The first emphasizes how multiple equilibria may exist when there are well-defined classes. The second scenario points out the role of new commodities and class formation in stimulating economic growth, and the third deals with distributional conflict in the long run.

The analysis begins with a restatement of Pasinetti's (1962) class-based growth model, which tends either to a Cambridge equilibrium where the formula growth rate = (capitalists' saving rate) × (profit rate) holds, or else to a Solow-type neoclassical equilibrium, depending on initial differences in savings propensities between classes and the profit-sensitivity of the investment function, in conditions reminiscent of those separating wage- and profit-led regimes in chapters 3 and 4.

Next, a model is developed in which a new sector producing "luxuries" (e.g., scooters and televisions in India today) appears in the economy. If such products are consumed by a new "middle" class and the saving counterpart of the investment required for the new sector comes from that class, then a positive feedback loop is set up via investment demand. It can lead to faster growth and increased overall inequality in the presence of economies of scale, a possibility already noted in chapter 10.

The last example draws on recent Marxist models for rich countries, focusing on the question of why their growth slowed after 20 years of historically unprecedented expansion in the wake of World War II. Different schools emphasize the effects of changes in the income distribution on either investment incentives or labor militancy. The implications of these differing views are illustrated in the Kaleckian framework used throughout this book.

2

Short-Run Model
Closures and Steady
State Growth

In this and the following chapter we look from different angles at how to specify causal relationships among price and quantity variables in a one-sector macroeconomic model. As argued in chapter 1, defining relevant social classes and stating how they influence determination of prices and quantities is fundamental to the structuralist approach—its implications are explored for very simple model structures here.

We begin by analyzing the comparative static properties of the models in the short run, presupposing that they are in "equilibrium" in the sense that a consistent solution to a model's equations exists and is actually in force.[1] Section 2.1 takes up the basics of macroeconomic adjustment, and section 2.2 considers additional mechanisms through which equilibrium may be attained. The discussion is first set up in algebraic terms, and then illustrated with diagrams in section 2.3. The figures also help illustrate how short-run model solutions extend to the long period in which equilibrium is conventionally represented by a growth model in steady state. Appendix 2.A informally brings an extension of Ramsey's (1928) optimal saving model into this discussion, while appendix 2.B explores the interesting bypath of potential long-run instability in the popular overlapping generations growth model, a variant of the Mill-Marshall-Solow specification discussed in the main text.

2.1 Macro Causality in the One-Sector Economy

Structuralists usually assume that macroeconomic causality runs broadly from demand injections to leakages under conditions of passive money supply.[2] They treat the extended functional distribution and at least some sectors' outputs as endogenous in their macro models, subject to rules such as markups and fix-price/flex-price distinctions (see chapter 9) regarding value adjustment. Neoclassicals, by contrast, typically presuppose full labor employment and capacity utilization under an active money supply that fixes the overall price level. They root their firms upon cost and input demand functions derived from clever optimization games.

Maintained hypotheses as diverse as these have notable effects upon the different models' qualitative results. For example, greater investment demand in a structuralist model will make output rise and/or the income distribution shift to generate the complementary saving supply. With available saving determined from full employment output, distribution, and prices (or the forces of "productivity and thrift") in a neoclassical world, an upward jump in investment is an impossible event. Such distinct outcomes arise throughout nonstructuralist and structuralist policy analyses, as we will see in discussing the contrasting effects under different causal schemes of exogenous changes in the income distribution as well as higher government spending, currency devaluation (in chapter 7), and other policy moves.

In the jargon, we want to define "closures" of a one-sector macro model, to adopt a methodology from Sen (1963) and a term from Taylor and Lysy (1979). Formally, prescribing closure boils down to stating which variables are endogenous or exogenous in an equation system largely based upon macroeconomic accounting identities, and figuring out how they influence one another. When one is setting up a practical model for any economy, the closure question becomes less abstract and of much greater economic interest, transforming itself to one of empirically plausible signs of "effects" and—more important—a perception of what are the driving macroeconomic forces in the system. A sense of institutions and history necessarily enters into any serious discussion of macro causality. We can easily run through the algebra here; the models in this book give examples of applied institutional perspective.

Table 2.1 sets the stage in an economy without foreign trade and in which monetary linkages are ignored. It contains two similar but not identical macro models—the neoclassical version to the right is more internally constrained or closed than the one with markup pricing. Properties of different closures can be illustrated by adding restrictions to the seven that appear, but first the table itself should be explained.

Consumption C, investment I, and government spending G are the only components of demand, meaning that the material balance condition in value terms (with output X at the price level P) is[3]

$$PC + PI + PG - PX = 0. \tag{1}$$

As written, this equation signifies that excess commodity demand vanishes.

Table 2.1
Basic macroeconomic relationships for a one-sector model

Markup pricing	Neoclassical cost function
(1.1) $P = (1 + \tau)wb = wb/(1 - \pi)$	$P = f(w, rP)$
(1.2) $L/X = b$	$L/X = f_\omega(\omega, r)$
(1.3) $u = X/K$	$u = X/K$
(1.4) $r = [\tau/1 + \tau)]u = \pi u$	$K/X = f_r(\omega, r)$

Investment-saving balance
(1.5) $g^s = sr = s\pi u$
(1.6) $g^i = g^i(r, u) = g^i(\pi, u)$
(1.7) $\gamma + g^i - g^s = 0$

Definitions
$\pi = rPK/PX = \tau/(1 + \tau), \qquad \omega = w/P = (1 - \pi)/b, \qquad \gamma = PG/PK$

In what follows, we interpret it both as an ex post accounting relationship that will be observed in well-defined national income and product accounts, and as a necessary condition for macroeconomic balance. In an economy closed to foreign trade, macro balance does *not* presuppose either full capacity use or full employment of labor (the two are *not* the same thing). Output can in principle be determined by either effective demand or input supply (including available foreign exchange if the economy is open to trade).

For simplicity, we consolidate incomes of firms and rentiers. Then (ignoring intermediate inputs and indirect taxes), the income statement is

$$PX = wbX + rPK, \tag{2}$$

where w is the money wage rate, b the labor/output ratio, r the profit rate, and K the capital stock (assumed to be made from the same "stuff" as output in this one-sector model).

The saving rate from profit incomes rPK is s. We set workers' saving to zero, without much loss of generality in analyzing current output-expenditure interactions so long as the saving rate from wages is well less than that from profits.[4] Total consumption becomes

$$PC = wbX + (1 - s)rPK. \tag{3}$$

Combining equations (1) through (3) gives

$$PG + PI - srPK = 0. \tag{4}$$

This equality of private saving to investment plus government spending (or, more generally, the current fiscal deficit or public dissaving[5]) is a familiar condition for macro balance. It is clearly not independent of the material balance condition (1)—one is derived by accounting manipulation from the other.

Closure rules in a one-sector system are easier to illustrate if the foregoing equations are restated in a normalized or "intensive" form, with all nominal income and expenditure flows divided by the value of the capital stock PK.[6] We let $g^s = srPK/PK = sr$ and $g^i = PI/PK$ stand, respectively, for the capital stock growth rate permitted by national saving and created by investment demand (ignoring depreciation). Also let $\gamma = PG/PK$ (i.e., government outlay relative to the capital stock). Then the macro equilibrium condition (4) can be written in the form $\gamma + g^i - g^s = 0$, or equation (1.7) of table 2.1. The growth rates possible from saving and investment appear in lines (1.5) and (1.6).

The arguments in the investment function are quite standard. We use the output\capital ratio $u = X/K$ to measure capacity utilization. As an argument in (1.6), u represents a contemporaneous version of the accelerator, introduced by Kaldor (1940) and Steindl (1952). It basically makes investment respond to short-run economic activity. The profit rate r in (1.6) can be interpreted as an index of expected future returns, on the basis of either common sense or by invoking firms' dynamic expectations and optimizations as in the q investment theory proposed by Tobin (1969) and acolytes and (with less fanfare) Minsky (1975). Alternatively, r is a proxy for firms' available cash flow when investment is largely self-financed under credit rationing. Since table 2.1 is set up for an economy without money, we postpone discussion of the effects of the interest rate on investment demand to appendix 2.A and chapter 5.

As the table headings indicate, we work with two pricing theories—contrasting assumptions about pricing rules and the presence or absence of full employment or capacity use will provide the gist for the discussion that follows. On the left, the markup rule after the first equality in row (1.1) simply states that output prices are based on variable costs (here, of labor) with producers taking a margin at rate τ.

Markup pricing equations have the advantage of fitting the data, at least in nonprimary goods producing sectors where producers' margins are often stable. There is no dearth of theoretical explanations for both the level and stability of τ. They may follow from considerations of market power (Kalecki 1971; Sylos-Labini 1984); efficiency wages (Bowles and Boyer 1990); setting prices high enough to generate corporate savings sufficient to finance the bulk of planned capital formation (Duesenberry 1958; Eichner 1980); or ease of internal coordination in multiproduct, multiplant firms (Semmler 1984). The presence of a markup can thus be supported by optimizing models or—more plausibly—by empirical observation of enterprises and common sense. Its rate may change with the current macro situation, institutional evolution, and redistributive policy, as the models in the following chapters emphasize.

Following down the left-hand column, in line (1.2) employment is L and the labor/output ratio is b, and the output/capital ratio u is formally defined in (1.3). With regard to (1.4), it is easy to see from (1.1) that the share of profits in output is $\pi = rPK/PX = \tau/(1 + \tau)$. Since the profit rate is the product of the profit share and the output/capital ratio u, (1.4) follows directly. This definition leads to the second formulation of markup pricing in row (1.1) which restates the identity $PX = wbX + \pi PX$. It also implies that investment in (1.6) can be treated in formal terms as a function of π (instead of r) and u, although, as Marglin and Bhaduri (1990) emphasize, one should be careful about the signs of partial derivatives when undertaking such terminological shifts.

The markup model (1.1)–(1.7) is a full macro system. It is of interest because markup pricing imposes few restrictions on supply. The markup rate τ and profit share π follow from institutions and policy, while the labor use coefficient b comes from technology and market custom. There is no mechanism stated so far via which τ (or other distributional parameters such as π) and b interact. Such independence of distribution and resource allocation does not occur in the neoclassical model of the right-hand columns of table 2.1 (as well as in markup formulations based on an efficiency wage such as Bowles and Boyer's).

Equation (1.1) in the neoclassical model is a cost function. When production takes place under constant returns to scale (the standard hypothesis), the function f will be homogeneous; that is, it can be written as

$$1 = f(\omega, r), \tag{5}$$

where $\omega = w/P$ is the real wage. This version is often called a "factor-price frontier" since it sets up an inverse relationship between the real wage ω and the profit rate r. We will see below that this characteristically neoclassical (or neo-Marxian) trade-off need not occur in a demand-driven markup model.

When some degree of input substitution is assumed, neoclassical equations (1.2) and (1.4) are based on a relationship known as Shepard's lemma (cf. Varian 1984, pp. 54–57), which states that factor input ratios are equal to the partial derivatives of the cost function, f_ω and f_r. Equation (1.2) ties the labor/output ratio to the real wage—if ω rises, L/X goes down. For a given output level, greater employment is necessarily associated with a lower real wage—another strong distributional result.

Finally, note that the cost function (1.1) and the marginal productivity conditions (1.2) and (1.4) imply (and are jointly implied by) the existence of a constant returns production function, $X = g(L, K)$. When marginal productivity rules for input demands are postulated, a neoclassical model can be set up around either a production or cost function. For comparison with markup pricing, the latter is more convenient to use.

The causal structure of both versions rests on determination of price and input-output relationships from (1.1)–(1.4), and the level of demand from (1.4)–(1.7). How the two sets of equations interact is determined by additional restrictions, or closure. We discuss three standard cases— models characterized by output adjustment, forced saving, and determination of investment by saving supply—and in the following section consider additional adjustment mechanisms through which rigidities of the last version can be relaxed.

Output Adjustment

Assume that in the markup model the nominal wage w is fixed by historical wage bargains and custom, the capital stock K by previous investment, and government spending G and (for the given K) the spending ratio γ by policy. Then with a fixed markup rate τ, the price level P and the income distribution follow from (1.1). The demand equations (1.5)–(1.7) and the distributional identity (1.4) jointly determine r and u. Output X follows from (1.3) and employment L from (1.2). We have a macro system in which causality runs toward employment and output from the side of demand; output is implicitly assumed to lie below the full capacity level κK determined by the available capital stock. A classic formulation of the markup causal scheme is by Kalecki (1971).

The neoclassical story is similar, but more tightly constrained. Only γ, w, and K can be predetermined—distributional variables such as τ, the profit share π, and the real wage ω are endogenous to the system. This complication is reflected in the fact that (1.1) must be combined with (1.4)–(1.7) to solve jointly for u, r, and ω. Output and employment follow from (1.3) and (1.2) as before, while (1.1) gives the price level. Without benefit of his characteristic subtlety, one can interpret Keynes's (1936) *General Theory* model of the real side of the economy as comprising the neoclassical equations (1.1)–(1.7) closed from the side of demand. Graphical solutions are presented below and in chapter 3.

Comparative statics of the two versions can be illustrated with three experiments: changing government dissaving γ, the money wage w, and the real wage ω.

In both versions a higher value of γ raises u and X through a multiplier process that converges so long as saving supply increases more strongly than investment demand as a function of u—a Harrodian stability condition explored in chapter 3. In the neoclassical model, (1.1) can be inserted into (1.4) to eliminate ω. The upshot is a positive relationship between r and u. But then from (1.1) stated as the factor-price frontier (5), ω must fall as u goes up. An increased demand injection is associated with greater output and a lower real wage, with decreasing returns setting in as more labor is combined with the available capital stock. Since the nominal wage is fixed, P must rise to reduce ω—the demand injection drives up the price level as well as output.

Neither the real wage decrease nor the price increase occurs in the markup model, since τ is set from the outside and diminishing returns do not set in so long as capacity exceeds output. A demand injection could cause real wage *increases* and price *de*flation (at least with respect to money wages) if the markup rate is an inverse function of u, as some evidence suggests (Schor 1985).

A change in the money wage w has no real effects in the markup system. From (1.1), P just adjusts in proportion, and the real side is unchanged. The neoclassical equations can easily be seen to depend only on ω or w/P; therefore the same conclusion applies. For a given level of effective demand (i.e., γ), the real wage is an outcome of the neoclassical model. Hence money wage changes will affect only the price level and not employment. This is basically Keynes's argument about the uselessness of money wage reduction in chapter 19 of *General Theory*, illustrated in detail in chapter 3.

Since the real wage is endogenous in the neoclassical system, it cannot be shifted exogenously in a thought experiment. In the markup model, if the rate τ is changed by macroeconomic shocks or policy (price controls, revised public enterprise charges, trade policy, etc.), the real wage will also move. As noted in chapter 1, a real wage increase may make capacity utilization go either up or down. It will fall if there is a small differential between rentiers' and workers' saving shares and/or the responsiveness of investment demand to the profit share is strong. When saving propensities from capital and labor incomes sharply differ, real wage increases will stimulate output if investment responds vigorously to the consumption surge that redistribution toward low-saving workers will trigger. Through the same linkage, capital stock growth may be faster. Finally, if u goes up more than π falls after redistribution, the profit rate r will rise. Such an outcome is ruled out by the inverse trade-off between ω and r imposed by the factor-price frontier in a neoclassical specification.[7]

Forced Saving

Forced saving occurs when u and X cannot vary, for instance, because the economy is at full capacity (u is at its "technical" maximum κ) or employment L is predetermined at a "full" level or otherwise. In what follows, we concentrate on closure by a fixed L, but the line of analysis extends to any supply-side restriction on output, such as due to available capital, foreign exchange (see chapter 8), or a labor supply function like $L = L(\omega, X, K)$. A surplus labor specification, for example, would make L highly elastic to the real wage, effectively setting ω. Such an assumption underlies the neo-Marxian growth model, illustrated graphically in section 2.3.

In the markup model setting employment exogenously adds a restriction to (1.1)–(1.7). In algebraic terms, the system becomes overdetermined, and some variable must become endogenous to meet the new constraint. If incipient excess demand with fixed output leads to upward pressure on prices, the obvious candidate for endogeneity is the markup rate τ, and thereby the price level P from (1.1). The causal structure is that L determines X in (1.2), and then (1.3) sets u. The demand equations (1.5)–(1.7) give the profit rate r that balances saving and investment at the supply-determined level of u. The markup rate then comes from (1.4) and P from (1.1). Through price movements relative to the fixed money wage (presupposing a greater saving propensity from profits than wages), the income distribution adjusts endogenously to force the creation of enough saving to meet the new injection of demand.

In the neoclassical version, (1.1) and (1.4)–(1.7) determine u, r, and ω as in the output adjustment closure. But then the model falls apart. Equations (1.2) and (1.3) give inconsistent values for X—the only recourse is that one equation be dropped. Two excisions generally appear in the literature. The first is to leave out the investment demand function, with implications to be taken up below. The other is to omit (1.2) and replace

(1.4) by the identity $r = \pi u$. These moves are tantamount to abandoning marginal productivity input demand functions and returning to the markup system.

This forced retreat underscores Kaldor's (1956) doubts about the usefulness of distribution theory based on marginal productivity; it also illustrates why implementation of a Schumpeterian innovation via credit creation and forced saving is a disequilibrium process from the neoclassical perspective. Alternatively, forced saving can be viewed as a macro adjustment scenario in which the neoclassical combination of output and price increases in response to higher demand degenerates into a pure price (and distribution) change when output is determined from the side of supply.

This last observation leads into comparative statics in the markup model. With u fixed, if the demand injection γ increases, then in (1.5)–(1.7) the profit rate is the free variable that goes up to provide the corresponding saving supply. From (1.4) and (1.1) the markup and price level rise and the real wage goes down. Reduced real spending on the part of wage earners caused by higher prices is the adjustment vehicle.

Since τ follows from effective demand, a money wage increase would just drive up the price level proportionally under forced saving. A worse outcome could befall an attempt at redistribution. Suppose in a simple case that investment is stable at the level $\bar{g}$ and that a tax $trPK$ is levied on profit income and transferred to wage earners. Saving-investment balance becomes $r = \bar{g}/s(1 - t)$. The profit rate rises along with the tax rate increase, and the real wage correspondingly falls.

Straightforward manipulation shows that the derivative of real posttransfer income per worker [which is $(w + trPK/L)/P$] with respect to t is $-t/(1 - t)$. If there is an existing tax-cum-transfer in place, increasing its rate worsens the position of wage earners. This is an example of the so-called paradox of thrift that accompanies forced saving. It bedevils any transfer attempt when output is at an upper bound.

In closing, note that although forced saving has been described here in terms of wages and profits, similar redistributional effects can occur among any number of saving flows. Applied models will include saving from one or more income classes, the rest of the world, and the government. Movements in financial surpluses (saving less investment) as prices shift will differ across these classes and institutions, allowing forced saving to occur. The presence of flows fixed in nominal terms—transfers and state spending are common examples—makes redistribution induced by changing prices even more important.

Determination of Investment by Saving

Forced saving provides one means for accommodating a labor supply function into the macro system. As we have already noted, dropping the independent investment demand function (1.6) is another. This artifice is widely used. For example, it is the heart of the Solow's (1956) neoclassical growth model which lies squarely in the Mill-Marshall tradition discussed in chapter 1.

Causal links are straightforward. In the markup model, K, L, w, and τ are predetermined. In table 2.1, P comes from (1.1), X from (1.2), u from (1.3), r from (1.4), and g^s from (1.5). In a savings-driven economy there is no room for (1.6), so that capital stock growth g^i comes from (1.7). The solution of the neoclassical version is similar, except that as usual there is no room for a predetermined distributional index such as τ. With w fixed, equations (1.1)–(1.4) solve jointly for P, X, r, and u, and the story thereafter goes as in the markup model.

Output, income distribution, and saving all come from the supply side in the neoclassical version of this closure, which emphasizes productivity and thrift. A higher value of γ reduces g^i from (1.7)—government spending "crowds out" investment demand. The real wage can't be altered, and a money wage increase reflects itself solely in higher prices.

The markup model also demonstrates a pure price increase from a higher money wage and investment crowding-out by γ. A real wage increase is represented by a lower τ. From (1.4) and (1.5) the profit rate and saving supply fall. Hence (1.7) shows that the growth rate must decline. Such outcomes are opposite those possible in the output adjustment closure discussed above. To reiterate, with potential results so different, empirical awareness and institutional understanding of the economy are required to judge how an apposite macro model should be closed.

2.2   Additional Adjustment Mechanisms

Since the publication of *The General Theory*, mainstream macroeconomics has devoted great efforts toward putting independent investment demand and labor supply functions into the same model—its theoretical pursuit of equilibrium full employment (ideally to be induced by real wage cuts) does not cease. In terms of table 2.1, this quest takes the form of adding endogenous variables or by postulating new adjustment mechanisms. The examples discussed in this section have all influenced neoclassical macroeconomic analysis. They appear less frequently in models designed by structuralists, who are not wedded to the idea that full employment of resources is an everyday aspect of the macroeconomic system.

Adding Endogenous Variables to the System

In table 2.1, suppose that the investment demand function (1.6) is reinstated along with predetermined employment but that γ is endogenous. Then all equations can be retained, with γ coming from (1.7). The interpretation is that the government regulates its spending to ensure full employment. Another possibility would be for the government to adjust some tax variable (e.g., the rate t in the tax-*cum*-transfer program discussed above) to the same end. The spending scenario is spelled out in Meade (1961), while Johansen (1960) implicitly used an endogenous income tax to permit both an independent investment function and full employment in the first practical computable general equilibrium macro model.

Loanable Funds

Changes in "the" interest rate (e.g., i) mediate an adjustment mechanism that has been suggested at least since Thornton's day. If the saving rate s rises as a function of i, while investment demand g^i declines, then all seven equations of table 2.1 comprise a well-behaved system. An exogenous increase in γ will make the left-hand side of (1.7) positive, and i will increase to restore equilibrium by cutting investment and inducing extra saving. Optimal saving models with a superficially independent investment function rely on such an adjustment mechanism, as we will see in appendix 2.A. They add a loan market subplot to the main theme of Mill, Marshall, and Solow's macroeconomic play.

The loanable funds story sounds sensible, but it is subject to at least two objections (both emphasized by Keynes). The first is structural. Rates of return to assets in principle are determined in markets for stocks, not by savings and investment flows. The more serious question is about the *strength* of interest rate effects. There is not much evidence in the Third World that overall saving responds to interest rate movements (although portfolio compositions certainly do). With much investment controlled by the state and large enterprises with good access to finance, interest rate effects on aggregate demand will be limited to only part of gross capital formation (housing construction?) and perhaps consumer purchases of durable goods. Empirical questions obviously arise, but low elasticities can cripple adjustment based on interest rate movements.

The Real Balance Effect

If output is predetermined and there is an independent investment function, consumption is the main demand component that must vary to permit macro equilibrium. If consumer demand is an inverse function of the price level, the linkage is straightforward: Increased investment crowds out consumption by driving prices up. As noted in the last section, forced saving provides such a linkage, but it lost theoretical favor (apart from Kaldor and colleagues) 50 years ago. In contemporary macroeconomics its place is taken by the real balance effect.

The story is familiar, although, as we will see, it leads toward an overdetermined model in a neoclassical specification. It rests upon an exogenous money supply, say, M. A price increase will reduce national wealth by eroding "real balances," M/P. Wealth-holders might be expected to try to restore their position by saving more; hence the saving rate becomes $s = s(M/P)$. A higher P cuts consumption by increasing the saving rate. Crowding-out by rising prices becomes feasible again.

Comparative statics of the real balance effect are worked out in chapter 3. The key result in a markup model is that money wage cuts can raise output from the demand side by reducing P—this is the reason why the real balance story is congenial to the mainstream. With neoclassical price formation, an even stronger result emerges. Marginal productivity rules plus full employment determine the real wage w/P. But if P varies to bring demand into line with predetermined supply by altering real balances, then there is no room in the neoclassical specification for independent determination of the money wage w! How wage changes are neutralized by neoclassicals in the long run is also taken up in chapter 3.

The Inflation Tax

The inflation tax is a dynamic version of the real balance effect, already sketched in chapter 1 and developed more fully in chapter 4. The effect at times is practically relevant, for example, in the consumption surges that have followed attempts to stabilize inflations by banning indexed contracts and imposing price controls (Taylor 1988a). For that reason it makes sense to merge an inflation tax with structuralist inflation theories emphasizing distributional conflict and propagation mechanisms in applied models. See chapters 4, 5, and 8.

Positive Effects of Inflation on Demand

Finally, inflation may activate demand. Suppose that i, the nominal loan rate of interest, is pegged or comes from the financial side of the economy. Then faster inflation reduces the real rate $i - \hat{P}$, perhaps stimulating capital formation. If this possibility is deemed relevant, it is easy enough to build into an investment function. The same observation obviously applies to effects of inflation on competitive imports, demand for consumer durables, the efficiency of tax collection,[8] or other variables.

2.3 Graphical Representations and Growth

The foregoing arguments are easy to summarize in diagrams. One approach is adopted here, and another in chapters 3 and 4. We first describe equilibrium in the short run and then show how growth models converging to steady state solutions emerge from the various closures.

Figure 2.1 illustrates macro equilibrium under a markup pricing specification. For simplicity we write the investment demand function as

$$g^i = g_0 + \alpha r + \beta u$$

$$= g_0 + \left[\alpha + \left(\frac{\beta}{\pi}\right)\right] r = g_0 + (\alpha \pi + \beta)u. \tag{6}$$

The topmost quadrant to the right plots potential capital stock growth as a function of the profit rate. Equilibrium is defined by the intersection of the schedules for saving leakages g^s and demand injections $g^i + \gamma$ (two levels of investment demand are shown). In the quadrant just below, capacity use is related to the profit rate by the rule $r = \pi u$ until a capacity limit $\bar{u}$ is reached. To the right of the kink at $\bar{u}$, r and π vary independently of u. The lowest quadrant shows that the real wage ω (and therefore the markup rate τ and profit share π) is constant for $u \leqslant \bar{u}$; then it becomes a decreasing function of r as forced saving applies with a binding output constraint. Finally, in the quadrant to the left, the labor/capital ratio $L/K = bu$ increases with u until $u = \bar{u}$. For later use, let λ stand for L/K.

The intersection of $g^i_1 + \gamma$ with g^s depicts a closure in which output adjustment reigns. A small increase in γ will shift the injection schedule up,

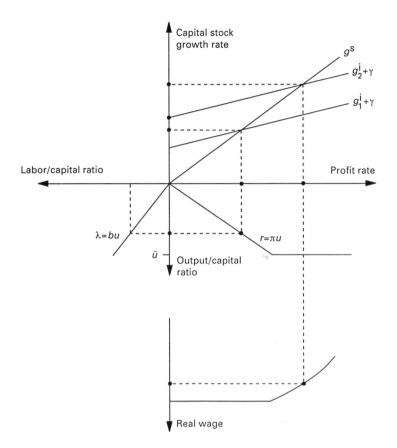

Figure 2.1
Markup macroeconomic equilibrium

causing g, u, and λ to rise with a constant real wage. With a predetermined π, the macro equilibrium will be stable when the condition $(s - \alpha)\pi - \beta > 0$ applies. An overly strong investment response to an increase in u can create short-run Harrodian instability, as noted in chapter 1. Figure 2.1 shows the stable case; instability would require $g_1^i + \gamma$ to have a steeper slope than g^s.

The intersection of $g_2^i + \gamma$ with g^s corresponds to a forced saving model. A higher γ initially shifts the injection schedule upward, causing g, r, and u to rise while ω declines. Final equilibrium is reached after an upward re-adjustment of $g_2^i + \gamma$ which is induced by the rise in π corresponding to the lower real wage. The new solution will be stable in the short run when $s > \alpha$. Through the coefficient α, excessive responsiveness of investment to a higher profit share is destabilizing when u is at an upper bound $\bar{u}$. Harrodian hyperinflation with an ever-increasing profit share can arise when this condition is violated, as discussed in chapters 3 and 4.

The model with neoclassical price formation is illustrated in the right-hand quadrants in figure 2.2; the story combines output and forced saving adjustments as discussed above. The main contrast with figure 2.1 is that the kinks at $u = \bar{u}$ have been replaced by smooth curves indicating that the profit rate is an increasing function of capacity utilization, while r and ω trade off inversely along the factor price frontier. An increase in γ now causes g, r, and u to rise and ω to decline.

The quadrant to the left shows that u ($= X/K$) rises smoothly with the labor/capital ratio λ along a neoclassical production function. This observation becomes of interest when we switch closures in the model. Suppose that instead of reading the diagram clockwise in an investment-determined scenario, we trace causality counterclockwise from a predetermined level of λ. Now u follows from the identity $\lambda = bu$, determining r which in turns sets ω and g^s. As we have already noted, there is no room in this Mill-Marshall-Solow reading for an independent investment function: g^i must adjust to satisfy the macro balance condition $g^i + \gamma - g^s = 0$. The injection schedule $g^i + \gamma$ can be viewed as sliding up and down until it meets g^s at the supply-determined profit rate r. The resulting capital stock growth rate g varies to ensure steady state stability in Solow's (1956) mainstream standard model.

In formal terms, the usual approach to stability analysis in growth models is to assume that short-run variables, such as the ones pictured in figures 2.1 and 2.2, converge "rapidly" to equilibrium as functions of one or more "state variables" set up as ratios of two growing quantities. The time

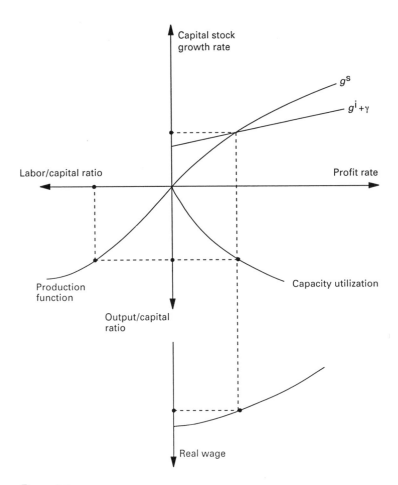

Figure 2.2
Neoclassical macroeconomic equilibrium

derivative of each state variable comes from short-run equilibrium. When it is equal to zero, both the numerator and denominator will be growing at the same rate—this is a steady state that can be used to characterize the economy in the long run. Two exercises in stability analysis are built into this procedure, namely, for the short-run adjustment and the steady state. The implicit time frame for the former might be months or quarters, and years or decades for the steady state. Presumably a steady state is not worth investigating if the economy is not stable in the short run.

For the Solow model the capital/labor ratio K/L is usually adopted as the state variable, but since it already appears in figures 2.1 and 2.2, we work with its inverse $\lambda = L/K$. The relevant differential equation is

$$\dot{\lambda} = \lambda[\hat{L} - g(\lambda)],\qquad\qquad\qquad (7)$$

where the employment (= population) growth rate $\hat{L}$ is predetermined, setting the "natural" rate of growth.

Suppose that $g < \hat{L}$. Then $\dot{\lambda} > 0$, and the consequent increase in λ will lead in figure 2.2 to higher values of u, r, and g in the counterclockwise reading. The upshot is that g is an increasing function of λ, so that in equation (7), $d\dot{\lambda}/d\lambda < 0$ around the rest point where $g = \hat{L}$. The implications are that λ is locally stable, and that marginal productivity rules and the cost function determine long-run distribution from its value at steady state.

Solow emphasized the role of real wage (and more generally, price) adjustment in leading to full employment steady state growth, but figure 2.2 suggests that wage changes are a sideshow in the southeast corner. Indeed, in the constant markup area of figure 2.1 (with causality running counterclockwise and the independent investment function suppressed), it can be seen that a reduction in λ will lead u, r, and g to decline in the short run. Thereby steady state growth equilibrium is stable in a price-*insensitive*, saving-driven model. Short- and long-run distribution both follow from the predetermined markup rate τ.

The moral is that the key to stability in saving-driven models is the determination of accumulation by saving supply (as an increasing function of capacity utilization or the profit rate), not flexible prices. Another reading of figure 2.2 would set the real wage in the southeast quadrant, say, from "class struggle" in a neo-Marxian closure of the sort discussed by Sen (1963), Marglin (1984), and Dutt (1990). Again, there is no room for an independent investment function, as u, λ, r, and g all follow from ω. Capital stock growth g will in general not be the same as the natural growth rate $\hat{L}$, which eventually may lead the model to break down.[9]

As we have discussed, forced saving permits an independent investment function to be combined with full employment. Kaldor's (1957) growth model is the dynamic version of this closure. Omitting an unconvincing (indeed, un-Kaldorian!) justification for the full employment assumption, his short-run story can be read from figure 2.1. Capacity utilization $\bar{u}$ follows from the full employment level of λ in a counterclockwise reading of the southwest quadrant based on the relationship $u = \lambda/b = \xi\lambda$, where ξ is the output/labor ratio or average labor productivity. The capital stock growth rate and the profit rate and share are determined by the intersection of $g_2^i + \gamma$ with g^s as outlined above. For a given level of u, the explicit solutions for π and g are

$$\pi = \frac{\gamma + g_0 + \beta u}{(s - \alpha)u} \tag{8}$$

and

$$g = \frac{s}{s - \alpha}(g_0 + \beta u) + \frac{\alpha}{s - \alpha}\gamma, \tag{9}$$

where g_0, α, and β are the parameters of the investment function (6) above. As argued in section 2.1, these relationships are inconsistent with marginal productivity distribution theory in the short run.

Kaldor's (1961) stylized facts about advanced economies included a stable output/capital ratio and profit rate combined with steady increases in labor productivity and the capital/labor ratio over time. He tied up the latter two observations in a "technical progress function" $\xi = f(K/L)$, or

$$\hat{\xi} = \phi_0 + \phi_1(g - \hat{L}) \tag{10}$$

in growth rate form: ϕ_0 is a trend rate of productivity growth, while ϕ_1 shows how productivity responds to growth in the capital/labor ratio.

The natural state variable for the Kaldor model is the output/capital ratio u. If its differential equation is stable, u presumably will not differ greatly from its value at steady state, fitting the stylized fact. Since $u = \xi\lambda$, using (10) its growth rate $\hat{u}$ is given by

$$\hat{u} = (1 - \phi_1)(\hat{L} - g) + \phi_0 \tag{11}$$

$$= (1 - \phi_1)\left[\hat{L} - \frac{s}{s - \alpha}(g_0 + \beta u) - \frac{\alpha}{s - \alpha}\gamma\right] + \phi_0.$$

So long as $\phi_1 < 1$ and $s > \alpha$, the second line shows that $\hat{u}$ is an inverse function of u, so the differential equation is locally stable and the economy converges to a steady state. From the first line of (11), the long-run, natural rate of growth when $\hat{u} = 0$ is

$$g = \hat{L} + \frac{\phi_0}{1 - \phi_1},$$

which depends only on population expansion and the parameters of the technical progress function. The steady state output/capital ratio and profit share follow, respectively, from equations (9) and (8) for g and π above. If there is no government dissaving ($\gamma = 0$), equations (1.5)–(1.7) of table 2.1 show that the Cambridge equation $g = sr = s\pi u$ determines long-run income distribution from the steady state values of r, π, and u. In other words, the profit rate and share are stable.[10]

All in all, Kaldor's logic elegantly ties together the stylized facts that he built in. As noted in chapter 1, it also anticipates by three decades recent neoclassical treatments of endogenous technical change. These start from the Ramsey (1928) growth model, an exercise in convex optimal control theory outlined in appendix 2.A. For its saddlepoint extremals to exist, the model requires a production function of the form $X = f(aK, bL)$ with constant or decreasing returns to scale in its "effective" capital and labor inputs aK and bL.

The neoclassical track follows Kaldor's equation (10) by noting that if the scale coefficients are tied to existing input stocks by rules such as $a = a(K, L)$, $b = b(K, L)$ which are *not* perceived by individual producing firms, there is an "externality" or "scale economy" that gives overall increasing returns in the production of X (Romer 1986; Lucas 1988). The Ramsey model can then be solved with the scale functions a and b parametrically prescribed.

Alternatively, one might make $\hat{a}$ or $\hat{b}$ depend on X, K, and/or L in a more dynamic story (Krugman 1987; Lucas 1988). Either way, since both productivity and inputs increase over time in a buoyant economy, R^2's for econometric equations incorporating these formulations will be high. As Kaldor willingly recognized, whether a regression fallacy or a causal relationship is reflected in the 'metrics is a doubt that only firm or plant level evidence can resolve. The answer, more often than not, is in the affirmative.

Finally—and with more relevance to developing economies—we can consider capital stock growth when there is an independent investment function and the labor force is *not* constrained by available supply. At present, the existence of readily employable labor is probably not a bad assumption in most of the advanced industrial economies of Western Europe and is certainly a good one in the developing world (especially for those countries afflicted with IMF-style austerity programs in recent years). There are two cases to consider—when output adjusts in Keynes/Kalecki fashion, and when it is limited by factors such as available capital stock or foreign exchange.

The first case comprises "stagnationist" growth models of the sort described in chapter 1.[11] Assuming that the investment function (6) applies and that the overall saving rate $s(\pi)$ depends on the profit share (as it will in chapter 3 when different, nonzero saving propensities from profit and wage income are considered), then the macro balance condition in the short run is

$$\gamma + g_0 + (\alpha\pi + \beta)u - s(\pi)u = 0.$$

Solving for u in this expression and substituting back into the investment function shows that the capital stock growth rate will be

$$g = \frac{(\alpha\pi + \beta)\gamma + s(\pi)g_0}{s(\pi) - (\alpha\pi + \beta)}. \tag{12}$$

With a given profit share or real wage, g from (12) is set in the short run. However, as we will see in the following chapters, there are reasons to believe that these distributional indicators move over time (as can other variables affecting growth such as the interest rate, exchange rate, asset stocks, etc.). As they change, then so will the growth rate; for example, in (12) g is a function of π which in turn evolves according to its own proper dynamics.

A steady state is reached in a stagnationist model when the dynamic process for the profit share (and other variables affecting g) reaches a point at which $\hat{\pi} = 0$ (and similarly for other state variables). Across steady states, g can vary, which is not the case in employment-constrained growth. Stagnationist models are useful for asking how certain policies affect prospects for sustained economic expansion. A question relevant for the 1990s is whether there is a natural way for austerity programs of the IMF type to lead an economy through a period of recession back to an acceptable rate of growth. The answer to this particular query usually turns out to be no.

If output is restricted by capital stock or foreign exchange, growth models involving short-run adjustment via forced saving and/or the inflation tax naturally apply; the growth rate will come from an equation like (9) with u predetermined in the short run. Again, u and other variables such as the inflation and exchange rates can adjust over time between different steady states across which g can vary; As we will see in chapters 4 and 8, hyperinflations and/or foreign exchange crises arise naturally in such models, as they do frequently in the developing world.

Appendix 2.A   The Ramsey Optimal Saving Model

In the 1830s the ingenious Irish mathematician William Rowan Hamilton devised an elegant formulation of Newtonian dynamics in dual sets of differential equations for a particle's location and momentum. The first set restated Newton's second law: Rate of change of momentum = force. The second said that the rate of change of the particle's position = momentum/mass. About a century later Frank Ramsey (1928) further restated Hamilton's problem in the calculus of variations for economists' benefit. In his version the particle's position becomes the size of the economy's capital stock (per capita); momentum becomes capital's asset price. How recent versions of the Ramsey model add loanable funds saving-investment equilibration to the Solow growth model is the topic of this appendix.

Following Abel and Blanchard (1983), we work separately with optimizing decisions of firms and households, although the institutional distinction between these two sorts of "agents" will prove to be slight. We measure all variables relative to the supply of labor L, which for simplicity is assumed not to grow (steady state growth is a minor extension of the stationary state, anyway). The capital/labor ratio $k = K/L$, $c = C/L$, ω is the real wage, and $g = I/K$ is the growth rate of capital. To finance investment, firms issue bonds Z with a short-term real interest rate i, and $z = Z/K$.

Both firms and households are assumed to share perfect foresight about an infinite future—the incredibility of this hypothesis has already been noted in chapter 1. If they can foretell all that lies ahead, firms might plausibly be supposed to maximize the present discounted value V of their real cash flow (output less investment and wages) per capita,

$$V = \int_0^\infty \rho[f(k) - gk - \omega]\,dt = \int_0^\infty \rho J\,dt, \tag{13}$$

subject to the restriction

$$\dot{k} = gk. \tag{14}$$

In (13), $f(k)$ is a neoclassical production function in which output per capita is determined by the capital stock per capita (presupposing full employment of labor), and ρ is a discount factor based on the changing bond interest rate over future time: $\rho = \exp[-\int_0^t i(t)dt]$. Since firms issue bonds to pay for investment, we have $\dot{Z}/L = k\dot{z} + z\dot{k} = \dot{K}/L = gk$. Bond purchases and interest payments show up below in the household budget constraint (21).

Following a standard recipe, we can collapse (13) and (14) into a simpler problem by letting ρQ stand for the "costate" variable dual to k, and defining the "present value" Hamiltonian

$$H = \rho(J + Q\dot{k}) = \rho[f(k) + (Q - 1)gk - \omega].$$

Newton's second law of motion for the economy at hand is

$$\frac{d(\rho Q)}{dt} = -\frac{\partial H}{\partial k} = -\rho[f'(k) + (Q - 1)g], \tag{15}$$

where $f'(k)$ is the marginal product of capital, df/dk. That is, the capital asset price (or capital's "momentum") ρQ declines more rapidly as the marginal product $f'(k)$ is higher.

The accumulation equation dual to (15) is (14) once again:

$$\frac{dk}{dt} = \frac{\partial H}{\partial(\rho Q)} = gk. \tag{16}$$

Equations (15) and (16) apply Hamiltonian mechanics to the firm's planning. Both formulas depend on the capital stock growth rate g, which according to optimal control theory *should* be determined by the rule $\partial H/\partial g = 0$. But here a small fly creeps into the ointment: The Hamiltonian H is *linear* in g. Hence there is no simple way to solve the condition $\partial H/\partial g = 0$ for the capital stock growth rate. Fancy mathematics involving upper and lower bounds on g (e.g., $g \geqslant 0$ and $g \leqslant \bar{g}$, where $\bar{g}$ could be some sort of "absorptive capacity" limit on investment) and "singular arcs" can be invoked; a typical solution would have the firm investing heavily with $g = \bar{g}$ for some period of time, and then settling back to enjoy its profits in endless balanced growth. In the jargon, this is a "bang-bang" solution that bangs into the upper bound and then bangs back to the singular arc with $\bar{g} > g > 0$.

Although such punctuated capital stock growth might make perfect sense for a firm (especially if its technology involves decreasing costs, as we will see in chapter 10), it is implausible at the macro level. Mainstream aggregate growth theory muffles the bangs with "installation costs" $h(g)$ associated with capital formation. So long as $h(g)$ is conveniently non-linear,[12] its presence in the Hamiltonian permits an interior solution for g. This revision of Ramsey's original model, first popularized by Eisner and

Strotz (1963), may make empirical sense, but it also should be recognized for what is it: a mathematical shock absorber designed to smooth accumulation dynamics over time.

Cash flow, including installation costs, is $J = f(k) - gk[1 + h(g)] - \omega$. When this accounting is incorporated in the Hamiltonian, the condition $\partial H/\partial g = 0$ gives the formula

$$Q = 1 + h(g) + gh'(g).$$

Inverting this relationship makes g an increasing function of Q:

$$g = \phi(Q). \tag{17}$$

This equation is tantamount to the q theory of investment proposed by Tobin (1969). Substitution into (16) gives

$$\dot{k} = k\phi(Q), \tag{16'}$$

so the asset price determines the rate of accumulation.

The evolution of Q itself is determined by plugging (17) into (15) as rewritten to take into account installation costs. The differential equation becomes

$$\dot{Q} = iQ - [f'(k) + g^2h'(g)]. \tag{15'}$$

Equations (15') and (16') summarize dual Hamiltonian dynamics for the optimizing firm, involving joint determination of k and Q over time.

The accumulation equation (16') is naturally integrated forward in time from an initial level of capital stock k(0). The asset price equation (15') can be integrated backward from a "transversality condition" at $t = \infty$, which need not concern us here. If the economy always has been and ever will be at a stationary state, then (15') has a solution

$$Q = \frac{f'(k) + g^2h'(g)}{i}, \tag{18}$$

so the capital asset price is just the marginal product of capital $f'(k)$ (augmented by a term $g^2h'(g)$, which says each unit of investment is cheaper to install when the existing capital stock is bigger), capitalized over an infinite horizon at the (constant) market interest rate i.

Before turning to household behavior, it makes sense to restate this result in the language of table 2.1. Following Minsky (1975), we can define a variant capital asset price P_k directly as capitalized profits per unit of capital stock:

$$P_k = \frac{Pr}{i},$$

where P is the price of output and r is the profit rate defined by (1.4). Minsky simply postulates that investment demand g^i is an increasing function (subject to unforeseeable shocks) of $(P_k - P)/P = (r - i)/i$. In linearized form, we have

$$g^i = g_0 + \alpha r - \theta i, \tag{19}$$

an extension of (1.6) with an interest rate term appearing in a natural way and unexpected shocks and animal spirits fitting into g_0. Adding an accelerator would make empirical sense. The content of equation (19) is the same as that of (16') and (18) combined. However, it should be recognized that if future short-term interest or profit rates are expected to differ from their current values, then the appropriate discount integrals should be applied.

Returning to the Ramsey formulation, the immortal, identical households that make up the citizenry are supposed to choose their consumption levels by maximizing their lifetime utility

$$U = \int_0^\infty \exp(-\varepsilon t) u(c) \, dt, \tag{20}$$

subject to the intertemporal budget relationship

$$\dot{z} = \frac{\omega + \delta - c}{k} + z(i - g), \tag{21}$$

where $u(c)$ is a utility function, ε is a subjective discount factor, and δ stands for any dividends per capita that firms may distribute when their cash flows are high.

We omit details about the Hamiltonian dynamics of (20) and (21), which in any case are presented by Abel and Blanchard (1983) and Blanchard and Fischer (1989). Under strong enough assumptions—in particular, one that the household utility function takes the frequently postulated form $u(c) = c^{1-j}/(1-j)$—optimized consumption per head can be expressed as

$$c = \xi(i)\left[Qk + \left(\frac{\omega}{i}\right) \right]. \tag{22}$$

That is, c is proportional to total wealth comprising the value of capital per head Qk and capitalized wage income ω/i.

From equation (18) for Q, c will depend positively on the marginal product of capital (or the profit rate r in the model of table 2.1). Depending on the balance of income, substitution, and wealth effects, $\partial c/\partial i$ can take either sign, but we conventionally assume that it is negative. These signs mean that household savings decline with the profit rate (an anomaly pursued further in appendix 2.B) and rise with the interest rate. That is, we can write the savings function as

$$g^s = \sigma(r, i)u, \tag{23}$$

with $\partial\sigma/\partial r < 0$ and $\partial\sigma/\partial i > 0$. In table 2.1's terms the full employment assumption that we have been making all along sets $u = \bar{u}$ while marginal productivity conditions would fix the profit share π. From (19) and (21) the macroeconomic balance condition (1.7) comes out as

$$\gamma + \alpha\pi\bar{u} - \theta i - \sigma(\pi\bar{u}, i)\bar{u} = 0, \tag{24}$$

with the interest rate i as the adjusting variable. Equilibrium is locally stable since the derivative of the excess demand function to the left of the equals sign in (24) with respect to i is negative. We have a full employment economy sustained in equilibrium via changes of the interest rate in the market for bonds issued by firms, or loanable funds. A more interesting story about how inflation can arise from loanable funds imbalances when they are intermediated by a banking system is set out in chapter 4.

Finally, note that Abel and Blanchard show that the separate optimizations of firms and households are equivalent to the single planner's problem of maximizing household utility

$$U = \int_0^\infty \exp(-\varepsilon t)u(c)\,dt,$$

subject to the restrictions

$$c + gk[1 + h(g)] - f(k) = 0$$

and

$$\dot{k} = gk.$$

As is usual in neoclassical models, this "command economy" optimizing problem can be implemented by decentralized "agents," provided that they keep their accounting straight and faithfully carry out their assigned maximization tasks. This equivalence between planning and the market is often credited to the cleverness of the invisible hand in guiding a market economy to optimal growth. In the present context competitive forces are supposed to lead the interest rate (or the structure of present and future short-term rates, if we are out of the stationary state) to adjust in the market for loanable funds to ensure that saving is equal to investment at full employment. Investing firms are differentiated from saving households only by capital stock installation costs, a pale reflection of the institutional structure of capitalism that Keynes among others emphasized.

This 1980s vintage Ramsey model advances one step beyond postulating that saving determines investment à la Solow, but it is still basically driven by forces of supply. With his predilection for loanable funds, John Stuart Mill would have heartily approved. Upon reading Abel and Blanchard's summary observation that their Hamiltonian mechanics " ... provide a consistent theoretical framework in which to embed standard IS relations ... ", Keynes and Kalecki might have begged to differ. Indeed, Keynes dedicated chapter 14 of *The General Theory* to arguing that interest rate equilibration of the market for loanable funds was precisely what his model was *not* about. If unemployment is not postulated away, then u is not necessarily equal to $\bar{u}$ in (24), and the loanable funds formulation is underdetermined. While he was writing *The General Theory*, Keynes was acutely aware that macro equilibrium with less than full capacity use or employment is a state of the world that economics has to confront. His younger friend Ramsey's exercise of a few years earlier (along with all its mainstream successors) happened to leave the possibility of underutilized resources out.

Appendix 2.B   The Overlapping Generations Growth Model

As we have noted in section 2.3, long-run stability in a savings-driven growth model requires that capital accumulation be an increasing function of the profit rate. The story is that an upward blip in employment or the labor/capital ratio leads immediately to a higher output/capital ratio and profit rate, thereby increasing saving and accelerating growth. With capital accumulation running faster, the labor/capital ratio begins to fall, offsetting the initial shock. Interestingly enough, this stabilizing feedback loop can break down in the popular overlapping generations (OLG) model, as Marglin (1984) points out. The fundamental problem is that the model makes the saving-warranted growth rate g^s an *inverse* function of the profit rate r.

Considering different generations is about the only concession mainstream theory makes to potential social conflict. The OLG model's dispute is between the young and old about the division of total product—next to adultery à la *Madame Bovary* the most banal contest that humans have contrived. When the mainstream comes to build differentiated social groups into its models, the standard way it separates them is by savings propensities, copying the structuralists with their wage and profit income flows. We will see how a distributional outcome favoring the dissaving elderly can create an unstable steady state.[13]

The story in the well-known Diamond (1965) version of the model is that each "agent" lives two periods, working the first and subsisting on accumulated saving before s/he (it?) dies at the end of period two. Faced with such a life history, an agent optimizes two-period consumption. A simple statement of the choice problem is to maximize a Cobb-Douglas utility function

$$U = C_1^{1-\beta} C_2^{\beta}$$

subject to the intertemporal budget constraint

$$C_1 + \frac{C_2}{1+r} = \omega,$$

where the subscripts denote time periods. Note that future consumption is discounted at the profit rate r, so saving automatically takes the form of physical capital accumulation—we drop the distinction between households and firms maintained in appendix 2.A. The income available for saving and first-period consumption comes from the real wage ω; second-period consumption is paid for by first-period saving and accumulated profit income.

With this simple utility function, optimal saving per person working in period one turns out to be

$$\text{saving per person} = \frac{C_2}{1+r} = \beta\omega,$$

so in a saving-driven model the capital stock growth rate is

$$g = \frac{\beta\omega L}{K} = \beta\omega bu = \beta(u - r), \tag{25}$$

where as usual u is the output/capital ratio and the last expression follows from the identity $1 = \omega b + (r/u)$. Note that the direct effect of the profit rate is to *reduce* g in this expression, since a lower r corresponds to a higher ω from the factor price frontier, and saving rises with wage income.

For simplicity, we analyze stability of the growth model in continuous time.[14] Using (25) for g, the growth equation for the labor/capital ratio λ can be written as

$$\dot{\lambda} = \lambda[\hat{L} - \beta(u - r)]. \tag{26}$$

Interesting stories about the stability of this equation can be put under the umbrella of a CES (constant elasticity of substitution) cost function, plus associated marginal productivity conditions.[15] This specification gives the relationships

$$u = \alpha r^\sigma \quad \text{or} \quad du = \sigma\left(\frac{u}{r}\right)dr, \tag{27}$$

between the output/capital ratio and the profit rate, where σ is the elasticity of substitution between labor and capital and α is a constant. The profit rate responds more strongly to changes in u when σ is small. There is a constant profit share (with π equal to α) when σ equals one in the Cobb-Douglas special case. For values of σ near zero a small rise in u leads to a big increase in r, a response that becomes macroeconomically import since it amounts to an income redistribution toward the spending-prone elderly population.

To analyze stability of the model around a steady state where $\dot{\lambda} = 0$, we can combine (27) with Euler's theorem, which implies that $du/d\lambda = (1 - \pi)/b$, to show that the derivative $d\dot{\lambda}/d\lambda$ in (26) will be stably negative when $\sigma > \pi$. In words, the elasticity of substitution has to exceed the profit share for the growth equation to be stable.

In most economies typical CES econometrics gives σ in the range between one-third and two-thirds, while π could be one-half or more. Insofar as a neoclassical closure and the specific OLG model really apply, unstable or borderline stable growth would seem to be on the cards. A relatively low value of σ means that when λ and u rise, there is a strong distributional shift toward elderly agents who receive profit incomes but just spend them to consume. As a consequence overall saving and the growth rate g decline, λ becomes positive, and the economy diverges from steady state. In a savings-driven closure, macro adjustment via income redistribution cannot work, if the beneficiary group has a high propensity to consume. A generation of elders happily dissaving in their Winnebagos (in the United States at least) can lead a Mill-Marshall growth equilibrium to break down.

3   Real Wages and Output

In this chapter the arguments of chapter 2 become a critique of old wine, of a vintage that never runs dry. During the past decade many bottles of wage cuts and regressive redistribution more generally have been poured in stabilization programs in the developing world, with the International Monetary Fund usually playing sommelier. Structuralist economists in the imbibing countries, aware of the taste, have again thought through old questions about the effects of wage changes on output and inflation, with interesting and novel results. Their ideas are pulled together here, with an eye to the policy debate.

Sections 3.1 through 3.3 address the following questions: (1) In an economy closed to trade, do real wage increases cause output to fall or rise? (2) If output is at an upper bound (due to shortages of foreign exchange, capacity, or even labor) what are the roles of real wage and wealth changes in macroeconomic adjustment? (3) Taking effective demand into account, do money wage cuts stimulate employment? On institutional grounds, we argue that wage-cutting may be a counterproductive answer to all these policy questions in the developing world. Section 3.4 summarizes the reasons why, and appendix 3.A shows how the analysis here includes North Atlantic-style "disequilibrium" macroeconomics of the sort proposed by Barro and Grossman (1976), Malinvaud (1977), and Benassy (1986) as a special case.

3.1 Income Distribution and Output

As in chapter 2 the mode of argument is to impose different causal schemes on simple macroeconomic models, to ask which ones fit semi-industrialized stylized facts and institutions the best. The starting point is Kalecki's (1971) model of output adjustment in an economy closed to trade. In this section we take up extensions due to Rowthorn (1982) and Dutt (1984), who analyze how changes in the real wage affect output, the profit rate, and growth.

As we have observed, Kalecki believed that commodity output is not limited by available capital stock or capacity and that final goods prices are determined from variable costs (for labor only in the simplest model) by a markup rule:

$$P = (1 + \tau)wb, \tag{1}$$

where the notation is the same as in chapter 2: P is the price level, w the nominal wage rate, b the labor/output ratio, and τ the markup rate. We assume that w is fixed at any point in time, from institutions and a history of bargaining or class struggle. The markup rate is also instantaneously fixed but evolves according to policy and dynamic distributional processes of the sort discussed in chapter 4. The coefficient b is determined by technology and custom.[1]

In this section, for a given money wage w, we concentrate on the macroeconomic effects of changes in the real wage ω ($= w/P$) or profit share π. Both variables are assumed to be determined by historical forces and policy interventions. The latter can range from tax/transfer policies through actions such as price and import controls to labor market regulation and nationalization of firms. Shifts in distribution can be specified by changes in π, τ, or ω.

Any one of these parameters identifies the others. For example, $1 + \tau = 1/(1 - \pi)$. We use this formula to restate the markup rule (1) as equation (1.1) in table 3.1, which is a compact rendition of Kaleckian macroeconomics in an economy closed to foreign trade. Equation (1.2) expresses the real wage in terms of the profit share. The output/capital ratio u (which as usual we take as a measure of economic activity) is defined by (1.3). The profit rate r is identically equal to the product of the profit share and the output/capital ratio, equation (1.4).

Let g^i stand for investment demand, expressed as the growth rate of the capital stock (ignoring depreciation, g^i is the ratio of real investment to capital). Kalecki assumed that g^i depends on the profit rate r as an index of expected future earnings. Along a different track Kaldor (1940) and Kalecki's colleague Steindl (1952) introduced the output/capital ratio u as another variable affecting g^i. As argued in chapter 1, its influence can easily be rationalized by an accelerator. Dutt and Rowthorn picked up on the Kaldor-Steindl formulation, writing the investment function in the form appearing after the first equals sign in (1.5). The expression after the

Table 3.1
Closed economy macroeconomic relationships

(1.1)	$P = wb/(1 - \pi)$
(1.2)	$\omega = (1 - \pi)/b$
(1.3)	$u = X/K$
(1.4)	$r = \pi u$
(1.5)	$g^i = g_0 + \alpha r + \beta u = g_0 + (\alpha \pi + \beta)u = g^i(\pi, u)$
(1.6)	$g^s = [s_\pi \pi + s_w(1 - \pi)]u = s(\pi)u$
(1.7)	$g^i - g^s = 0$
(1.8)	$MV = PX$ or $\omega = wKu/MV$
(1.9)	$u = \bar{u}$
(1.10)	$s_\pi = s_\pi(M/P)$, $\quad s_w = s_w(M/P)$
(1.11)	$P = f(w, rP)$, $\quad b = L/X = f_\omega(\omega, r)$, $\quad 1/u = K/X = f_r(\omega, r)$
(1.12)	$\hat{w} = h(bu - \bar{\lambda})$

second equality follows from (1.4), and the function $g^i = g^i(\pi, u)$ with both partial derivatives positive can be postulated as a general description of investment demand.

Let g^s stand for the capital growth rate permitted by saving supply, that is, national saving divided by the value of the capital stock PK. In (1.6) saving comes from markup and wage income at rates s_π and s_w, respectively. If workers don't save ($s_w = 0$), (1.6) reduces to the familiar Cambridge equation, $g^s = s_\pi \pi u = s_\pi r$. More generally, we have $g^s = s(\pi)u$, with $s(\pi)$ an increasing function of π when $s_\pi > s_w$.[2]

Macro equilibrium based upon (1.1)–(1.6) occurs when excess commodity demand is zero, or (1.7). Before we use this equation to figure out the effect on output of changes in the income distribution, a word should be added about the formulas in (1.8). These complete the model with the simplest possible money market specification, omitting interest rate effects to force a sharp contrast (softened in chapter 5) between structuralist and monetarist views.

The first expression in (1.8) is the "equation of exchange," where M is the money supply and V velocity. The second equation restates $MV = PX$ in terms of capacity utilization and real and money wages. Either way, the system (1.1)–(1.7) solves for all variables appearing in (1.8) except M and V. The simplest Kalecki model presupposes endogenous money in the Banking School tradition discussed in chapter 1: The supply is "passive" in Olivera's (1970) phrase. Relative *and* absolute prices are being determined in the nonmonetary part of the economy by institutional forces; therefore

M and/or V must be endogenous. It is easy to verify that proportional changes in absolute prices leave the real equilibrium unchanged, so the model "dichotomizes" in the sense of Patinkin (1965).

An alternative approach is to assume that M is predetermined and that V is an institutional constant. Then for a predetermined real wage or income distribution, the money wage w has to be endogenous. This reading is crucial to orthodox recommendations to cut money wages to raise output, and to impose tight money to slow inflation (as shown, respectively, in section 3.3 and chapter 4). Empirically exogenous money is hard to find in face of the widespread wage resistance and indexation observed throughout the semi-industrialized world. Proactive monetary policy is usually only attempted in connection with aggressive stabilization packages. Then it is often abandoned when instead of slowing inflation, tight money forces economic activity to collapse.

We take macro equilibrium to follow from (1.1)–(1.7), with w predetermined and M and/or V tagging along from (1.8). The real wage is also predetermined, and output (or the output/capital ratio u) adjusts to assure demand-supply balance. Standard arguments show that this system will be stable when investment responds less strongly than saving to an increase in output.

Formally, the stability condition is[3]

$$\Delta = s_\pi \pi + s_w(1 - \pi) - g_u^i > 0, \tag{2}$$

where g_u^i is the partial of the investment function with respect to u. If this inequality is violated, short-run equilibrium will be unstable along Harrod's (1939) lines. His knife-edge was sharp precisely because of a strong accelerator.

To show the effect of a change in the profit share on output, we can differentiate the macro balance condition (1.7) to get

$$\frac{du}{d\pi} = \frac{g_\pi^i - (s_\pi - s_w)u}{\Delta}. \tag{3}$$

From (2) the denominator is positive. Equation (3) shows that income redistribution in favor of profits will stimulate economic activity if workers have a relatively high saving share and/or the effect of the profit share on investment is strong. From the linearized investment function in (1.5), the latter condition applies when the profit rate coefficient α is big. Real wage cuts boost output when saving propensities from different income flows are similar and/or investors react with agility to profit signals.

With regard to other key variables, one can show that the profit rate r *rises* with a higher real wage if β in (1.5) exceeds s_w. Redistribution toward labor stimulates consumer demand. A strong investment response to higher consumption offsets the lower value of π in (1.4) with a higher u. Similar reasoning applies to the capital stock growth rate. The sign of $dg/d\pi$ is positive if

$$\alpha s_w - \beta(s_\pi - s_w) > 0.$$

A lower real wage speeds growth in the absence of the accelerator. It slows the economy if the accelerator is strong ($\beta \gg 0$) and saving from wage income is lower than saving from profits. The present model arrives at steady state growth upon convergence of dynamic processes affecting the income distribution (discussed below); the condition just stated signifies that the growth rate in general differs across steady states.

The ambiguous effect of redistribution on output should first be explored. Following Marglin and Bhaduri (1990), an output increase in response to redistribution toward labor may be called "stagnationist" or "wage led"—redistribution favoring workers activates an otherwise stagnant system. The opposite case in which output is profit led becomes "exhilarationist" as a natural piece of jargon. (Neither term of course should be confused with our alternative use of "stagnationist" to describe an investment-driven, non-full employment growth model of the type discussed in this chapter.)

As we will see shortly, there is no certainty with regard to the shape or slope of the income distribution versus aggregate demand relationship, but one might "naturally" suppose that a higher profit share will stimulate capital formation more strongly when the share itself is low; that is, α in (1.5) is an inverse function of π or a direct function of ω. If so, the "output response" relationship between the real wage ω and the output/capital ratio u is illustrated by figure 3.1. Macro equilibrium always lies somewhere along the curve—the activity level is picked out by the profit share or real wage. As the schedule is drawn, the economy is wage led for low values of ω and profit led for high ones due to stronger profit effects on investment as the real wage rises. In section 3.3 more facile substitution of capital for labor as the wage increases is shown to be consistent with figure 3.1.

The stylized facts suggest that developing economies adjust to changes in the real wage in wage-led fashion when the level of output is free to vary. For example, this was the predominant finding in 18 country studies of recent stabilization programs sponsored by the World Institute for Development Economics Research (WIDER) (for a review of the evidence,

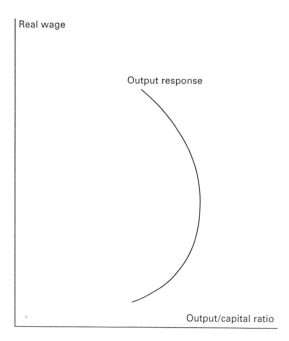

Real wage

Output response

Output/capital ratio

Figure 3.1
Relationships between the real wage and output with no capacity constraint

see Taylor 1988a). We can better assess the policy implications of this observation after working through adjustment mechanisms when output is fixed.

3.2 Macro Adjustment via Real Balance Changes and Forced Saving

Production is frequently subject to upper bounds in the developing world. The most common are lack of capacity, a shortage of foreign exchange, and weather and the seasonal cycle which determine supplies of food and export crops. At the one-sector level of aggregation, it is simplest to treat these restrictions as if they all merged into a generalized "capacity limit," such as the vertical line at the output/capital ratio $\bar{u}$ in figure 3.2.

In this diagram macro equilibrium lies on the thickened segments of the curves. The economy may operate below capacity either along the wage-led segment AB or in the profit-led range CD of the output response curve. Along the segment BC, production constraints bind. Below full capacity,

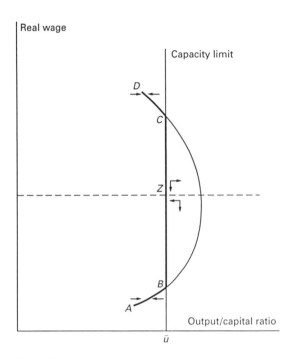

Figure 3.2
Modes of adjustment with and without a binding capacity constraint

adjustment of output toward the relevant curve is usually assumed to be rapid, as shown by the small arrows.

The interesting question is how demand is limited to supply when capacity limits start to bind, for example, due to progressive income redistribution in a stagnationist economy, expansionary policy that shifts the entire output response curve to the right, or an adverse supply shock that makes $\bar{u}$ decline. Three mechanisms are likely to be important in practice—forced saving, real balance effects, and (in an open economy) changes in net imports.

In the model of table 3.1, forced saving kicks in when the capacity constraint (1.9) is added to the preceding equations. There is the usual overdetermination problem with one more equation than there are variables. This problem resolves itself, however, insofar as an incipient excess of aggregate demand over capacity makes prices rise. If the money wage is not fully indexed to inflation, the markup τ and profit share π increase, becoming endogenous and equilibrating macroeconomic variables. The real wage declines, reducing demand, output, and very possibly the rate of capital stock growth in a wage-led system.

Short-run inflationary adjustment via workers' forced saving (or "automatic lacking" in Dennis Robertson's 1933 phrase) toward limited capacity is stable in the stagnationist case—the segment BZ in figure 3.2.[4] If the economy is profit led—segment ZC—price increases raise profits, stimulate investment, and lead toward hyperinflation in response to an initial increment in demand. Harrodian instability shows up in divergent prices instead of output levels.

The transition from a wage-led regime like AB to forced saving or even hyperinflation may be unpleasantly brusque. Supply shocks are always a danger; expansionary fiscal policy and wage increases can be pursued only over a certain output range. "Beyond" the capacity limit $\bar{u}$, further attempts at redistribution become counterproductive—the paradox of thrift begins to apply, as discussed in chapter 2. But suppose that the government redoubles its distributional efforts as it begins to see them fail in the face of accelerating inflation and further declines in the real wage. Then, at full capacity use, the economy jumps abruptly from stagnationist to state-led exhilarationist adjustment, as illustrated in figure 3.3. A sudden macroeconomic regime shift from wage-led growth toward hyperinflation has caused more than one government with an initially successful redistributive program to fall in the developing world.

A formal treatment of inflation dynamics under forced saving is postponed to chapter 4. There, we also take up the analagous problems of regulating aggregate demand arise when inflation is braked by price freezes and de-indexation in a "heterodox shock" anti-inflation package. If wages rise along with output along Phillips curve lines, then the demand increase due to abolition of the inflation tax by the heterodox move can trigger renewed inflation and expansion, absent other stabilizing policies.

Although it hovers in the background (as in figure 3.5 below), forced saving lost its star role in mainstream macroeconomics between 1930 and 1936, the respective publication years of Keynes's *Treatise on Money* and *General Theory*. As Amadeo (1989) points out, the Keynes of the *Treatise* along with the rest of his "post-Wicksellian" generation (Robertson, Schumpeter, the Swedes) emphasized macro adjustment via inflationary income redistribution around a steady state in which market and "natural" rates of interest are equal and there is full employment. Wicksell (1935), Robertson (1926), Keynes, and other post-Wicksellians recognized the possibility of output changes in response to demand, but only with *The*

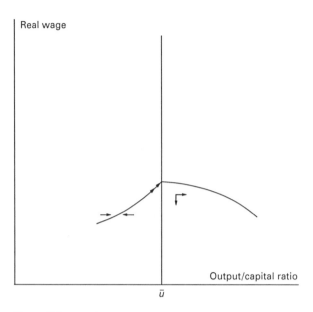

Figure 3.3
Harrodian hyperinflation in response to redistributive policy pushing aggregate demand
"beyond" the capacity limit $\bar{u}$

General Theory did this mode of adjustment as opposed to forced saving
come to dominate the debate.

As observed in chapter 2, forced saving under a capacity constraint
creates an inverse relationship between the price level and real consumption demand. When such a curve was again needed after World War II, it
found its mainstream rationale not in real wage reduction but in lower real
wealth. The relative importance of ideological and empirical reasons for
this shift in emphasis is an inquiry beyond our scope here. But it is clear
that a real balance or quantity theory explanation for a stagnationist real
wage–output relationship is an essential component of the orthodox argument for cutting money wages to stimulate employment, as we will see
in section 3.3. For this or other reasons the real balance effect became
the accepted justification for a downward-sloping schedule for aggregate
demand.

The adjustment scenario has already been sketched in chapter 2. An
initial price increase when capacity limits are reached will reduce "real
balances," (i.e., the money stock divided by the price level). With the real
value of their assets reduced by this change, wealth-holders save more to

compensate, cutting consumption. From an investment function like (1.5), capital formation follows in train.

The real balance process runs parallel to forced saving. In practice, the two modes of adjustment are hard to tell apart. However, in the model world, the real balance effect is easy to incorporate by adding (1.10) to the full capacity specification. The saving rates s_π and s_w inverse functions of M/P, the real value of the nominal money stock M. But P is directly related to τ and π (a higher markup goes together with higher prices and lower real balances), so the saving rates rise with π. Another negative term $-u[\pi(\partial s_\pi/\partial\pi) + (1 - \pi)(\partial s_w/\partial\pi)]$ appears in the numerator of (3). Stagnationist adjustment to distributional changes becomes more likely, since markup increases cut demand by reducing both real wages and wealth.

A third way to evade capacity limitations is to bring in imports freely —such a move could be treated formally in the model structure here by including imports relative to capital stock as a negative term in (1.7). Macro adjustment via wholesale importation is important in practice (recall France under early Mitterrand where household durable goods highly prized by wage-earners led the import surge after progressive redistribution, the United States under Reagan's expansionary fiscal policy, and countless external crises in the Third World) and bears mention in passing.

In semi-industrialized economies two problems with the easy import strategy arise. First, thanks to import-substituting industrialization as discussed in chapter 7, many goods are effectively nontraded—they cannot be imported "competitively" since protective policies don't permit foreign goods to compete freely with national products. Excess demand for local goods will make their prices rise, and we are back to forced saving. Second, foreign exchange has to be available from reserves or capital inflows to finance extra purchases abroad. Such plentitude of yen or dollars is rare in the Third World.

3.3 Real Balances, Input Substitution, and Money Wage Cuts

So far, wage-cutting is no panacea. If capacity limits don't bind, policies aimed at shifting the income distribution in favor of profits may well reduce output and employment. When the economy tends toward demand levels exceeding capacity, real wage reductions induced by inflation will help restore equilibrium but will be less necessary when real balance effects are strong.

In view of these observations, why does wage restraint remain a central orthodox theme? At least as far as output responses are concerned, the answer hinges upon positing the real balance effect as the *unique* macro adjustment mechanism, in conjunction with neoclassical input substitution. To see the logic, we proceed by stages, first observing that Keynes in *The General Theory* was perfectly willing to accept marginal productivity rules but still thought that cutting money wages would not effectively raise employment. As Amadeo (1989) emphasizes, the policy only works smoothly in models that suppress Keynes's ideas about effective demand while dropping dichotomy by letting absolute price changes influence macro equilibrium in a very specific fashion.

Keynes stressed the low efficacy of reducing the *money* wage. Already in light of the markup equation (1), such a policy does not affect the real side in Kalecki's formulation. Prices just fall in proportion to wages, the profit share and real wage are unchanged, and macro equilibrium remains wherever it was along the heavily shaded schedule in figure 3.2.

The General Theory differs from Kalecki by building in the "first classical postulate" that the real wage equals the marginal product of labor under a regime of decreasing returns to additional employment. Following the right-hand column in table 2.1, a standard way to fit this view into our equations is to drop the markup rule (1.1) of table 3.1, and use the neoclassical supply specification appearing in (1.11) instead. In effect we replace imperfect competition in the product market and a constant marginal (=average) product of labor with perfect competition and a marginal product that falls when output rises.

In (1.11), $P = f(w, rP)$ is a linearly homogeneous cost function consistent with an aggregate production function having constant returns to scale in capital and labor—it can be restated as the factor-price frontier in the form $1 = f(\omega, r)$. Input demands follow from Shepard's lemma, where f_ω and f_r stand for partial derivatives. Keynes did not bring capital explicitly into his story about decreasing returns, but (1.11) with K predetermined translates his analysis into current textbook language.[5]

To see how the argument works, assume for a moment that the real balance effect is inoperative. In terms of the real wage ω, the macro balance equation (1.7) can be written as

$$g^i(\omega, u) - [s_\pi - (s_\pi - s_w)\omega b]u = 0, \qquad (4)$$

where the profit share π is replaced by the real wage in the investment function since one depends monotonically on the other. If (1.11) is in force, the elasticity of π with respect to ω is $-(1 - \sigma)$, where σ is the elasticity of substitution between capital and labor (interpreted as a local measure of curvature of the cost function).

Equation (4) is our familiar output response curve, redrawn in figure 3.4. The (1.11) model makes the labor/output ratio b a decreasing function of ω, with elasticity $-\sigma$. When σ is less than one, a stagnationist response to a real wage increase is likely to occur. The labor/output ratio falls by less than the real wage goes up; hence the wage share ωb rises while the profit share π falls. With a weak response of investment to the decrease in π and a big difference in saving propensities, the result is higher demand.

Although such reasoning goes beyond the limits of pure competition, one might further assume that a higher real wage will stimulate firms to explore more aggressively possibilities for using less labor. In that case σ will be positively correlated with ω. The profit share (and investment demand) will decline less as the real wage rises. With a high value for σ, an exhilarationist response to redistribution is likely, especially if investment demand responds strongly to profit signals when the real wage is high. A positive dependence of σ on ω can produce an output response curve shaped like the one sketched in figures 3.1 and 3.4.

The textbook model also implies a relationship between the output/ capital ratio and the real wage. Lower labor cost means that more workers

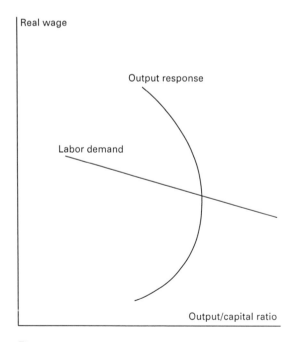

Figure 3.4
Keynesian determination of output and the real wage

can be profitably employed, leading u to rise. This linkage underlies *The General Theory*'s real side macro closure. It combines (1.11) with (1.2)–(1.8) in table 3.1. For simplicity we retain the hypothesis of passive money, eliding Keynes's emphasis on interest rate effects.

The graphical solution is instructive. The negatively sloped "labor demand" curve representing (1.11) in figure 3.4 uniquely picks out macro equilibrium, determining output and the real wage. Of course shifts in the output response schedule (from changing investment demand or fiscal moves) modify the equilibrium position. Higher exogenous demand moves the output response curve to the right, causing the real wage to fall.

Reducing the money wage has no effect in this formulation precisely because the *real* wage is determined in figure 3.4. A lower w makes P drop in proportion, given effective demand. In a nutshell, this is Keynes's key argument against the effectiveness of money wage cuts.[6] The conclusion does not depend the slope of the labor demand schedule, as Keynes (1939) admitted after Dunlop and Tarshis showed that in the United Kingdom and United States the real wage rose with output over the business cycle. He was willing to scrap the first classical postulate and accept procyclical real wage variation as an empirical matter, so long as his reasoning about money wage changes went through.

Now we can reintroduce the real balance effect, which makes the saving rates s_π and s_w functions of real balances M/P, not the real wage w/P. Cutting the money wage reduces P through the cost function, raises M/P, and stimulates demand since wealth-holders feel richer. If the linkage is strong, Keynes's aggregate demand argument (leaving out interest rate effects which we do not consider here) is undone.

Strong assumptions about model causality and empirical legitimacy are built into the real balance story. The causal question is whether money supply M is determined prior to the price level P. In inflationary semi-industrialized economies, passive money is usually the rule. The empirical doubt is whether the postulated positive effect of price changes on saving rates in (4) overrides the other linkages in that equation.

The standard mainstream model answers both queries in the affirmative, dropping effective demand. The quantity theory of money is transferred from the asset market to the real side of the system, and pressed into force as a shorthand representation of dominant real balance effects in demand. The model comprises equations (1.2)–(1.4), the second version of the quantity equation in (1.8) with predetermined M and V, and (1.11). Effective demand equations such as (1.5)–(1.7) don't get around much any more.[7]

In this setup it is easy to verify from (1.8) that for a given money wage, the real wage increases along with capacity utilization. Higher output means that the price level must fall (and real wage rise) from the equation of exchange. The direction of macro causality is the reverse of the one pursued heretofore. It supports a "monetarist stagnationist" theory of aggregate demand.

Equation (1.8) appears as the "velocity" schedule in figure 3.5. Its cross with the labor demand curve (the same as in figure 3.4) determines macro equilibrium. The new twist is the dependence of the velocity relationship in (1.8) on the money wage w. Cutting w shifts the curve downward to the dashed position, reducing the real wage and raising output. A bigger money supply also leads u to rise and ω to fall due to a higher price level. With their relative importance depending on how easily new workers can be utilized (i.e., on the value of a parameter like σ), both employment gains and forced saving play roles in adjustment to the bigger money supply. After 50 years, mainstream macroeconomics has now returned close to post-Wicksell/pre-*General Theory* views about how equilibrium is attained.

The return extends to the long run, with a "natural" rate of employment replacing Wicksell's rate of interest. It is easy to turn figure 3.5's short-run adjustment into a process leading to the natural rate in steady state, following Friedman (1968), and later Fischer (1977) and John Taylor (1980). Suppose that for reasons of "expectational errors" (Friedman) or "fixed contract periods" (Fischer and Taylor), the money wage responds to labor market disequilibrium according to a Phillips curve differential equation such as (1.12), in which bu is the current labor/capital ratio, and $\bar{\lambda}$ is the ratio corresponding to zero wage pressure or the natural rate.

For a given capital stock, employment is an inverse function of w from figure 3.5. The implication is that if bu drops below $\bar{\lambda}$, then w begins to fall, leading to real wage reduction, new hiring, and restoration of equilibrium at $bu = \bar{\lambda}$. At this long-run stable position, u is at its natural rate level and ω comes from (1.11). Hence from (1.8) the money wage is also determined. All nominal prices follow from $MV = PX$; there is no room in a monetarist steady state for institutional influences on either the real or money wage. As observed in chapter 2, macro adjustment relying on real balance effects is institutionally overdetermined.[8]

Structural inflation processes make these results largely beside the point in semi-industrialized countries—(1.8) as an aggregate demand equation lacks verisimilitude in the Third World. Periods of extreme stabilization efforts apart, wage and price increases have their own dynamics, forcing money supply and/or velocity to become accommodating variables in the

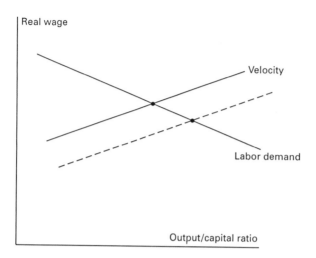

Figure 3.5
The effect of a money wage cut when aggregate demand is determined by the equation of exchange

equation of exchange. Meanwhile, other forces that *do* affect economic activity continue to apply. They are best described by equations like (1.5)–(1.7), as extended in chapters 7 and 8 to deal with foreign trade.

3.4 Political Economy

At the risk of oversimplification, the main conclusions can be summarized in terms of discrepancies between structuralist and neoclassical/monetarist views:

1. When output is the chief macroeconomic adjusting variable, real wage increases can either stimulate or hold down capacity utilization and the growth rate. Outcomes depend on interactions between distribution and demand in a Kaleckian framework, as discussed in section 3.1. Taylor (1988a) argues on the basis of the 18 WIDER country studies that developing economies may well be "stagnationist" in the sense that increasing the real wage activates an otherwise stagnant system. Besides output, the profit and growth rates may also increase in response to a higher real wage.

2. Orthodox views frequently run the opposite direction—wage reductions push up production from the side of supply. In part, an issue of money versus real wages is involved. If effective demand determines output, Keynes's key argument in chapter 19 of *The General Theory* (summar-

ized in section 3.3) applies—money wage cuts will pull down prices in proportion and leave the real part of the economy unchanged. To get away from price-quantity dichotomy, some mechanism must transform shifts of the money wage into *real* wage changes. One possibility is that the price level is held stable. The equation of exchange and trade theory's law of one price both act in this direction. Their relative importance vis-à-vis saving-investment linkages may be weak in the Third World, since the money supply is likely to be passive under ongoing inflation and the process of import substitution undermines the importance of price arbitrage for traded goods.

3. When output restrictions bind, adjustment via forced saving and/or the real balance effect becomes central. Wage-led output responses to institutionally determined distributional shifts give way to changes in wealth and income positions which help the economy achieve inflationary equilibrium. The model in section 3.2 illustrates how a transition from stagnation to forced saving can easily put an end to expansionary, re-distributive economic experiments. Their end may come sooner if output increases bid up wages in a stagnationist economy, for then an inflationary, expansionary spiral can only continue up to the point at which capacity limits begin to bind. The details are presented in the following chapter.

Appendix 3.A   "Disequilibrium" Macroeconomics

During the 1970s mainstream economists proposed "disequilibrium" macro models combining nominal price rigidity with output adjustment along either aggregate demand or supply curves. Work along these lines has recently diminished (less in Europe than in the United States), and from our perspective the "disequilibrium" approach's main interest is as a failed attempt on the part of neoclassically minded economists to break out toward structuralism. Perhaps with more exciting macro shocks around the North Atlantic at some point in the future, a renewed effort will make the grade. One has to observe changes like real wage reductions of up to 90 percent in parts of Africa and Latin America over the past ten years to understand the relevance of phenomena like forced saving and wage-led output adjustment to the practical world.

Barro and Grossman (1976) introduced "disequilibrium" models, and they were elaborated by Malinvaud (1977), Benassy (1986), and many others. The latter authors distinguished several adjustment modes, which we can illustrate using figure 3.2. The different segments there can be labeled as follows:

Segment	Structuralist nomenclature	Neoclassical nomenclature
AB	Wage-led output adjustment	Keynesian adjustment
BZ	Forced saving	Repressed inflation
ZC	Harrodian hyperinflation	Not considered
CD	Profit-led output adjustment	Classical adjustment

Broadly speaking, the neoclassical label for demand-driven changes is "Keynesian," and the term "classical" refers to an output reduction due to a higher real wage. In figure 3.2 such a response occurs because of a fall in aggregate demand along segment CD. The neoclassical taste of course is for marginal productivity input demand relationships like those in equation (1.11) of table 3.1. These are incorporated in figure 3.4, which is modified in figure 3.6 to illustrate two classical adjustment regimes when the "short-

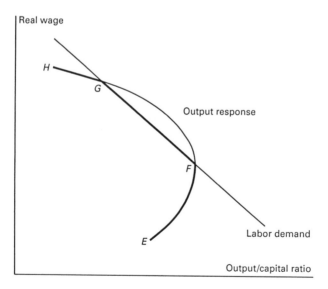

Figure 3.6
"Disequilibrium" macroeconomic adjustment regimes

side rule" determines market clearing: Output is limited by segments of the output response or labor demand curves lying furthest to the left (so that output is at the lesser of two possible levels for a given real wage).

Neoclassical authors prefer segment FG on a downward-sloping marginal-productivity based "labor demand" curve as a classical regime, but there is no reason why demand could not limit output in what we call "profit-led" fashion along GH as well. Segment EF is a Keynesian or wage-led regime, and in figure 3.6 the possibility of Harrodian hyperinflation in which regressive redistribution stimulates demand with output at an upper bound is suppressed.

4   Real Wages and Inflation

In this chapter the model of chapter 3 is extended to deal with inflation. Section 4.1 provides the background, setting out structuralist views about how steady price increases are rooted in social conflict and rely upon propagation mechanisms such as contract indexation to maintain their march. When indexation fully takes over inflation, it becomes self-perpetuating or "inertial" in a sense defined below. Section 4.2 crosses structural wage increases with the inflation tax at full capacity use to give "the" monetarist inflation theory, deriving ultimately from Wicksell. In section 4.3 output adjustment is introduced, to give a more structuralist flavor to the story and permit discussion of "heterodox shock" programs which attempt to eradicate inflation by price and wage controls and contract deindexation. Brief conclusions appear in section 4.4. Appendix 4.A presents a version of the section 4.2 model incorporating a positive response of velocity to the inflation rate (it is assumed constant in the text), and appendix 4.B shows how responsiveness of saving and investment to the interest rate can help stabilize inflation in Wicksell's model.

4.1   Structuralist Inflation Theories

Inflation is a dual process. It unavoidably has a monetary dimension. But at the same time prices are determined by costs, meaning that social conflict over values of inputs such as the nominal wage and exchange rates and rules for contract indexation combine to force up the price level. As observed in chapter 1, different schools of economists have emphasized one or the other aspect, but for full understanding of inflation in any economy, one has to look at both theories as they relate to the institutions in place. The book by Taylor (1988a) and the studies from WIDER upon which it is based go into institutional analysis for developing economies. Carlin and Soskice (1990) review somewhat similar "new Keynesian" inflation and distribution models worked out for industrialized countries in the 1980s.

In this section we set out the structuralist view about cost inflation in a one-sector economy with markup pricing. Price excursions coming from demand pressure in flex-price sectors are ignored, even though they can be fatal to inflation stabilization in practice (as discussed in section 4.3 below). Contract indexation with changing adjustment periods is central to markup based inflation theory and is modeled more simply in discrete time. We revert to continuous time when we take up macro dynamics in section 4.2.[1]

A simple indexation model for a closed economy was presented by Modigliani and Padoa-Schioppa (1978), and we begin with that. Prices in period t (denoted by a subscript) are assumed to be set according to the lagged markup rule

$$P_t = h(1 + \tau)w_t b + (1 - h)P_{t-1}, \tag{1}$$

where a fraction h of current wage cost is passed into prices via the markup. The lagged price P_{t-1} feeds into the current level with a coefficient $1 - h$.

Wages are fully indexed between periods according to the formula

$$w_t = \bar{\omega}P_{t-1}, \tag{2}$$

where $\bar{\omega}$ stands for a highest instantaneous real wage that workers get. At the beginning of period t, w_t is set according at (2), and then real payments erode as prices rise during the period (a year, a quarter, or perhaps even less). Avoiding wage erosion is the workers' game in this model, as we will see in detail shortly.

The price inflation rate coming from (1) and (2) is

$$\hat{P}_t = \frac{P_t - P_{t-1}}{P_{t-1}} = h[(1 + \tau)\bar{\omega}b - 1] = hF, \tag{3}$$

so inflation runs at a steady rate when $F > 0$ (i.e., when desired markup and peak real wage claims conflict). Also $\hat{P}_t$ will be larger, the more important is current markup pricing as reflected by the coefficient h. If the markup rate and profit share are increasing functions of capacity utilization (which as we observed in chapter 3 may not be true, especially when output is well below full capacity), the model is illustrated in figure 4.1. There will be ongoing inflation at any capacity utilization level u exceeding $\bar{u}$. Moreover one can show that

$$\frac{w_t}{P_t} = \frac{\bar{\omega}}{1 + \hat{P}_t},$$

so the real wage that workers actually get is lower as inflation runs faster.

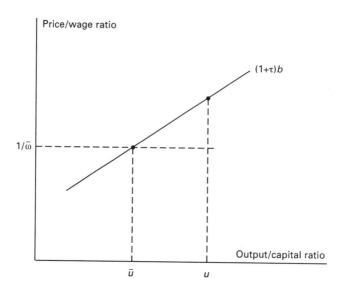

Figure 4.1
Conflicting claims with price and wage indexation

As trending prices settle in, pressures to shorten indexation periods almost always develop. With an annual rate of up to 30 percent (say), workers may accept yearly readjustment, but if inflation is much more rapid, they are likely to press for semiannual or quarterly contracts. At 100 percent per year (just under 6 percent per month), monthly readjustments may come into play. The analytical question is: what is the impact of shortening indexation intervals on the inflation rate? Our first major conclusion is that more frequent indexation makes inflation speed up.

Suppose that there are N indexation periods per year (from now on we use t and $t - 1$ to stand for the end and beginning of a year, respectively). Let $\psi = 1/N$ be the length of a period, and let h_ψ stand for the producers' price adjustment coefficient per period. One can show that $h_\psi = 1 - (1 - h)^\psi$, where h is the annual adjustment rate. Rewriting (3) shows that the inflation rate over the last adjustment period in a year is

$$\hat{P}_\psi = \frac{P_t - P_{t-\psi}}{P_{t-\psi}} = h_\psi F,$$

and the annual rate Z becomes

$$Z = \frac{P_t - P_{t-1}}{P_{t-1}} = [1 + [1 - (1 - h)^\psi]F]^{1/\psi} - 1. \tag{4}$$

Using (4) with $F = 0.3$, one can construct the following table showing how shortening the indexation period makes inflation accelerate:

Number of wage	Annual inflation rate	
adjustments per year	$h = 0.5$	$h = 0.8$
1	0.15	0.24
2	0.18	0.36
3	0.20	0.42
4	0.20	0.46
6	0.21	0.51
12	0.22	0.56

In practice, workers can of course enhance their wage claims by raising the real wage peak $\bar{\omega}$, but reducing the indexation period is a ploy at least as frequently used. From (3) and (4) both moves drive up the inflation rate.

To pursue the discussion further, we set aside markup dynamics for the moment and follow Ros (1988) in asking how the peak real wage in fact gets set. To that end, let ω stand for the *average* real wage over the indexation period. Figure 4.2 is a diagram familiar in inflation-prone countries, showing how ω oscillates under an indexation scheme in which wages are readjusted every ψ units of time. If we let $\lambda = \psi/2$ and inflation is steady, then ω is given (approximately) by the formula

$$\omega = \bar{\omega}\left(\frac{P_{t-\lambda}}{P_t}\right), \tag{5}$$

while the annual inflation rate is

$$Z = \left(\frac{\bar{\omega}}{\omega}\right)^{1/\lambda} - 1. \tag{6}$$

Finally, suppressing institutional detail, historical discontinuity, and partial irreversibility at one blow, we assume the indexation period is fixed according to a simple rule of the form

$$\lambda = \frac{\lambda_0}{1 + Z}. \tag{7}$$

Lying behind the real wage peak $\bar{\omega}$ is a *target* real wage ω^* that workers wish to receive. This target in fact will evolve over time in light of changing bargaining positions, the employment situation, government policy, and many other factors—long-run growth and distributional implications are sketched in chapter 11. But for determination of labor contracts in the

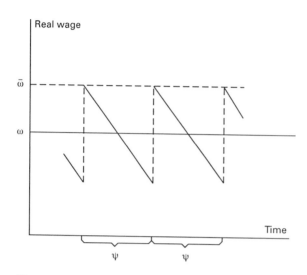

Figure 4.2
Real wage fluctuations under inflation

fairly short run, we can assume that when the inflation rate changes the peak wage is adjusted according to a formula such as

$$\bar{\omega}_t = \bar{\omega}_{t-\psi} \left(\frac{\omega^*}{\omega_t} \right)^{\nu},$$ (8)

where we adopt the timing conventions that the observed real wage ω_t over the period between $t - \psi$ and t is compared to the target, while $\bar{\omega}_t$ is the new wage peak set for the period between t and $t + \psi$.

We start from a nonconflict situation in which there is ongoing inflation but the wage target has in fact been attained between $t - 2\psi$ and $t - \psi$, as illustrated in figure 4.3. Suppose that there is a crop failure, devaluation, or some other such shock at $t - \psi$. Inflation accelerates during the next period, and the average real wage falls below its previous (and target) level ω^*. Workers respond with increased money wage claims, pressing for an increase in the peak from its old level $\bar{\omega}_{t-\psi}$ to a new level $\bar{\omega}_t$. In (8) the exponent ν measures how successful they are in this quest.

Different inflation theories can be conveniently parameterized by values of ν. To see the details, let Z_t and $Z_{t+\psi}$ stand for the annualized inflation rates over the periods ending at the times indicated by the subscripts. Combining (6) and (8) gives the expression

$$1 + Z_{t+\psi} = (1 + Z_t) \left[\left(\frac{\omega_t}{\omega_{t+\psi}} \right) \left(\frac{\omega^*}{\omega_t} \right)^{\nu} \right]^{1/\lambda},$$ (9)

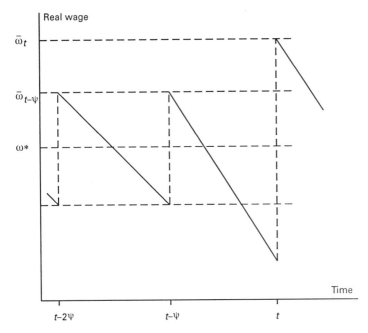

Figure 4.3
Adjustment of the peak real wage to acceleration in inflation

tying real wage adjustments to the change in the inflation rate between periods.

Inertial inflation occurs when the peak real wage is fully adjusted to allow workers to regain their target wage when inflation speeds up. If the inflation rate does not jump again at time t, then (9) simplifies to give

$$\frac{\omega_{t+\psi}}{\omega_t} = \left(\frac{\omega^*}{\omega_t}\right)^v . \tag{10}$$

For $v = 1$, the peak wage moves upward to allow workers to recover the target in the period between t and $t + \psi$ They suffer only a one-period, transitional real income loss as inflation accelerates. There is inertia in the sense that when steady inflation returns, workers regain 100 percent indexation at their target real wage.

The problem with this scenario is that it ignores both markup dynamics as in (3) and shortening of the indexing period as in (7). Both factors are likely to provoke a new jump in the inflation rate, with subsequent adjustment of the wage peak $\bar{\omega}$, another upward movement in the inflation rate, and so on. If these developments do *not* transpire, then equation (9) with $v = 1$ in fact describes an inflation equilibrium of the form

$$1 + Z_{t+\psi} = (1 + Z_t)\left(\frac{\omega^*}{\omega_{t+\psi}}\right) \tag{11}$$

with $\omega_{t+\psi} = \omega^*$ and $\bar{\omega}_{t+\psi} = \bar{\omega}$. However, as Amadeo and Camargo (1989a) stress, this situation is unstable in the sense that any adverse price development, for example, originating in flex-price sectors or foreign trade, can easily provoke price increases to speed up.

This general conclusion also applies to heterodox shock[2] anti-inflation packages. They basically build upon (11) as an exact description of inflation in attempting to drive price increases directly to zero by freezing prices and wages and deindexing contracts at a stroke. Unfortunately, we will see in section 4.3 that there are likely to be unfavorable demand effects from the shock, and chapter 8 brings in balance of payments complications as well. The policy conclusion is that even if inflation is inertial, it cannot be attacked solely from the side of costs. Contract deindexation may be a necessary condition for stopping inflation, but other policies have to be applied as well. And beyond "policy" in the usual sense of the word, unless conflicting income claims are ameliorated inflation is likely to recur.

Conflict inflation is exacerbated when workers' wage aspirations are not fully met. When $v < 1$, equation (8) shows that the wage peak is increased less than proportionately to the real wage loss between times $t - \psi$ and t; hence workers' real income losses persist. Suppose that they resort to pressing for a shorter indexation period along the lines of (7). Figure 4.4 illustrates how two inflationary equilibria become possible. The "wage inflation" schedule represents (6), and the "indexing rule" is (7); the curves can intersect twice. The lower equilibrium at point A is stable while B is unstable. At B an inflationary shock leads Z_t to rise, provoking a large increase in the indexation frequency $1/\lambda$, another upward jump in inflation, and so on. Such a divergent process is often invoked in structuralist interpretations of hyperinflations such as the one in Germany in the early 1920s (Franco 1986). If, due to an upward jump in the peak wage or an increase in the overall frequency of indexation, the wage inflation schedule lies completely above the Indexing rule, not even the unstable equilibrium at B can exist.

Finally, it bears emphasis that h in (1) and v in (8) are only parameters; their values depend on economic history and the nature of any inflationary shock. In practice, less intense reaction to small shocks seems to be the rule: h and v may be bigger when nominal price movements are large in terms of recent experience. For example, in an economy open to foreign trade, a maxi-devaluation of 100 percent is a strong economic signal. It may

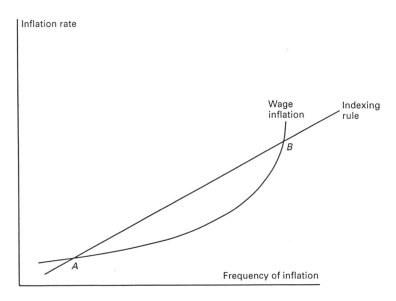

Figure 4.4
Interaction between conflict inflation and the frequency of indexation

well provoke bigger or faster price and wage responses than ten mini-devaluations of $2^{0.1} = 7.177$ percent spread over weeks or months.

This observation suggests the advantages of gradualism in policies aimed at manipulating (or "reforming") relative prices, for example, reconstituting the real exchange rate after it has gotten badly overvalued. Reform inevitably means that some nominal prices go up. The overall inflationary impact is likely to be smaller (and hence the real effects greater) when the price excursions are small and sequenced over time. A "crawling peg" exchange rate policy is one example of this approach—each nominal devaluation is small and scaled to the underlying inflation rate. As we will argue in diverse contexts below, a crawling peg and related gradualist policies smooth transitions and give better distributional and inflationary results than more heroic attempts at price reform.

4.2   The Inflation Tax and Forced Saving

Orthodox anti-inflation programs traditionally rely on wage reduction and monetary restraint. Their rationale combines supply-determined output, a given short-run money supply, forced saving, and the inflation tax. We work through a simple model here to show how the orthodox approach hinges upon cutting the real wage, even though inflation is assumed to result from excessive money emission.

The inflation tax and forced saving were the key adjustment mechanisms in the macroeconomics of authors such as Wicksell (1935) and Robertson (1933) The equations in table 4.1 restate their model using machinery we have in place—the formulation draws from Cardoso (1979), Taylor (1979), Lopes and Bacha (1983), and Taylor (1983). Its approach is monetarist in the sense that the rate of price inflation is determined solely by demand conditions as stated by the equation of exchange. Price increases *caused* by higher costs fit uneasily into monetarist schemes, and are reintroduced in section 4.3.

The financial side of the economy is treated as a Wicksellian pure credit banking system. Its consolidated balance sheet is $A = D + M$, where A stands for advances (credits, loans) from the banks, D is desired deposits, and M is an endogenously adjusting money supply. Equation (1.1) states the banks' balance sheet in flow terms (where we go back to continuous time and a "dot" above a variable denotes its time derivative).

The driving force in the system is bank credit A, which rises with capital formation and government spending. As in chapter 3, we can parameterize investment demand $g^i(\omega, u)$ in terms of the real wage, with $g^i_\omega < 0$ and $g^i_u > 0$. We also introduce government real spending (or, better, dissaving, since we leave tax terms out of the model equations) in proportion to capital, $G = \gamma K$, and further we assume that firms distribute all profits to rentiers so that enterprise saving is nil. Under such circumstances bank credit is the only means for financing fiscal expenditure and investment demand. Equation (1.2) shows that banks make new advances A for just these ends.

Table 4.1
A monetarist inflation model

(1.1)	$\dot{A} = \dot{D} + \dot{M}$
(1.2)	$\dot{A}/PK = g^i(\omega, u) + \gamma$
(1.3)	$\dot{D}/PK = [s_\pi - (s_\pi - s_w)\omega b]u = s(\omega)u$
(1.4)	$\mu V = PX$
(1.5)	$\dot{\mu}/PK = [(\mu/P)\dot{P} + \mu\dot{X}]/PK = (u/V)(\hat{P} + g^i)$
(1.6)	$u = \bar{u}$
(1.7)	$\dot{M}/PK - \dot{\mu}/PK = 0$
(1.8)	$\hat{w} = \varepsilon\hat{P} + \delta(\omega^* - \omega)$
(1.9)	$\hat{P} = -\hat{\omega} + \hat{w}$

New deposits D come from voluntary saving parameterized by the real wage ω, in (1.3). Combining (1.1)–(1.3) shows how money creation depends on the excess of government dissaving and investment over desired saving:

$$\frac{\dot{M}}{PK} = \gamma + g^i(\omega, u) - s(\omega)u. \tag{12}$$

Equation (12) underlies a cumulative process inflation, when put together with the quantity theory and an assumption of full capacity use, equations (1.4) and (1.6), respectively. Wicksell used a money supply equation like (12), but he made the variables on the right-hand side functions of the interest rate, thereby tying inflation to a discrepancy between the rate currently fixed by the banks and the price-stable "natural" rate. We shift the emphasis here to distributional questions, postponing consideration of interest rate adjustments to appendix 4.B.

Before deriving the inflation rate $\hat{P}$, it makes sense to ask how the difference between $\gamma + g^i$ (demand injected by the government and investors) and $s(\omega)\bar{u}$ (saving leakages) reflects itself into the rest of the economy when u is at its capacity level $\bar{u}$. To that end, note that commodity supply-demand balance is given by

$$\bar{u} = \xi\bar{u} + g^i + \gamma,$$

where ξ is the share of consumption spending in total demand.

Comparison of this equation with (12) shows that

$$\xi\bar{u} = [1 - s(\omega)]\bar{u} - \frac{\dot{M}}{PK}, \tag{13}$$

so consumption lies below output less desired saving by the increase in money supply $\dot{M}/PK$. Consumers seem to be forced off their preferred spending level $[1 - s(\omega)]\bar{u}$ by monetary emissions which from (12) result from excess commodity demand. Either lack of market power or irrationality on the part of households appears to be involved.

Fortunately for the orthodox perspective, it is possible to provide (13) with a rational-actor justification. The argument is built around the equation of exchange, (1.4), used now to describe the demand for money, μ, instead of commodity aggregate demand as in section 3.3. The quantity theory states that μ is proportional to the value of transactions PX through the velocity coefficient V.

In the discussion that follows, we consider only the special case in which V stays constant (V is made a function of $\hat{P}$ in appendix 4.A). As will be clear from the jumping inflation rates in figures 4.5 and 4.6 below, this hypothesis is a simplified version of rational expectations about the cost of holding money. In those diagrams, inflation $\hat{P}$ moves to satisfy the growth rate version of the quantity equation, $\hat{\mu} = \hat{P} + \hat{X}$, which presupposes that $\hat{V} = 0$.

The quantity theory in growth rate form directly implies (1.5). The lead term in the brackets after the first equals sign is the loss in real balances μ/P induced by the instantaneous price change $\dot{P}$. The second term $\mu\hat{X}$ shows the amount of money that output growth $\hat{X}$ stimulates wealth-holders to acquire to continue to satisfy the equation of exchange. As already observed in chapter 1, the loss in wealth is called the "inflation tax" (or "induced lacking" in Robertson's words); offsetting it by saving is a rational choice. The increase in money balances to keep up with growth is often called "seigniorage." If we assume that the increase in money demand matches the increase in supply as in (1.7), then the inflation tax and seigniorage just add up to the term $-M/PK$ subtracted in the consumer demand function (13).[3]

Since we are in a full capacity model ($u = \bar{u}$), the inflation tax and seigniorage are really just transfers from wealth-holders to the state. If the level of output can vary, they have aggregate demand effects, as we will see next section. Their strength depends on velocity, as the expression after the second equals sign in (1.5) shows. Since the stylized fact is that V drifts up with inflation, seigniorage and the tax yield decline.

Equation (1.7) states that excess money supply growth is zero. In an economy where people only hold money or purchase goods, the appropriate substitutions show that (1.7) is equivalent to a statement that excess commodity demand vanishes:

$$\left(\frac{V}{\bar{u}}\right)\left\{\gamma + \left[1 - \left(\frac{\bar{u}}{V}\right)\right]g^i(\omega, \bar{u}) - [s_\pi - (s_\pi - s_w)\omega b]\bar{u}\right\} - \hat{P} = 0. \qquad (14)$$

This formula neatly summarizes monetarist views about inflation. Its meaning is that an excess of demand injections over leakages (with investment spending partly offset by the seigniorage yield it creates) directly translates into a higher level of $\hat{P}$: The leakage that adjusts to bring macro balance is the inflation tax. Distributional changes affect the strength of the pressure on prices. A higher real wage ω reduces investment demand g^i but also cuts into saving from profits. Presumably the orthodox view with regard to this matter is stagnationist; that is, progressive redistribution raises excess demand and increases $\hat{P}$. A surge in investment or state spending in response to a lower real wage could lead to a profit-led aggregate demand increase and potential dynamic instability (called "Harrodian hyperinflation" in chapter 3), as we will see below.

Structuralist views about the dynamics of inflation follow Robertson in emphasizing earnings lags, redistribution, and forced saving. The discussion in section 4.1 can be extended to incorporate three dynamic hypotheses. The first, implicit but so far unstated, is backward-looking contract indexation. We have seen that when high levels of inflation persist for a time, contracts which periodically increase "micro" prices like the money wage in response to last period's overall inflation rate tend to appear. The procedure makes sense, since recent inflation can be measured unambiguously (modulo index number problems)—it provides a point of reference around which all parties can disagree.[4]

The second issue is the proportion of price increases that should be redeemed for wage-earners: Should the "pass-through coefficient" of past price inflation into money wage growth be 100 percent or less? In section 4.1 we assumed full indexation with changing lags and wage peaks, but partial (or zero!) indexation is often applied, especially under orthodox inflation stabilization schemes.

Finally, factors besides conflicting income claims influence money wage formation. The level of economic activity or employment is one important consideration, although it is not relevant in the present model where capacity utilization is fixed at $\bar{u}$. We continue to assume that workers push for higher money wage growth when their real earnings decline. Specifically, money wage inflation $\hat{w}$ will run faster when ω is less than the target level ω^*.

In a formal specification we concentrate on conflicting claims and the pass-through coefficient. The continuous time wage equation is (1.8), in which we define ε as the pass-through coefficient, and δ measures the extent of wage pressure resulting from low real earnings. Backward-looking indexation with lags could be modeled by replacing the actual inflation rate $\hat{P}$ by an expected rate determined through adaptive expectations. This extension is eschewed, since it just adds a differential equation for the expected inflation rate without affecting the model's basic results. Finally, we assume that $\varepsilon < 1$, in recognition of the fact that indexation mechanisms are never perfect—even with 100 percent indexation, a finite contract period means that the real wage falls when inflation accelerates, as we have seen. Incomplete indexation can be highly regressive when ε is reduced brusquely in orthodox programs to stabilize inflation.

Plugging (1.8) into the definitional equation (1.9) gives

$$\hat{\omega} = (\varepsilon - 1)\hat{P} + \delta(\omega^* - \omega), \tag{15}$$

which states that distributional changes are mediated by monetary forces through the effect of $\hat{M}$ on $\hat{P}$ via (1.5) and (1.7). Equations (14) and (15) describe dynamics of the inflation rate and real wage. The economy (aside from jumps) is always on the "Inflation" locus representing (14) in figures 4.5 and 4.6—that is the result of assuming $\hat{V} = 0$. Setting $\hat{\omega}$ to zero in (15) gives a "distribution" schedule along which the real wage is constant.[5]

To see how the model works, consider the effects of an increased demand injection γ—the government permanently starts spending more. Figure 4.5 illustrates the outcome when a higher real wage spurs demand.

The fiscal expansion shifts the Inflation schedule to the right. At the current real wage, the inflation rate immediately jumps upward from A to B—the inflation tax brings aggregate demand into line with supply. Thereafter forced saving under incomplete indexation ($\varepsilon < 1$) takes over, leading ω and $\hat{P}$ to decline to a new equilibrium at C.

Reversing this process shows that lower government spending would raise the real wage, if it occurred in isolation. However, orthodox anti-inflation programs always involve wage restraint (i.e., reduction of the parameters ω^*, ε and δ in (1.8)). Such moves rotate the distribution schedule clockwise, reducing both ω and $\hat{P}$ directly through a forced saving process. Incomplete wage indexation emerges as a key component of orthodox anti-inflation policy—it reduces $\hat{P}$ along the inflation locus and is crucial to holding down money emission by increasing net saving supply. Nominal wages growing more slowly than prices are the mirror image of tight money, as in most quantity theory models. The resulting real wage loss implies that the capital stock growth rate will also slow under orthodox stabilization, with typical parameters for wage-led aggregate demand (an argument developed more fully in chapter 5).

Outcomes of a fiscal expansion in the exhilarationist case in which a higher real wage reduces inflation by cutting back on investment demand are illustrated in figure 4.6. In the upper diagram $\hat{P}$ is not very sensitive to changes in ω. Instead of overshooting its equilibrium level after fiscal expansion as in figure 4.5, inflation undershoots. After its initial upward jump, $\hat{P}$ continues to increase, cutting back on demand via both the inflation tax and forced saving.

In the lower diagram in which $\hat{P}$ is highly sensitive to ω, undershooting extends to instability. After an initial upward jump, price growth continues to accelerate. Forced saving steadily bids up the profit share, stimulating investment spending. Harrodian hyperinflation is caused by highly profit-responsive investment demand.

In perhaps a more realistic (and certainly more policy-relevant) scenario, fiscal expansion can also set off hyperinflation along the lines depicted in

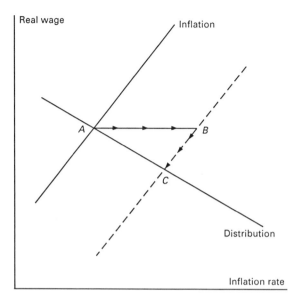

Figure 4.5
Effects of an increased demand injection in a Wicksell/Robertson model of inflation with a stagnationist aggregate demand response to the real wage

figure 3.3. The state may keep trying to offset ever-increasing demand or real wage reductions, perhaps initially induced by a change from an output adjustment to a forced saving regime under progressive redistribution or a supply shock. When capacity limitations bind, the paradox of thrift means that attempts to restore workers' real purchasing power via state spending or transfers can create an unstable price spiral. The situation will only be worsened if the tax system is not indexed to inflation, so that the Olivera-Tanzi effect begins to bite.[6]

All these factors can apply in practice: Late in the Allende and Garcia periods in Chile and Peru, respectively, real wages had fallen by three-quarters or more in inflations of the type illustrated in figure 4.6. The same thing happened in Nicaragua in the late 1980s, except that defense spending as opposed to frustrated expansionary and redistributive policy was the driving force.

4.3   Inflation Control When Output Can Adjust

The model just discussed is attractive in several ways. It has a plausible endogenous mechanism to generate the money supply. In growth rate

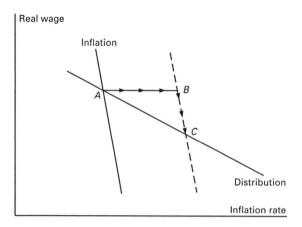

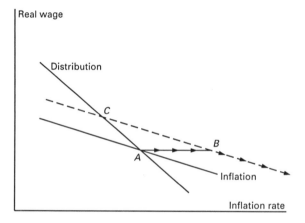

Figure 4.6
Cases of stable (*upper diagram*) and unstable (*lower diagram*) adjustment to an increased
demand injection in a Wicksell/Robertson model in which the aggregate demand response
to a real wage increase is exhilarationist

terms, it avoids price-quantity dichotomy since the inflation rate affects the real wage from (1.8) or (15), and ω in turn feeds back into growth of output and the money supply through saving supply and investment demand.

The main problem with the economy described in table 4.1 is that it always operates at full capacity $\bar{u}$. In practice, when wage-cutting and demand reduction are pursued, output invariably falls below its potential. Capacity utilization u (without the "bar") becomes endogenous in (14), meaning that we have to come up with another theory for $\hat{P}$. Structural inflation driven by class conflict and labor cost is the obvious alternative. A simple model of how cost-based price increases interact with effective demand is set out in table 4.2.

The first three equations parallel those of table 4.1. In (2.4) V is assumed endogenous in the short run, in line with the Banking School principles that structuralists prefer. Velocity adjusts to meet changes in u, which instead of sticking to a predetermined level $\bar{u}$ now becomes a "jump" variable responding to effective demand. In (2.5) we assume that $\hat{\mu} = \hat{P} + g^i$, so that growth of money demand $\hat{\mu}$ depends on the inflation rate and capacity growth. Equation (2.6) states that the money market clears in flow terms, or that excess demand for output is equal to zero. The implications are that velocity has no definite level but will vary in a range no wider than capacity utilization, maintaining its famous approximate stability in the long run.[7]

The next step is to determine output as a function of the inflation rate and other variables. Straightforward substitutions show that (2.6) is equivalent to

$$\gamma + \left[1 - \left(\frac{u}{V}\right)\right] g^i(\omega, u) - s(\omega)u - \left(\frac{u}{V}\right)\hat{P} = 0. \tag{16}$$

Table 4.2
A structuralist inflation model

(2.1)	$\dot{A} = \dot{D} + \dot{M}$
(2.2)	$\dot{A}/PK = g^i(\omega, u) + \gamma$
(2.3)	$\dot{D}/PK = [s_\pi - (s_\pi - s_w)\omega b]u = s(\omega)u$
(2.4)	$V = uPK/M$
(2.5)	$\dot{\mu}/PK = (u/V)(\hat{P} + g^i)$
(2.6)	$\dot{M}/PK - \dot{\mu}/PK = 0$
(2.7)	$\hat{P} = -\hat{\omega} + \hat{w}$
(2.8)	$\hat{w} = \varepsilon\hat{P} + f(\omega, u)$
(2.9)	$\hat{\omega} = h(\omega, u)$

This equation describes the output response curve, augmented to take into account fiscal, seigniorage, and inflation tax effects.

Output adjustment in the short run will be stable if

$$\Gamma = s_\pi \pi + s_w(1 - \pi) - \left[1 - \left(\frac{u}{V}\right)\right] g_u^i > 0,$$

a condition more easily satisfied than (2) in chapter 3 because seigniorage reduces excess aggregate demand. With $\Gamma > 0$, (16) shows that u will increase when government dissaving γ rises or the inflation rate $\hat{P}$ falls; in other words, cutting the inflation tax stimulates aggregate demand.

Inflation itself will depend on rates of growth of the money wage and the markup rate or real wage, as can be seen from (2.7) which is a growth rate version of markup pricing. To specify inflation dynamics, we have to set out separate differential equations for w and ω (or τ). Two widely quoted theories for money wage changes were advanced above—the Phillips curve appearing as equation (1.12) in table 3.1 and the combination of class conflict with indexation appearing as (1.8) in table 4.1. Putting the two together gives (2.8), where the signs of the partial derivatives are $f_u > 0$ and $f_\omega < 0$. The more completely indexed the economy, the closer the pass-through coefficient ε will be to one.

Real wage dynamics are harder to specify—there are not many stylized facts to be found. Common sense suggests that real wage movements are self-stabilizing—a low level of ω releases forces that make $\hat{\omega} > 0$, while real wages decline when they are already high. The real wage is also likely to change in response to the level of activity. Conventional wisdom dating from Dunlop and Tarshis (recall the discussion in section 3.3) suggests that ω varies with the cycle. We arrive at the differential equation (2.9), with $h_u > 0$ and $h_\omega < 0$. A steady state in the present model is defined by a constant real wage in (2.9); the possible (u, ω) combinations are described by an upward sloping curve. Its slope will be shallow for a stable wage, and vertical at some $\bar{u}$ if inflation is only steady at a "natural" unemployment rate as discussed in connection with figure 3.5. The natural rate hypothesis looks restrictive in light of a wage equation like (2.9).

Combining (2.7) through (2.9) gives a price inflation equation of the form

$$\hat{P} = \frac{1}{1 - \varepsilon}[f(\omega, u) - h(\omega, u)]. \tag{17}$$

With $f_u > h_u$ and $f_\omega < h_\omega$ inflation increases with the level of activity and decreases with the real wage, although other outcomes are possible. Suppose that demand is strong enough and/or the real wage low enough to make $f(\omega, u)$ positive. Then more extensive indexation as reflected in a high value of ε means that inflation runs faster in a steady state in which $h(\omega, u) = 0$. When ε is near to one, inflation is close to being inertial in the sense that it largely depends on indexation, with low levels of wage pressure producing very high inflation rates.

As we have already discussed, heterodox shock anti-inflation programs were based on inertial theory, the notion being that freezing wages and markups while simultaneously getting rid of all indexation mechanisms (i.e., setting ε close to zero) will make inflation go away. Section 4.1 showed how inertial models underplay the social conflict underlying many inflations. The present formulation indicates that they also leave out aggregate demand.

In both Argentina and Brazil when heterodox shocks were tried, consumer purchases jumped upward. In Brazil a stagnationist response to real wage increases leading into the freeze no doubt played a role. But more fundamentally, cutting $\hat{P}$ from triple- to single-digit annual rates drastically reduced the inflation tax. The implications for u can be seen from (16). Slower inflation leads consumers to spend more; accelerator feedbacks through investment amplify the output response by making the multiplier $1/\Gamma$ large.[8]

Monetarists did not anticipate these results, perhaps because they habitually assume that output is determined from the side of supply. Structuralists also did not foresee them, perhaps dismissing inflation taxes as a monetarist ploy. The shocks' outcomes suggest that each school has an incomplete model of inflation. Or to put it another way, a comprehensive theory must incorporate elements from both.

Higher demand has implications for macro stability since it feeds into real wage dynamics in (2.9). That equation is stable if the slope $\partial u / \partial \omega$ of the output response curve is less than $-h_\omega / h_u$. From our assumptions on signs ($h_\omega < 0$, $h_u > 0$), long-run equilibrium will be stable when $\partial u / \partial \omega < 0$ (i.e., when real wage increases make output fall). However, instability problems can arise in a stagnationist economy, if the real wage is strongly procyclical and/or its self-stabilizing tendencies are weak.

Figure 4.7 illustrates possible outcomes. The upper diagram shows a stable adjustment. The output response curve comes from figure 3.1, while the real wage schedule represents the steady state condition $\hat{\omega} = 0$. The schedule's slope is shallow for small (large) absolute values of $h_u(h_\omega)$. By voiding the inflation tax, a heterodox shock makes the output response curve shift to the right. Capacity utilization immediately increases from

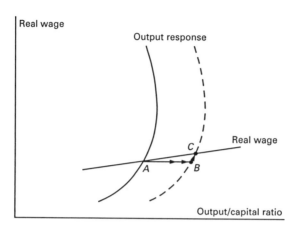

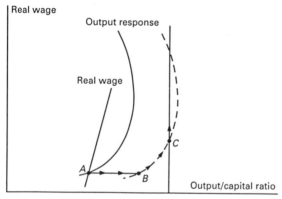

Figure 4.7
Stable (*upper diagram*) and unstable (*lower diagram*) real wage and output adjustment after a heterodox anti-inflation shock

A to B, and then drifts up to C as the real wage gradually increases. From (17) inflation may reappear if distributional effects don't offset the Phillips curve, but with a low value of ε, the price acceleration will be weak. The capital stock growth rate could also accelerate between steady states A and C in a wage-led economy.

The lower diagram illustrates a more unpleasant course of events. Real wage dynamics are unstable, with output increases in response to progressive redistribution accelerating money wage inflation. The freeze leads to an initial output jump, and then u and ω just continue to rise. The diagram shows them ultimately hitting the capacity limit $\bar{u}$ at point C. The economy shifts over to a forced saving/inflation tax adjustment mode —social pressures for re-indexation would surely emerge. As Winograd (1987) emphasizes, other policies—for example, interest or exchange rate manipulation—are needed to divert the economy from the forced saving segment of figure 4.7.

Other events may trigger an unstable inflationary process, for example, income redistribution and/or fiscal expansion. Managing a stagnationist economy is a difficult task, especially since it has no natural rates of capacity use and inflation to rely on. The same policies work differently, depending on the macroeconomic adjustment regime. Using diagrams like figure 4.7, Amadeo and Camargo (1989a) show how changing demand and labor market conditions shifted the curves in such a way as to make inflation stabilization immensely difficult throughout the 1980s in Brazil.

4.4 Political Economy

Our findings can be briefly summarized as follows:

1. The models of section 4.1 suggest that inflation is rooted in conflicting income claims and contract indexation. If indexation dominates, price increases may become inertial, in the sense that real wage targets, for example, are satisfied while at the same time last period's overall inflation is an unbiased predictor of current price growth. However, upward price shocks can easily push inflation to a higher plateau by forcing the real wage below the target and causing money wage claims (and therefore prices via the markup) to jump up. In practice, the inflationary response to large shocks (e.g., a strong signal such as a maxi-devaluation) may be more acute than when shocks are small as in a gradualist policy such as a crawling peg. In this structuralist model reduced demand will not strongly affect inflation because it will just lead output to fall in the short run.

2. Inflation according to monetarist models such as the one in section 4.2 has other causes. It is fundamentally due to excessive demand stimulation, with the inflation tax and seigniorage playing important adjustment roles. Unwittingly, the orthodox take a stagnationist stance in such models, believing that by increasing demand pressure, higher real wages speed inflation. Their stabilization schemes typically rely less on demand reduction than on cutting wages to ratify tight money and accentuate forced saving. In the exhilarationist case (real wage cuts stimulate demand), forced saving can give rise to unstable, ever-accelerating inflation. Redistributive attempts to offset wage shocks by transfers and state spending could conceivably trigger such a process.

3. Output decreases always occur under anti-inflation programs based on wage reduction and demand restraint, so the economy soon ceases to operate at full capacity. Inflation, however, usually continues in response to conflicting social claims and indexation mechanisms as emphasized in structuralist theory. Price freezes and de-indexation (combined in a "heterodox shock") are a recent response to this problem. By eliminating the inflation tax, they run the risk of stimulating demand and driving the economy back toward inflationary adjustment. In stagnationist economies—perhaps typical of the Third World—delicate policy choices always arise.

Appendix 4.A   Inflation-Dependent Velocity

As we have noted, velocity tends to rise when inflation accelerates, as the opportunity cost of holding noninterest-paying money goes up. If we stick to a strict quantity theory of money demand (an assumption relaxed in the following chapter), the obvious way to build this stylized fact into algebra is to treat velocity as a function of the inflation rate, say,

$$V = V_0 + v\hat{P},$$

in which the usual econometric estimates make v and V_0 positive constants with values between one and ten. With this specification, the growth rate version of the equation of exchange becomes

$$\hat{\mu} + \left(\frac{v}{V}\right)\left(\frac{d\hat{P}}{dt}\right) = \hat{P} + \hat{X},$$

which (when $u = \bar{u}$ and the money market clears) can be restated in the form

$$\frac{d\hat{P}}{dt} = \left(\frac{V}{v}\right)[\hat{P} - (\hat{\mu} - g^i)]$$

$$= \left(\frac{V}{v}\right)[\hat{P} - Q(\hat{P}, \omega)] \tag{18}$$

in which

$$Q(\hat{P}, \omega) = \left(\frac{V}{\bar{u}}\right)\left\{\gamma + \left[1 - \left(\frac{\bar{u}}{V}\right)\right]g^i - s(\omega)\bar{u}\right\}.$$

Equation (18) should be compared to (14) in section 4.2, which states that $Q(\hat{P}, \omega) - \hat{P} = 0$: With constant velocity, $\hat{P}$ jumps to meet any gap between money supply growth $\hat{M}$ and capacity (= output) growth g^i. In (18) the *change* in the inflation rate ($d\hat{P}/dt$) rather than inflation itself is the jump variable. When inflation exceeds the growth rate of money supply less output growth, velocity has to rise to satisfy the tautological equation of exchange. The entelechy behind (18) is that a higher V requires a higher $\hat{P}$: Inflation *accelerates* when its current rate exceeds the rate warranted by money supply growth. We are clearly dealing with a potentially unstable dynamic process, since there is a positive feedback of $\hat{P}$ into $d\hat{P}/dt$.[9]

To see how inflation evolves, we have to combine (18) with (15) restated in the form

$$\frac{d\omega}{dt} = \omega(1 - \varepsilon)\left[-\hat{P} + \left(\frac{\delta}{1 - \varepsilon}\right)(\omega^* - \omega)\right] \tag{19}$$

in a two-dimensional dynamic system. Around a steady state where $d\hat{P}/dt = d\omega/dt = 0$ and $\omega > 0$, the Jacobian of (18) and (19) takes the form

$$\begin{bmatrix} (V/v)[1 - v(\dot{M}/PX)] & -(V/v)(\partial Q/\partial\omega) \\ -(1 - \varepsilon)\omega & -\delta\omega \end{bmatrix}.$$

Instability is signaled by the facts that typically output exceeds money emission by a wide margin ($PX \gg \dot{M}$), while v is not so large as to make $v(\dot{M}/PX)$ exceed one; in other words, the northwest entry representing the partial derivative $\partial(d\hat{P}/dt)/\partial\hat{P}$ is positive.

A saddlepoint solution to (18) and (19) is possible when the determinant of the Jacobian (or the product of its eigenvalues) is negative: a condition satisfied in the stagnationist case in which $\partial Q/\partial\omega > 0$. Figure 4.8 illustrates the dynamics when there is a fiscal expansion shifting the "Inflation" locus along which $d\hat{P}/dt = 0$ to the right. The inflation rate immediately jumps

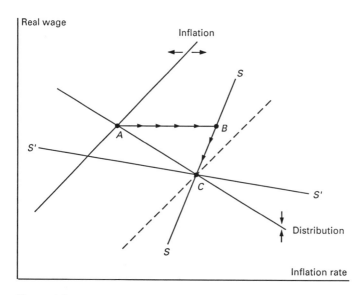

Figure 4.8
Inflation dynamics in the Wicksell/Robertson model when velocity depends on the
inflation rate (the stagnationist case)

from point A to B along the saddlepath SS, and then converges to a new
equilibrium at C. Tracing arrows for dynamic trajectories (an exercise
omitted here to avoid cluttering the diagram) shows that all other solutions
diverge toward the unstable separatrix S'S'.

Comparing Figures 4.5 and 4.8 shows that inflation and wage dynamics
with constant and inflation-sensitive velocity are similar in the stagnationist case—the initial upward jump in the inflation rate is a bit smaller
when V depends on $\hat{P}$. In the exhilarationist case, both a saddlepoint and
an unstable hyperinflation remain possible, with dynamics under variable
velocity qualitatively similar to the scenarios illustrated in figure 4.6.

Appendix 4.B   Interest Rate Effects on Inflation

Knut Wicksell (1935), who pioneered cumulative process inflation models
like the one in section 4.2, argued that inflation is set off when the interest
rate in a "pure credit" banking system is pegged too low. That is, if
the nominal rate i is controlled by the banks, and if $j = i - \hat{P}$ stands for the
inflation-deflated or "real" rate, then the aggregate demand equation (14)
should be restated as

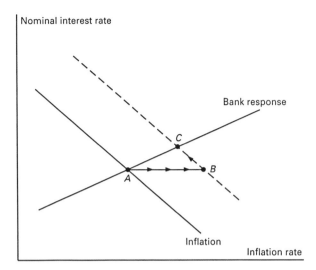

Figure 4.9
Interest rate adjustment in a cumulative process inflation model

$$\gamma + \left[1 - \left(\frac{\overline{u}}{V}\right)\right]g^i(j) - s(j)\overline{u} - \left(\frac{\overline{u}}{V}\right)\hat{P} = 0, \tag{20}$$

to capture the inflation story Wicksell had in mind. A reduction in i (and thereby j) increases investment g^i and reduces saving s, as in the model of appendix 2.A. In that discussion we assumed that the interest rate adjusted freely to clear the market for loanable funds. But now we follow Wicksell in assuming that i is momentarily pegged by the banks, so excess aggregate demand must be restrained by a higher inflation tax due to more rapid money emission.

Equation (20) is represented by the "inflation" schedule in figure 4.9. Its negative slope means that increases of both the interest and inflation rates reduce aggregate demand. For $\hat{P}$, the implication is that the saving leakage due to an increased inflation tax exceeds the increment in investment less saving resulting from a lower real interest rate as $\hat{P}$ goes up:

$$\frac{\overline{u}}{V} > \left[1 - \left(\frac{\overline{u}}{V}\right)\right]\left(\frac{dg^i}{dj}\right) - \overline{u}\left(\frac{ds}{dj}\right)$$

in formal terms. In the following discussion, we assume that this condition is satisfied.

Wicksell argued that after inflation persists for a time, banks (or the Central Banker) will voluntarily raise the interest rate to limit loan demand

and cut down on losses of reserves, say according to a rule such as

$$\frac{di}{dt} = \theta\hat{P} + \phi(i^* - i), \tag{21}$$

where i^* is a target rate. Alternatively, they might seek to stabilize the real rate,

$$\frac{di}{dt} = \theta'\hat{P} + \phi[j^* - (i - \hat{P})],$$

but this equation reduces to (21) with $i^* = j^*$ and $\theta = \theta' + \phi$, so we can consider either case. If the real rate is targeted, then $\theta > \phi$ in (21), a condition that turns out to be interesting below.

The "bank response" curve in figure 4.9 represents the condition $di/dt = 0$, giving a positive relationship between i and $\hat{P}$. An autonomous increase in aggregate demand (e.g., from higher public dissaving γ) immediately makes the inflation rate jump upward from A to B, and then banks begin to raise interest rates until a new steady state is reached at C. Inflation will be forced back closer to its initial level insofar as the bank response schedule is steep, namely, $\theta \gg \phi$ in (21), but for finite parameters $\hat{P}$ will increase at least somewhat.

The diagram also shows that the nominal interest rate will be higher in the new steady state, while a bit of manipulation indicates that the real rate will increase when $\theta > \phi$. But then investment g^i will decline, and so will the steady state rate of growth. In other words, if banks respond aggressively to inflation by raising interest rates (in particular, if they try to stabilize the real rate j by raising the nominal rate i), then they may force investment to be reduced enough to make fiscal dissaving crowd out growth in the medium run. There is no automatic transition from inflation stabilization to renewed capital formation.

Two further observations can be added. First, even if forced saving à la equation (15) is combined with interest rate adjustment in (21), one can show that inflation still will rise in a new steady state after γ increases (with finite parameters). The adjustments of ω and i shown in figures 4.5 and 4.9 do *not* combine to offset an inflationary shock fully.

Second, such persistent inflation means that the desired levels ω^* and i^* of the real wage and interest rates are not attained. In particular, Wicksell's natural rate of interest becomes a moving target, depending on the underlying inflationary trend (a result of the interactions of aggregate demand with wage indexation and bank responsiveness, in the present model)—a point perhaps first raised by Myrdal (1939, 1967).

5

The Interest Rate, Inflation, and Financial Instability

In this chapter we blend relationships brought out in chapters 3 and 4 into an investment-driven stagnationist growth model, incorporating interest rate and output variation in the short run. Macroeconomic equilibrium is illustrated with an IS/LM system; in a longer run the emphasis is on forces that can make the growth rate differ across steady states. The model's basic assumptions are that capacity utilization is never at an upper bound and that the real wage and the velocity of base money with respect to the capital stock adjust between steady states. A further state variable representing investors' confidence makes the model a convenient vehicle to demonstrate how financial instability along the lines suggested by Minsky (1975, 1986) can arise, a possibility elaborated further in chapters 6 and 7.

We begin in section 5.1 with a description of the monetary (or LM) side of the economy, and the real (or IS) side is added in section 5.2. They are linked not only by the usual effects of interest rates on investment and of output on money demand but also by (1) the fact that higher interest costs on loans to firms to finance working capital may increase prices in a form of cost-push; (2) the possibility that output increases can either raise or lower interest rates, by "crowding-out" or "crowding-in" loans to firms, respectively; and (3) positive effects of output and the interest rate on the inflation rate, which in turn shifts money and commodity excess demand functions. Comparative statics of the model are worked out in section 5.3, and changes in the real wage and velocity across steady states are discussed in section 5.4. Section 5.5 introduces Minsky-style financial instability (i.e., macroeconomic divergence from real/financial equilibrium, cyclical fluctuations, or even mathematically chaotic dynamics of macro variables) resulting from cycles in confidence exacerbated by financial crowding-in. Section 5.6 presents brief conclusions.

5.1   Asset Markets

In contrast to the flow model of money demand and supply in chapter 4, we work with stocks of financial assets—the advantage is presumably greater verisimilitude because asset returns are determined in markets for stocks and not just flows. Table 5.1 presents a simple asset market structure of the type that one might observe in semi-industrialized countries. The banking system dominates the picture: Its assets are base money H (which in a closed economy essentially takes the form of government liabilities placed with the banks) and loans to firms L_b. Deposits held by the public comprise the banks' liabilities.

Firms are assumed to finance their capital stock PK by borrowing from either banks (L_b) or the public (L_p). The public holds its wealth W only in the form of loans to firms and deposits, since there are no markets for equity or government obligations.[1] By consolidating entries in table 5.1, one can see that wealth is the sum of the value of capital stock and base money:

$$W = PK + H. \tag{1}$$

Since the public holds only two assets, we need just one market equilibrium condition. We use the one stating that excess demand for deposits should equal zero,

$$\delta(PK + H) - \xi H = 0,$$

in which δ is the fraction of wealth held as deposits and ξ is the deposit/base money ratio, controlled by the monetary authorities as their policy tool.

Table 5.1
Financial structure

Banking system	
Base money H	D Deposits from the public
Bank loans L_b	
Firms	
Capital stock PK	L_b Loans from banks
	L_p Loans from the public
The public	
Bank deposits D	W Wealth
Loans to firms L_p	

The deposit equilibrium can be rewritten as an LM curve,

$$\delta(i, \hat{P}, u)(V + 1) - \xi = 0, \tag{2}$$

in which $V = PK/H$ is the "velocity" of base money with respect to the value of the capital stock. We will use V as a state variable in dynamic analysis below, but in the short run it is predetermined since its components P, K, and H all come from history. The arguments of δ are the nominal interest rate i, inflation rate $\hat{P}$, and output/capital ratio u. We consider the signs of their impacts in turn.

The interest rate varies to clear the loan (and implicitly, deposit) market. Typically the partial derivative $\partial \delta / \partial i$ is assumed negative: An increase in the nominal interest rate paid by firms for loans pulls wealth-holders from deposits. From (2) the sign of this response implies that in partial equilibrium, a less restrictive monetary policy in the form of an increase in ξ will raise total deposits and reduce i. Higher velocity, a symptom of financial disintermediation in the sense that there is less monetary "coverage" of the capital stock, has the opposite effect.

Neither the theoretical literature nor econometric practice is terribly clear about the direction of the effect of inflation $\hat{P}$ on deposit demand. In chapter 4 households were assumed to flee money when inflation speeds up: The implication from (2) is that desired loans to firms increase so that the nominal interest rate falls. Alternatively, if the public wants to reduce loans to firms when the real interest rate $i - \hat{P}$ declines, then in partial equilibrium, $\partial \delta / \partial \hat{P} > 0$ and i has to increase along with $\hat{P}$.[2] For completeness, we consider both possibilities below even though an increased demand for money as the inflation rate declines seems the empirically more relevant case in the developing world.

With regard to capacity use, the usual hypothesis is that when u increases then so does transactions demand for money, meaning that δ goes up. To restore financial equilibrium, i has to rise. But alternatively, we have seen that the profit rate rises along with the capacity utilization rate. The wealth-holding public may then view firms as more promising investments, with portfolio preferences shifting from deposits to loans. In that event i would decline. These two possibilities, respectively, represent loan crowding-out and crowding-in by higher output; as we will see, strong crowding-in can lead to financial instability along Minskyian lines.[3]

5.2   The Commodity Market and Inflation

Investment theories popular since about 1980 typically postulate that capital formation rises in response to an increase in P_k or the price of capital in place, defined as the capitalized value (over an infinite future, for simplicity) of expected future profits per unit of capital stock:

$$P_k = \frac{Pr}{i - \hat{P}}$$

where we take the current real interest and profit rates as proxies for their expected future values. As we have seen in appendix 2.A, such a formulation appears in Minsky (1975) and underlies mainstream q investment theory as proposed by Tobin (1969). Minsky assumes that investment g^i depends on the premium of P_k over the commodity price level P (i.e., the cost of new capital goods). Linearizing this profitability linkage and bringing in a direct effect of capacity utilization on investment along Kaldor-Steindl lines gives the following relationships:

g^i = investment/capital stock

$$= g_0 + (\alpha\pi + \beta)u - \theta(i - \hat{P})$$

$$= g_0 + \left[\alpha + \left(\frac{\beta}{\pi}\right)\right]r - \theta(i - \hat{P}), \tag{3}$$

where π as usual stands for the profit share. Basically (3) adds a real interest rate term $-\theta(i - \hat{P})$ to the investment function used in chapters 2 through 4.

Together with government dissaving relative to capital stock (or γ) and a saving function as in previous chapters, (3) gives the IS schedule

$$\gamma + g_0 + (\alpha\pi + \beta)u - \theta(i - \hat{P}) - s(\omega, \hat{P})u = 0, \tag{4}$$

which can be solved together with the LM curve (2) and an inflation equation to be described shortly to give short-run equilibrium. The aggregate saving rate $s(\omega, \hat{P})$ is assumed to rise with a reduction in the real wage ω (from forced saving) and an increase in $\hat{P}$ (the inflation tax). We don't include an interest rate effect on saving, in line with empirical evidence for developing economies (Giovannini 1985). As in appendix 4.B we assume that faster inflation reduces aggregate demand; that is, the inflation tax dominates the increase in investment due to a lower real interest rate.

Price inflation is determined from the side of costs. Its rate is

$$\hat{P} = -\hat{\omega} + \hat{w} + \eta i, \tag{5}$$

which is the same as equation (2.7) in table 4.2 except for the addition of the term ηi. The reason to include the interest rate in the inflation equation is that the cost of loans for working capital is large in many developing economies, say, 10 to 20 percent of GDP in nominal terms when inflation is at double or triple digit annual rates. Firms will be strongly tempted to pass interest rate increases along into higher prices, which will then feed through wage increases into ongoing inflation: (5) is a reduced form representation of this process. The effect shows up in many developing economies (Taylor 1988a), and its analytical implications are discussed below.[4]

For the growth rates of the money and real wages, we adopt equations (2.8) and (2.9) from table 4.2,

$$\hat{w} = \varepsilon\hat{P} + f(\omega, u), \tag{6}$$

and

$$\hat{\omega} = h(\omega, u) \tag{7}$$

with the justifications presented in chapter 4.

Equations (2) through (7) make up a short-run macroeconomic system in the variables i, g^i, u, $\hat{P}$, $\hat{w}$, and $\hat{\omega}$, depending on the state variables V and ω. Treating the state variables as predetermined, we discuss several comparative static exercises of policy interest in the following section.

5.3 Comparative Statics in the Short Run

Equations (5)–(7) solve to give a reduced form expression for the inflation rate,

$$\hat{P} = \psi(u, i, \omega), \tag{8}$$

where the first two partial derivatives are positive and the last one may be negative. A higher inflation rate affects the LM function (2) with an ambiguous sign (depending on whether inflation increases or reduces demand for deposits) and reduces aggregate demand in the IS equation (4). We assume that feedbacks of u and i into themselves via $\hat{P}$ do not destabilize signs of responses in (2) and (4), and thus present diagrams with reduced form IS and LM schedules with changes in the inflation rate built in.[5]

Figure 5.1 illustrates the crowding effects already mentioned. In the upper diagram, a rightward shift of the IS curve (e.g., from more government dissaving or a heterodox anti-inflationary shock) makes the interest rate rise. Depending on the strength of interest rate and capacity utilization effects in the investment function (3), the capital stock growth rate g^i might

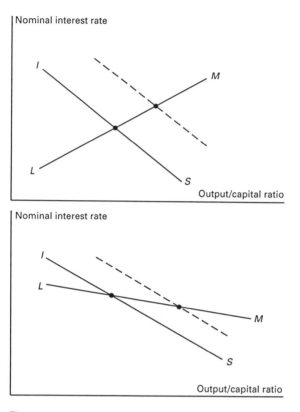

Figure 5.1
Financial crowding-out (*upper diagram*) and crowding-in (*lower diagram*) in an IS/LM system

well decline. This potential trade-off between government spending and growth (which could be accentuated by monetary policy, as in appendix 4.B) figures in mainstream stabilization programs based on models that emphasize interest rate linkages and downplay effects of output increases and public spending on entrepreneurs' animal spirits.[6]

Financial crowding-in is illustrated in the lower diagram of figure 5.1, in which higher capacity utilization stimulates loans to firms, making the interest rate decline. The LM curve has a negative slope, so that higher aggregate demand increases u and reduces i. The capital stock growth rate correspondingly speeds up. If these linkages spark investors and shift g^i strongly upward, there is a risk of instability due to a positive feedback of increased output into aggregate demand growth over time. Minskyian scenarios along these lines are explored below.

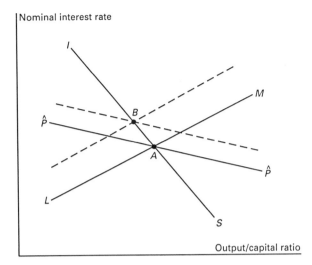

Figure 5.2
Stagflationary short-run effects of tight monetary policy when there is strong interest rate
cost-push

Stagflationary effects of tighter monetary policy due to interest rate
cost-push are illustrated in figure 5.2. The $\hat{P}\hat{P}$ schedule through the initial
equilibrium A is a contour curve or isoinflation locus showing values of the
output/capital ratio and interest rate that produce a given inflation rate
from (8). The slope is negative since increases in both u and i raise $\hat{P}$. There
is an infinite family of contours like $\hat{P}\hat{P}$, each corresponding to a given
inflation rate. As one skips from one to another heading northeast, inflation
goes up.

Point B shows a new equilibrium with tighter money. The interest rate
goes up and output declines, as usual. As the figure is drawn, the inflation
rate also rises. The condition for this outcome is that the $\hat{P}\hat{P}$ curves have a
shallower (less negative) slope than the IS schedule, corresponding to a
relatively strong effect of i on $\hat{P}$ in (8).[7] Figure 5.2 represents a situation
apparently common in developing countries: Both econometrics and discussions of political economy often point to higher interest rates, reduced
output, *and* faster inflation in the wake of tight money. This unfortunate
combination of policy outcomes is not inevitable, but it is a possibility to
be borne in mind. It will not occur if i does not strongly affect the inflation
rate so that the $\hat{P}\hat{P}$ curves are steep.

Figure 5.3 shows a final comparative statics exercise illustrating the
effects of a heterodox shock that drives the inflation rate sharply down-

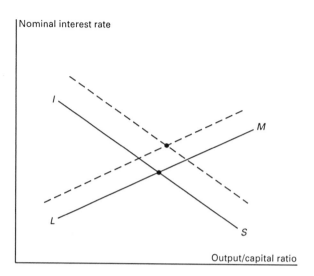

Figure 5.3
Effects of a heterodox shock in the short run

ward. If demand for money rises, the interest rate is likely to increase as discussed above (i.e., the LM curve shifts upward). With a reduced inflation tax, aggregate demand increases and the IS curve shifts to the right. The outcomes are a higher i and (probably) a higher u as well. How these changes feed into medium-term dynamics is discussed in the following section.

5.4   Comparisons across Steady States

The real wage ω and velocity V are the state variables that evolve to shift temporary equilibria of the sort we have been discussing.[8] Across steady states defined by $\hat{\omega} = \hat{V} = 0$ with positive ω and V, the growth rate, inflation rate, capacity utilization, and so on, can all differ. We explore some of the possibilities in the discussion that follows.

Real wage dynamics are given by (7). The direct partial derivative $\partial h / \partial \omega$ is assumed negative (i.e., real wage changes are self-stabilizing). However, in an economy with a consumption-led demand response to income redistribution a higher real wage makes output rise. Wage homeorhesis can be overcome through the compound derivative $(\partial h / \partial u)\,(du/d\omega)$ stating that ω grows faster in response to output expansion in the IS/LM system. We thus have to consider both stable and unstable real wage dynamics $(\partial\hat{\omega}/\partial\omega$

negative and positive, respectively) as in figure 4.7. High velocity resembles tight money in driving up the interest rate and cutting capacity
use, making the total derivative $\partial\hat{\omega}/\partial V < 0$ in (7).

The growth rate of velocity follows from its definition: $V = PK/H$ and
therefore $\hat{V} = \hat{P} + \hat{K} - \hat{H}$. Since the increase in base money stems from
government dissaving ($\dot{H} = \gamma PK$), the equation for $\hat{V}$ becomes

$$\hat{V} = \hat{P} + g^i - \gamma V, \tag{9}$$

where $\hat{P}$ and g^i come from (8) and (3), respectively. The steady state value
of velocity is $(\hat{P} + g^i)/\gamma$. For relatively small shifts in the inflation and
growth rates, long-term velocity will be little changed—the characteristic
observation in advanced economies. Moreover V increases with $\hat{P}$. With
triple digit inflation and fiscal dissaving more than 10 percent of GDP, V in
steady state might be expected to be on the order of ten, a magnitude in
accordance with stylized numerical facts.[9] As we have observed several
times, treating V as a state variable instead of a tautological constant
describing money demand is not a whimsical approach.

The sign of the partial derivative of $\hat{V}$ with respect to ω in (9) is
ambiguous for various reasons—whether the economy is wage or profit
led, the sign of the effect of ω on $\hat{P}$, and so forth. We will typically assume
a positive response, representing a wage-led system.

An increase in V itself is likely to reduce $\hat{V}$; in other words, γ is usually
positive, the growth rate will decline with tighter financial markets, and a
Cavallo/Patman inflation response to higher interest costs is not likely to
be destabilizing. If indeed $\partial\hat{V}/\partial V < 0$, velocity is a stable state variable.

Since we assume that $\partial\hat{V}/\partial\omega > 0$, then $\partial\hat{V}/\partial V < 0$ means that the
"asset market" locus along which $\hat{V} = 0$ has a positive slope in the dia-
grams of figure 5.4. The "distribution" locus along which $\hat{\omega} = 0$ has a
negative or positive slope depending on whether real wage adjustment is
stabilizing or destabilizing as discussed above. The two cases are shown in
the upper and lower diagrams, respectively.

The pictures illustrate medium-term implications of a heterodox shock.
The shock increases output and the interest rate in the short run, from
figure 5.3. If real wage adjustment is stabilizing, the higher u has to be
offset by a higher ω to hold $\hat{\omega}$ equal to zero: The distribution schedule
shifts up. With regard to velocity, by cutting $\hat{P}$ dramatically, the shock is
likely to make $\hat{V}$ negative. Hence V itself must fall to restore steady state
equilibrium: The asset market schedule shifts to the left.

The outcomes of these shifts in a new steady state are a higher real wage
and an ambiguous change in velocity. Because of the wage increase a

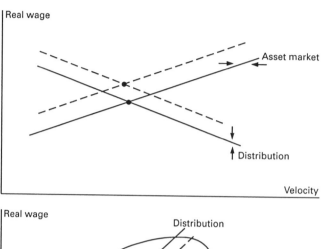

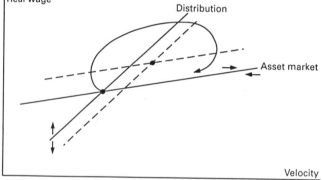

Figure 5.4
Effects of a heterodox shock across steady states when real wage dynamics are stable, (*upper diagram*) and unstable (*lower diagram*)

stagnationist economy is likely to end up growing faster, but if velocity rises, there could be renewed inflationary pressure from high interest rates. With luck, the shock could bring good results.

As already noted in chapter 4, one problem that arises with heterodox shocks is that the real wage may not be self-stabilizing if its growth rate rises with capacity utilization in a stagnationist economy. The lower diagram of figure 5.4 then applies, and there can be an unstable adjustment spiral as shown. If capacity limits begin to bind as the real wage and output go up, then the shock package is likely to fall apart when it fails to produce definitive results in the medium run.

Figure 5.5 depicts long-run effects of a tight money policy when the Cavallo-Patman effect is strong. By reducing activity in the short run, the policy makes $\hat{\omega} < 0$; ω itself must fall to restore equilibrium. Since inflation

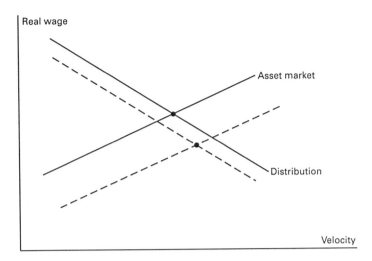

Figure 5.5
Long-run effects of tight money when there are strong interest rate cost-push and stable real wage dynamics

accelerates, $\hat{V}$ becomes positive. Velocity itself must rise as an offset; that is, the asset market schedule shifts to the right. The new steady state has an unambiguously lower real wage; hence in a wage-led economy there is slower growth.

The steady state value of V in figure 5.5 can shift either way. One key question is whether after monetary policy is tightened, V evolves toward a level low enough to restore the original interest rate. If not, the secular inflation rate can be higher—slower growth will in part offset faster price increases in holding velocity relatively stable. In an investment-driven growth model there is no reason for the adverse effects of short-run stagflationary policy not to persist over time, as we have already seen in appendix 4.B. Experience of several developing countries in the 1980s (e.g., Mexico until capital flight grudgingly reversed late in the decade) verifies the relevance of this theoretical conclusion.

5.5   Financial Instability

When there is financial crowding-in as in the lower diagram of figure 5.1, a destabilizing investment response is a possibility in a demand-driven economy. This is the gist of Minsky's financial instability hypothesis, which we illustrate formally here.

The easiest way to tell the story is to introduce a new state variable ρ, representing investors' confidence—we let expected future profits r^e be represented by the sum,

$$r^e = r + \rho.$$

The current profit rate r is given by enterprise cash flows while expected additional profits ρ will depend on the state of the economy. In the last line of (3), investment is now assumed to depend on r^e instead of r.

It is reasonable to assume that confidence rises when actual profit rates are high or real interest rates low. With crowding-in the two events run together, so we settle for a simple differential equation of the form,

$$\dot{\rho} = \phi[j^* - (i - \hat{P})], \tag{10}$$

where j^* is a reference real interest rate.

When there is financial crowding-in, the lower diagram of figure 5.1 suggests that an increase in ρ will shift the IS schedule to the right and reduce the nominal interest rate. If inflation does not slow markedly (i.e., $\hat{P}$ is driven by forces besides the Cavallo-Patman effect), the real rate will decline as well, so $\dot{\rho} > 0$ from (10). We have positive feedback of ρ into its own growth rate and potential dynamic instability.

Suppose that aggregate demand declines in response to a higher real wage (the economy has profit-led macroeconomic adjustment). A rise in ω will then shift the IS curve to the left and drive up the interest rate in the lower diagram of figure 5.1, making $\partial\dot{\rho}/\partial\omega < 0$. At the same time an increase in ρ increases u and hence $\hat{\omega}$ from (7). The phase diagram for (7) and (10) in this case appears in figure 5.6. Complications resulting from changes in velocity from (9) are taken up below.

The scenario is that there is a downward shock to confidence from an initial equilibrium at A. After the shock economic activity declines, and both confidence and the real wage fall. The latter change restores investment demand, leading to financial crowding-in and reduction of interest rates. The trajectory crosses the "expectations" locus along which $\dot{\rho} = 0$, confidence begins to rise and recovery gets fully underway. As the two trajectories that are sketched in the diagram illustrate, in a model described wholly by linear differential equations, there can be either cyclical convergence back to equilibrium or outright instability with ever-widening wage and expected profit rate fluctuations.

With nonlinear dynamics, elementary catastrophe theory suggests a third potential outcome. As $\partial\dot{\rho}/\partial\rho$ is increased parametrically from a value

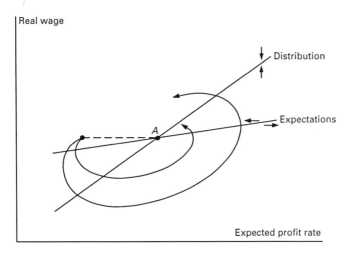

Figure 5.6
Potential dynamic instability when there is financial crowding-in in the short run

permitting cyclical convergence through the point at which $\partial\dot{\rho}/\partial\rho + \partial\dot{\omega}/\partial\omega = 0$ [where the trace of the Jacobian of (7) and (10) vanishes at equilibrium as the real parts of its two complex roots go to zero], there could be a Hopf bifurcation to a limit cycle with permanent, bounded fluctuations of ρ and ω. The existence of such an attracting cycle "between" the stable and unstable trajectories depends on nonlinearities in the functions (7) and (10) which could damp the system's divergent tendencies. Such cycles are explored further in the following chapter.

In a wage-led economy a higher real wage shifts the IS curve to the right and reduces the interest rate in figure 5.1, making $\partial\dot{\rho}/\partial\omega > 0$ and giving the expectations locus a negative slope. The Jacobian determinant for (7) and (10) becomes negative, the signal of saddlepoint dynamics: A downward jump in ρ leads to an ever-negative $\dot{\rho}$ associated with first a falling and then a slowly rising real wage until the model equations cease to make sense. However, changes in velocity can have intriguing effects in this situation.

Regardless of distributional changes, V and ρ interact qualitatively in the same fashion as ω and ρ in figure 5.6. After the shock, $\hat{V} < 0$ from (9) as growth and inflation decline. This increase in financial intermediation means that the real interest rate falls, helping to restore economic activity and ultimately ρ. During the recovery rising values of ρ and ω raise $\hat{P}$ and g. Velocity rises and the interest rate goes up, braking expansion.

Depending on the relative strengths of the braking effect in the upswing and stimulation from low interest rates in the trough, trajectories for ω, ρ, and V can be folded over each other as in an Olde English taffy machine. Because $\partial\dot\rho/\partial\rho > 0$, the first two variables spread away from each other in their plane and velocity fluctuations add folding action in the third dimension. In fancier language, the trajectories can cycle around a well-known "strange" or chaotic attractor—the Rössler band.[10] The outcome would be endless, unpredictable variations of all three state variables. This eventuality could only be explored after parametric specification of all the model's functional forms.[11]

5.6   Political Economy

In investment-driven models the growth rate can vary across steady states. The discussion in this chapter shows that

1. Austerity in the form of tight money can easily reduce capacity utilization in the short run *and* the growth rate over time. There is not a natural transition from recession to renewed growth, especially in a wage-led economy in which regressive income redistribution does not activate investors' confidence and aggregate demand.

2. If higher interest rates increase the inflation rate because of working capital cost-push (the Cavallo-Patman effect), then persistent tight money can also worsen inflation over time. The real wage and velocity will adjust across steady states to permit a stagflationary secular equilibrium.

3. As we have seen already in chapter 4, heterodox shock policies can run off the rails if real wage responses to increased aggregate demand from a reduced inflation tax are not strongly self-stabilizing.

4. If there is financial crowding-in, then investors' reactions to lower real interest rates à la Minsky can provoke real/financial instability, cyclical fluctuations of investors' confidence, the real wage, and velocity, or even chaotic dynamics among these variables over time. Further examples of such financial fragility are presented in the following chapter.

6

Regressive
Redistribution,
Speculation, and
Financial Collapse

Regressive income redistribution or windfall gains in wealth can cause output stagnation and a surge in speculative finance. Tight monetary policy can make these outcomes worse. This chapter develops the economics behind such effects in a stagnationist growth model incorporating choice among speculative and nonspeculative assets by firms or rentiers who benefit from policy and distributional shifts.

At least four historical cases—the United States in the 1920s, and more recently Chile, Argentina, and Kuwait—exemplify events the model reflects. In the United States, according to Galbraith (1961) and Sylos-Labini (1984), there was substantial income concentration in the decade before 1929—the nonlabor share rose by about six percentage points. The causes in part were rising productivity and a stagnant real wage. Although semiluxury sectors such as residential construction and automobiles flourished, basic industries such as food and textiles were flat. As Sylos-Labini puts it, the implication about the use of higher profit incomes was that "... at home the investment opportunities were increasing very slowly. Therefore those incomes were invested to some extent abroad (up to 1927) and to an increasing extent in speculative activities, namely, in the stock market which experienced a gigantic boom and eventually collapsed" (pp. 221–222). Finance for the boom came from margin trading and some degree of chicanery, as Galbraith recounts.

In Chile in the late 1970s a similar scenario played out, according to Arellano (1985). Income concentration imposed from above was the key to both macroeconomic stabilization and political restructuring under the Pinochet regime while tight money kept interest rates high. For both reasons goods production stagnated although imports and supplies of services shot up. Companies nationalized under Salvador Allende were sold off to financial groups (with nicknames like Piranhas and Crocodiles) close to the new government. Their shares soon became the object of a speculative boom, since as in the United States real investment opportunites were scarce. When the groups started borrowing from banks under their control to support their own firms' share prices, the boom was well on the way toward its early 1980s crash.

Across the Andes in Argentina, speculation centered on foreign exchange. As analyzed by Frenkel (1983), an initial slowing of a pre-announced crawling peg made domestic assets attractive, inducing capital inflow. Credit multiplication of reserve increases by the banking system rapidly expanded visible wealth. Interest rates fell, igniting a boom. However, with ongoing inflation the real exchange rate became increasingly overvalued, raising the local currency value of foreign exchange at the same time as domestic financial disintermediation grew worse. Confidence in local assets collapsed—the ensuing capital flight deprived the economy of investible resources for over ten years.

Finally, in Kuwait a couple of years later household wealth had reached unprecedented heights. Non-oil GDP was stagnant as the government reined in public spending when oil prices began to fall. Excess private funds went into speculation, on real estate and shares of companies "incorporated" elsewhere around the Persian Gulf. The boom was fueled by post-dated checks that could be cashed in advance—an effective device for blowing up nominal wealth. Indeed, the ratio of financial sector assets to GDP rose from 0.98 in 1979 to 2.14 by 1982 (compared to typical values between 1.2 and 1.5 in industrialized economies). As in the other examples this financial balloon was blown up by speculators in a lax regulatory environment, which was dramatically tightened after it burst.

Common themes in these experiences include the following:

1. *The real side of the economy.* Regressive redistribution reduces economic activity. In the simplest story, real wage cuts make output fall. Investment demand, driven by an accelerator, is low at the same time as potential saving goes up. Idle funds find their outlet in speculation. High interest rates from tight money strengthen the forces leading to these results.

2. *The financial side.* Prices of the speculative assets rise as portfolios shift from productive ends. Financial means are found to bid up speculative demands and prices further, making nominal wealth endogenous in the short run. Financial disintermediation—increasing velocity and a rising ratio of speculative to productive assets—may follow, especially if money is tight.

3. *Dynamics.* A cumulative process based on rising investor confidence in speculation and increasingly fragile enterprise balance sheets unfolds until

disintermediation surpasses feasible bounds. There can be limit cycles or chaotic dynamics. Other possibilities include a crash or cyclical convergence to a new equilibrium, perhaps on a faster growth path where confidence boosts domestic demand, accelerating investment to absorb higher potential saving. The outcomes depend on how strongly an increase in velocity or the shifts in the portfolio shares of real and speculative assets accentuate or reduce confidence in nonproductive holdings.

A model similar to the one in chapter 5 is used to analyze these linkages. It is presented as follows: Section 6.1 describes the financial part of the economy, introducing a speculative asset and a velocitylike state variable to measure intermediation. Section 6.2 presents the real side, along with an IS/LM apparatus used to investigate the comparative statics of income redistribution and monetary restraint in section 6.3.

On the basis of this short-run specification, two forms of speculation are discussed. Section 6.4 sets up joint dynamics of the velocity variable and an indicator of confidence in the speculative asset which depends on expected capital gains. Section 6.5 is based on the hypothesis that firms resort increasingly to "inside" debt finance when their net cash flows and capital gains from speculative holdings go up. In both cases dynamics of the speculative price depends on how effectively disintermediation brakes portfolio shifts from other assets. Appendix 6.A shows that these scenarios are not fundamentally changed when workers have visible saving, directed toward money as opposed to other assets. Adding the corresponding state variable—the ratio of workers' deposits to base money—complicates but does not alter the basic results.

6.1   The Financial Side of the Economy

Table 6.1 expands on table 5.1 in showing the economy's balance sheets in which two groups of households made up of rentiers and workers (who receive profit and wage incomes respectively) undertake transactions with firms and banks. In the first panel the banks' assets are base money and loans to firms; they accept deposits from both sorts of households. As before, we do not consider equity holdings and posit that firms finance their capital by borrowing from banks and rentiers.

The main difference with chapter 5 is that wealth-owners now have access to a third asset. Besides their loans and deposits, they also hold a speculative good Z that has a market-clearing prize P_z. It can be thought of as comprising objects such as foreign exchange, collectables, real estate,

Table 6.1
Financial structure

Banking system	
Base money H	D_π Deposits from rentiers
Bank loans L_b	D_w Deposits from workers
Firms	
Capital stock PK	L_b Loans from banks
	L_π Loans from rentiers
Rentier households	
Bank deposits D_π	W_π Wealth of rentiers
Loans to firms L_π	
Value of speculative P_zZ	
asset ("gold")	
Worker households	
Bank deposits D_w	W_w Wealth of workers

and speculative shares—we will call Z "gold." Workers are more cautious than rentiers with their wealth—they put it only in banks. This assumption is consistent with the two-class income division. Less affluent people have a high share of their incomes coming from wages and typically hold wealth in unsophisticated forms.

For the bulk of the discussion, we will set workers' wealth to zero to keep the algebra in hand—the appendix takes up the general case. With only rentiers holding wealth, the sum of asset market excess demands (equal to zero in equilibrium) is

$$(\delta W_\pi - \xi H) + [(\xi - 1)H + \lambda W_\pi - PK] + (\zeta W_\pi - P_zZ) = 0. \tag{1}$$

In this equation rentiers' wealth W_π is split among deposits, loans to firms, and gold in the proportions δ, λ, and ζ, respectively—the restriction $\delta + \lambda + \zeta = 1$ on these functions is required for market balance. Monetary policy takes the form of controlling the deposit/base money ratio ξ. In the absence of excess reserves, the supply of loans from banks is $(\xi - 1)H$.

Canceling terms in (1) gives the wealth "identity" in this model as

$$W_\pi - H - PK - P_zZ = 0, \tag{2}$$

so that the primary assets are base money, the value of the capital stock, and the value of gold. From (1) we need only specify two asset excess demand functions explicitly. It is easiest to work with deposits and gold.

The equations are

$$\delta(i, u, \rho)W_\pi - \xi H = 0,\tag{3}$$

and

$$\zeta(i, u, \rho)W_\pi - P_z Z = 0.\tag{4}$$

The arguments in the demand functions are the interest rate i that firms pay for short-term loans, the freely variable output/capital ratio u which is an indicator of the level of economic activity, and the expected return ρ to holding gold. Inflation is not considered explicitly in this chapter, so $\hat{P}$ does not show up as an argument of δ and ζ.

The first thing to note from these equations is that rentiers' wealth W_π need not evolve steadily in response to their saving but can jump in the short run. If ρ increases, meaning that speculation suddenly becomes more attractive, the gold price P_z rises to clear the market in (4). But then from (2), the value of wealth itself goes up. Speculation is self-propelling because it makes people feel richer. Nominal wealth expansion also provides room in the financial system for loans within a bank/industry group, postdated checks, or excessive margin accounts like those that appeared during the booms in Chile, Kuwait, and the United States. These novel financial vehicles intermediate between increases in $P_z Z$ and W_π, creating the unhealthy financial "layering" that crisis theorists like Minsky stress. At the same time there can also be nonspeculative wealth expansion,[1] but for simplicity we ignore this channel here.

Solving (2) and (4) together gives a reduced form for wealth,

$$W_\pi = \frac{H + PK}{1 - \zeta},\tag{5}$$

and plugging (5) into (2) does the same for deposit demand,

$$\frac{\delta(i, u, \rho)}{1 - \zeta(i, u, \rho)}(1 + V) - \xi = 0,\tag{6}$$

where as in chapter 5, $V = PK/H$ is the "velocity" of base-money with respect to the value of the capital stock.

Equation (6) amounts to an LM curve, more complicated than equation (2) in chapter 5 because of the endogeneity of W_π. Using subscripts to denote partial derivatives, we assume that δ_i and δ_ρ are negative while δ_u is positive. In the gold demand function, $\zeta_i < 0$, $\zeta_u < 0$ (if higher transactions balances are drawn in part from hedge assets), and $\zeta_\rho > 0$.

Overall deposit demand to the left of (6) falls with the interest rate i and rises with the level of activity u (if the positive effect of u on δ is stronger than the negative one on ζ, as is likely). Expansionary monetary policy is represented by an increase in ξ; with constant u and σ, it makes i decline. A *lower* value of V has the same effect; as we have seen in chapter 5, lower velocity represents enhanced intermediation by banks. Also as in that chapter, V is a proper state variable, since it does not jump. Its growth reflects steady evolution of base money H, the physical capital stock K, and the price level P. We will see in sections 6.4 and 6.5 that V has potentially important stabilizing effects on the macro system.

6.2   The Real Side

The real part of the economy is modeled as in chapters 3 through 5, with the output/capital ratio u as the adjusting macro variable. The markup rule for the price level takes its usual closed economy form:

$$P = (1 + \tau)wb = \frac{wb}{1 - \pi}. \tag{7}$$

The growth rate of the capital stock is g^i, equal to the ratio of investment to capital if we ignore depreciation. We adopt a linearized investment function as in appendix 2.A and chapter 5,

$$g^i(r, u, i) = g_0 + \alpha r + \beta u - \theta i = g_0 + (\alpha \pi + \beta)u - \theta i, \tag{8}$$

in which the nominal interest rate i instead of the real rate $i - \hat{P}$ is used to measure capital cost, again since inflation is ignored.

To specify the growth rate of capital permitted by available saving, let s_f, s_r, and s_w stand, respectively, for savings rates from firms' net cash flow, distributed profits, and wage income, and L ($= PK$) be the total of firms' outstanding loans. Then overall saving supply S is

$$S = s_f(\pi PX - iL) + s_r[(1 - s_f)(\pi PX - iL) + iL] + s_w(1 - \pi)PX,$$

where it is assumed that the interest that firms pay on their loans all finds its way directly or through bank deposits into the hands of rentiers (we omit the algebra needed to carry workers' interest income along). Defining two new parameters as $s_\pi = s_f + s_r(1 - s_f)$ and $\mu = s_f(1 - s_r)$ and dividing S by PK shows that the growth rate warranted by saving is

$$g^s(\pi, u, i) = [s_\pi \pi + s_w(1 - \pi)]u - \mu i. \tag{9}$$

If $s_r < 1$, then $\mu > 0$ and rentiers' consumption from interest income cuts back on potential saving, contrary to the usual supposition. Also, if $s_w = \mu = 0$, (9) reduces to the familiar Cambridge growth equation, $g^s = s_\pi \pi u = s_\pi r$.

Let government real spending as a proportion of the capital stock be γ. Then with taxes omitted for simplicity, macro equilibrium is defined by the condition $\gamma + g^i - g^s = 0$, or

$$\gamma + g_0 + (\alpha \pi + \beta)u - (\theta - \mu)i - [s_\pi \pi + s_w(1 - \pi)]u = 0. \tag{10}$$

Our usual short-run stability condition for (10) is

$$s_\pi \pi + s_w(1 - \pi) - (\alpha \pi + \beta) > 0,$$

in other words, higher capacity utilization stimulates more saving than investment. When this inequality holds, (10) shows that u is an increasing function of γ. The sign of $\partial u / \partial \pi$ depends on the quantity $\alpha - (s_\pi - s_w)$, as in chapter 3. By ignoring workers' wealth, we are already assuming that s_w is negligible. Given the usual econometric finding that profitability effects in investment demand are weak, we assume that $\partial u / \partial \pi < 0$; in other words, the economy responds in wage-led or stagnationist fashion to income redistribution in the short run. Finally, so long as $\theta > \mu$, interest rate increases cut back on aggregate demand. We follow convention in assuming this condition holds, in fact setting μ implicitly to zero in the following discussion.

6.3 Comparative Statics

Equations (10) and (6) constitute an IS/LM system in u and i, illustrated in figure 6.1. The leftward shift in the IS curve (dashed line) is the result of an increased profit share π or lower public spending γ. The upward shift in LM comes from contractionary monetary policy (a lower ξ) or disintermediation in the form of higher velocity V. All these changes reduce the level of activity u, and tight money plus redistribution could well increase i. With a strong accelerator, growth will also slow from (8).

With regard to gold, a lower u reduces deposit demand and makes ζ rise. The outcome is a higher speculative price P_z, especially if gold and loans to firms are *not* close portfolio substitutes. An increase in ρ, the expected return to holding gold, decreases the ratio $\delta/(1 - \zeta)$ in (6) when

$$\delta(\zeta_\rho + \delta_\rho) + \lambda \delta_\rho < 0.$$

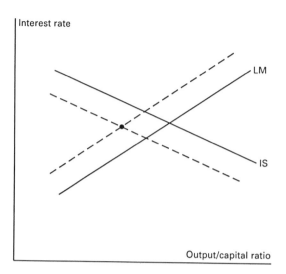

Figure 6.1
Determination of macroeconomic equilibrium in the short run: Regressive redistribution
shifts the IS curve leftward; tight money shifts the LM curve upward. An increased return
to holding gold shifts the LM schedule downward.

If deposits and gold are close subsitutes, ζ_ρ and $-\delta_\rho$ will be nearly equal;
that is, the second term will dominate and deposit demand will fall. The LM
curve shifts downward, meaning that happy speculation reduces the interest rate and increases growth along with capacity use. Of course easy
substitution between money and gold is an empirical hypothesis and need
not always hold. However, facile shifts among specific speculative and
nonspeculative assets underlie many models of financial crisis, not least the
one in Minsky (1975).[2]

6.4   A Confidence Boom

Recent models generate financial crises in two ways. One is through an
indicator of rentiers' confidence such as ρ which feeds positively into
itself over time. This is the route taken by Frenkel (1983) and Taylor and
O'Connell (1985), and pursued in this section. It leads to a boom from
speculation by rentiers in assets outside corporate balance sheets.[3] The
alternative approach emphasizes the debt structure of firms, such as in
Foley (1986b, 1987) and Franke and Semmler (1989). Instability comes
from positive responses of investment and borrowing by firms to increased
values of speculative assets such as shares or real estate held by the

enterprises themselves. With a set of balance sheets slightly revised from table 6.1, this more "inside" road to a crisis is mapped in section 6.5.

Recall that ρ stands for the expected return to holding the speculative asset. In practice, wealth-holders' confidence depends on myriad factors—the credibility of government promises about key variables such as the exchange rate, the overall political situation, anticipated actions of powerful entities outside the country such as international banks, and the attitude of regulatory authorities toward veiled swindlers (as in the recent Savings and Loan crisis in the United States) are only a few. But for holding "gold" one of the major motivations is surely the expected capital gain. A reasonable proxy is the current rate of gold price increase $\hat{P}_z$ (where as usual a "hat" over a variable signifies its growth rate). We assume that

$$\rho = \rho(\hat{P}_z), \tag{11}$$

and denote the positive derivative by ρ'.

Now from (4) and (5), P_z itself is given by

$$P_z = \phi(i, u, \rho)(1 + V)Q, \tag{12}$$

where the new symbols are $\phi = \zeta/(1 - \zeta)$ and $Q = H/Z$. From (11) and (12) it is easy to see that P_z and its growth rate $\hat{P}_z$ are positively related. This linkage is the source of financial instability here and also underlies the extensive neoclassical literature on bubbles. However, we shall not be interested in rational leaps to saddlepaths (enough of that in appendix 4.A) but rather in how the rest of the financial system may or may not tame speculation in gold.

In differential form, $\hat{P}_z$ depends on P_z and other variables as follows:

$$d\hat{P}_z = \frac{1}{\phi_\rho \rho'}\left[\frac{dP_z}{Q(1 + V)} - (\phi_i di + \phi_u du) - \phi\left(\frac{dQ}{Q} + \frac{dV}{1 + V}\right)\right]. \tag{13}$$

For an instantaneously given gold price P_z, a regressive redistribution/tight money experiment will accelerate its rate of inflation $\hat{P}_z$ by increasing i and reducing u. The "story" is that the expected gold return rises to meet the new economic situation. Disintermediation, or a higher V, has the same positive effect on $\hat{P}_z$ through i and u, but its direct impact in (13) is clearly negative. A higher V is more likely to slow $\hat{P}_z$ when V itself is small (i.e., the degree of financial intermediation is high). An increase in the money/gold ratio Q reduces $\hat{P}_z$. All these effects as well as the positive feedback of P_z into P_z will be stronger when gold demand is relatively insensitive to ρ, or ρ to $\hat{P}_z$.

In a full dynamic specification we must also consider the evolution of the ratio variables V and Q. Let a "dot" over a variable denote its time derivative. Since $V = PK/H$, we need differential equations for P, K, and H. The price level only jumps in response to changes in τ or π, so an expression for $\dot{P}$ is unnecessary—if inflation were an issue, it would be easy to add a cost- or demand-based price growth process as in chapter 5. The growth of the capital stock is $\dot{K} = g^i K$ from the investment function. Lacking taxes and state bonds, the government just monetizes its spending so that $\dot{H} = \gamma PK = \gamma VH$.

These assumptions together give an equation like (9) in chapter 5,

$$\dot{V} = V(g^i - \gamma V). \tag{14}$$

A higher value of V makes g^i fall and increases the growth rate of base money (for $\gamma > 0$). On both counts it is likely that $\partial \dot{V}/\partial V < 0$ (a certainty around a steady state at which $V = g^i/\gamma$). Since regressive redistribution and tight money both reduce investment g^i, they also make $\dot{V}$ decline. Finally, a higher gold price P_z and a lower money/gold ratio Q increase $\hat{P}_z$ and ρ, raising g^i and thereby $\dot{V}$.

The money/gold ratio Q is a nuisance state variable that will largely be ignored in the informal stability analysis that follows. However, we should indicate its dynamics briefly. We want to analyze a steady state in which no state variable goes to zero or infinity. Growth in the economy is determined by capital accumulation; to keep the gold supply from diverging, we assume that it is created (by real estate developers, artists, and imaginative financiers) in proportion to the capital stock (i.e., $\dot{Z} = \sigma K$). This formula leads to the differential equation

$$\dot{Q} = Q\left(\frac{V}{P}\right)(\gamma P - \sigma Q). \tag{15}$$

At a steady state where $Q = \gamma P/\sigma$, $\partial \dot{Q}/\partial Q$ is clearly negative and $\dot{Q}$ is unaffected by P_z and V.

Around a steady state, the 3×3 equation system (13)–(15) has partial derivatives signed as follows:

	P_z	V	Q
$\hat{P}_z$	$+$	$\pm$	$-$
$\dot{V}$	$+$	$-$	$-$
$\dot{Q}$	0	0	$-$

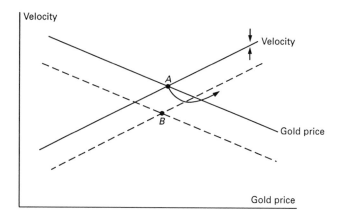

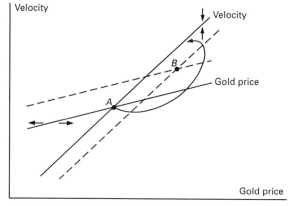

Figure 6.2
Unstable (*upper diagram*) and possibly stable (*lower diagram*) adjustment in a model with rentier speculation

Application of Routh-Hurwitz criteria suggest that system will be stable when equations (13) and (14) for $\hat{P}_z$ and $\dot{V}$ are well behaved. Hence we concentrate on this subsystem. Figure 6.2 illustrates the possibilities, with the "velocity" and "gold price" schedules respectively representing the loci along which $\dot{V} = 0$ and $\hat{P}_z = 0$.

In the upper diagram the effect of V on $\hat{P}_z$ in (13) is positive, and the equations demonstrate saddlepoint instability since the negative determinant of the Jacobian signals the presence of a positive real eigenvalue. A regressive monetarist shock, reducing output and driving up the interest rate, shifts the equilibrium from A to B. The gold price begins to rise while slow output growth makes $\dot{V} < 0$. When the trajectory crosses the shifted velocity schedule, both variables diverge—disintermediation and a gold boom go hand in hand until the model has to change. A jump of P_z (and nominal wealth) to reach a saddlepath leading to B is possible but implausible under reasonable institutional assumptions.

In the lower diagram higher velocity slows the increase in the price of gold, basically by driving down the return ρ in (4) for a given P_z. The spiral path may be diverging or converging, depending on the strength of the positive feedback of P_z into its own growth. If stable, the economy may

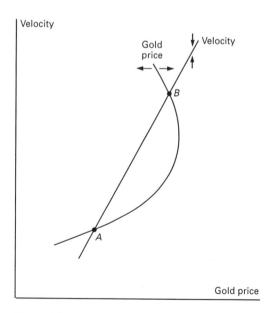

Figure 6.3
Global phase portrait of the model with rentier speculation

come to the new equilibrium B with faster potential output growth. Disintermediation ultimately cools speculative fever, while the gains in wealth it creates may spill over into higher investment demand and better real performance. Such outcomes are possible but seem a slender thread on which to hang orthodox policy.[4] The boom-and-crash financial fluctuations en route to the new steady state could be extreme.

Finally, figure 6.3 presents a possible global phase portrait. For the reasons just discussed, equilibrium B is unstable while the economy may possibly find a rest point at A (which lies below B because the negative effect of V on $\hat{P}_z$ is stronger for small values of V).

6.5   A Debt-Led Boom

Firms, along with rentiers, may hold speculative assets. Chilean conglomerates bidding up their own shares-are one example; Korean firms that hold real estate as collateral for bank loans (Kim 1987) are another. A higher gold price may lead firms to invest more, in turn forcing them to try to buy more gold as they seek collateral, igniting a borrowing boom. To work out the details, we begin with a revised set of balance sheets, shown in table 6.2. The main difference from table 6.1 is the shift of $P_z Z$ from rentiers' to firms' portfolios.

The modified financial accounting means that we also have to restate IS and LM relationships. Since rentiers now hold only deposits and loans to firms, the LM equation can be written as

$$\delta(i, u)\left[\left(\frac{1}{V}\right) + 1 + P_z D\right] - \left(\frac{1}{V}\right)\xi = 0, \tag{16}$$

in which D (for "debt") stands for Z/PK, the ratio of gold to productive capital which firms ultimately finance by borrowing. Equation (16) differs from (6) in that rentiers' wealth W_π is normalized by PK instead of H and gold's expected return ρ and portfolio share ζ have been dropped. Also W_π is no longer a jump variable. Speculative asset changes will now be represented by smooth changes in firms' balance sheets.

In place of (8) we write the investment function as

$$g^i = g_0 + (\alpha\pi + \beta)u - \theta i + \varepsilon P_z D,$$

in which the last term shows that firms' capital formation is stimulated by an increased value of their speculative holdings—heightened animal spirits or better loan collaterals could be the underlying cause.

Table 6.2
Financial structure

Banking system	
Base money H	D_π Deposits from rentiers
Bank loans L_b	
Firms	
Capital stock PK	L_b Loans from banks
Value of speculative $P_z Z$ asset ("gold")	L_π Loans from rentiers
Rentier households	
Bank deposits D_π	W_π Wealth of rentiers
Loans to firms L_π	

Adding government spending and subtracting (9) from this equation gives the IS curve as

$$\gamma + g_0 + (\alpha\pi + \beta)u + \varepsilon P_z D - (\theta - \mu)i - [s_\pi \pi + s_w(1 - \pi)]u = 0, \quad (17)$$

replacing (10). The IS/LM system is still represented by figure 6.1. The additional comparative static result is that an increase in $P_z D$ shifts the LM curve upward and the IS to the right. The outcomes are a higher interest rate and an ambiguous change in capacity use.

Rather than letting $\hat{P}_z$ jump to meet changes in other variables as it does in (13), we now simply assume that $\dot{P}_z$ varies to meet evolutionary movements in the demand and supply of gold. Total enterprise borrowing L (the sum of L_b and L_π) grows according to a behavioral equation to be presented shortly. With L, PK, and Z all fixed at a point in time, P_z must be given by $P_z = (L - PK)/Z$ from the consolidated balance sheets of all firms. Its change over time becomes

$$\dot{P}_z = \left(\frac{1}{Z}\right)[\dot{L} - (Pg^i + P_z\sigma)K], \quad (18)$$

since $\dot{K} = g^i K$ and $\dot{Z} = \sigma k$.

Firms increase their debt to pay for new capital formation and acquisition of speculative assets. The investment function has already been specified. We now assume that demand for gold rises in response to its expected capital gain and also when firms have a high cash flow (this latter effect can also be included in the investment demand function without changing the model's results). Let λ stand for cash flow relative to capital stock:

$$\lambda = \frac{\pi PX - i(PK + P_z Z)}{PK} = \pi u - (1 + P_z D)i. \tag{19}$$

Then we write the change in total borrowing of firms as

$$\dot{L} = Pg^i K + \left[\phi \left(\frac{\dot{P_z}}{P_z} \right) + \psi \lambda \right] P_z Z - vL, \tag{20}$$

in which ϕ and ψ are coefficients for the effects of expected capital gains and high cash flow on firms' desired increases in speculative holdings. New loan demand $\dot{L}$ is also assumed to increase less rapidly when the total loan stock L is high, reflecting credit rationing by banks or the firms' own prudent behavior.

Equations (18)–(20) can be solved simultaneously for $\dot{P_z}$ and $\dot{L}$. Either P_z or L/PK could be used as a state variable along with V and D to determine the evolution of the economy. For comparison with the previous model, we choose P_z. Its differential equation is

$$\dot{P_z} = \frac{1}{(1 - \phi)D} \left\{ P_z \left[(\psi \lambda - v)D - \frac{\sigma}{P} \right] - v \right\}, \tag{21}$$

and for the system to make sense, we assume $\phi < 1$. Near a steady state where $\dot{P_z}$ vanishes, (21) shows that P_z grows more rapidly when cash flow λ, the gold/capital ratio D, and its own level are high. The latter two results depend on a sufficiently high value of $\psi \lambda$, and indeed the condition $\psi \lambda > v + g^i$ is also necessary for P_z to take on a positive value at steady state.

More generally, behavior of $\dot{P_z}$ depends on how λ responds to shifts in the state variables. From (19) λ declines when i and $P_z D$ rise, or u falls. The IS/LM equations show that cash flow is lower with higher values of P_z, D, and V, unless the parameter ε giving the response of investment demand g^i to a higher value of $P_z D$ is improbably large. Moreover the partial derivatives of λ with respect to P_z and D become more negative as these variables increase. Hence from (21), $\dot{P_z}$ may respond positively and then negatively to P_z as the gold price itself becomes larger. In the discussion that follows, we assume that this sign shift does in fact occur.

The differential equation for the gold/capital ratio D is

$$\dot{D} = \left(\frac{1}{P} \right) (\sigma - Dg^i). \tag{22}$$

Equations (21), (22), and (14) form a simultaneous system for P_z, D, and V with the signs of the Jacobian matrix as follows:

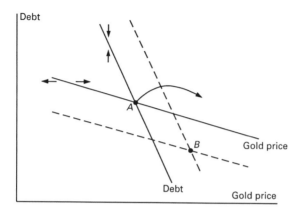

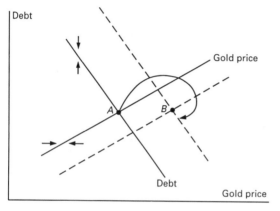

Figure 6.4
Unstable (*upper diagram*) and stable (*lower diagram*) dynamics in the model in which firms speculate

	P_z	D	V
$\hat{P}_z$	$\pm$	$+$	$-$
$\dot{D}$	$-$	$-$	$+$
$\dot{V}$	$+$	$-$	$-$

Velocity here on the whole exerts a stabilizing influence, so we do not consider it explicitly in analyzing how the model behaves.

The upper diagram in figure 6.4 shows the unstable case in which $\partial \hat{P}_z / \partial P_z$ is positive The "gold price" and "debt" loci, respectively, correspond to the conditions $\hat{P}_z = 0$ and $\dot{D} = 0$. An initial regressive shock at point A increases both $\hat{P}_z$ and $\dot{D}$. Hence, in a new steady state P_z must fall and D rise. After the shock, the gold price begins a speculative increase and $\dot{D}$ is also positive because investment g^i declines. From (22) the increase in D (plus higher investment from a higher P_z) finally makes $\dot{D}$ negative, but the system is unstable and never reaches a new equilibrium at B. In the stable case (lower diagram) an upward-sloping gold price locus "catches" the trajectory and brings the system to a new steady state at B—the cyclical convergence rests upon alternating gold booms and busts as cash flows rise and fall. As in the model of last section, a higher gold price may stimulate investment enough to lead to a faster growth rate at B.

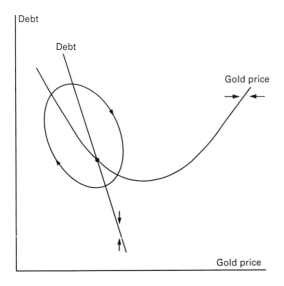

Figure 6.5
A limit cycle when firms speculate

The sign shift of $\partial \dot{P}_z / \partial P_z$ can also produce a limit cycle, as shown in figure 6.5. Here the alternation of cash flow increases, speculation, and then increasing debt leading to retrenchment never ceases. Such outcomes often arise in firm debt-led models of the type discussed here. Along with speculative adventures by rentiers, they help show how macroeconomic financial crises of the type discussed in the introduction continue to recur.

Finally, depending on nonlinearities, the three-dimensional system in P_z, D, and V could demonstrate chaotic dynamics. When $\partial \dot{P}_z / \partial P_z$ is positive, trajectories of the variables tend to spread in the (P_z, D) plane. These separating flows could then by "folded" by velocity interactions, potentially leading as in the model of chapter 5 to the sort of chaos exemplified by the Rössler band.

Appendix 6.A   Asset Accumulation from Wage Income

When wage-earners save and hold their wealth W_w in banks, an additional state variable $\eta = W_w / H$ enters the system. We examine its implications for the model of section 6.4; results for section 6.5 dynamics are similar.

In the short run the LM curve (6) takes the expanded form

$$\eta \left[1 - \frac{\delta}{1 - \zeta} \right] + \frac{\delta}{1 - \zeta} (1 + V) - \xi = 0.$$

Signs of responses as discussed in the text are not affected. A higher η increases deposit demand and drives up the interest rate. Because of their restricted portfolio preferences, more wealth in the hands of workers is contractionary—an interesting result. A rise in η also reduces P_z.

Since $\dot{W}_w = s_w(1 - \pi)uPK$ and $\dot{H} = \gamma PK$ follow regular growth processes, η is a proper state variable. Its differential equation is

$$\dot{\eta} = V[s_w(1 - \pi)u - \gamma\eta].$$

By increasing the interest rate, higher values of both η and V reduce u; the first effect means that η will be locally stable around a steady state. Its equilibrium value $s_w(1 - \pi)u/\gamma$ declines with a regressive redistribution, since π rises and u falls.

Stability analysis of the four differential equations involving V, P_z, Q, and η hinges on the positive feedback of P_z into $\dot{P}_z$ as in section 6.4. Subject to caveats about possible chaotic attractors in a higher-dimensional system, its dynamics are not strongly influenced by the presence of η in addition to V and Q.

7   Devaluation, Output, and Capital Flows

Chapters 7 and 8 are about models of developing economies open to foreign capital movements and trade. Dealing with economic openness adds twists to our previous discussions of both commodity and asset markets. On the asset side foreign exchange can easily become an object of speculation along the lines discussed in chapter 6. With regard to income distribution, three parties now enter the fray: profit recipients, workers, and the rest of the world. There are two key nominal prices—the exchange rate that is determined by policy[1] and the money wage that follows from institutional considerations. A change in one price with the other constant is bound to have effects on distribution and output, by altering the profit share, real wage, or real exchange rate. In the discussion that follows, we postulate a constant markup or profit share and concentrate on trade-offs between the real wage and exchange rates.

The analysis begins in section 7.1 with an ostinato theme in the structuralist tradition—that exchange rate devaluation may well cause at least short-run output contraction and price inflation in a developing economy open in typical fashion to foreign trade. A money wage increase, as it turns out, has the opposite effect on output. Section 7.2 takes up implications of these results, ignoring the effects of capital flows. Section 7.3 then brings in foreign exchange as an object of speculation and shows why capital movements make orthodox anti-inflation policies based on freezing the exchange rate likely to fail. Section 7.4 closes with the policy lessons one can draw about the manifold effects of devaluation in macroeconomic stabilization attempts.

In chapter 9 further aspects of exchange rate changes are discussed, using the fix-price/flex-price apparatus developed there. Section 9.3 shows that devaluation continues to act in ways similar to those discussed in this chapter when import quotas are in effect, as they often are under import-substituting trade regimes. Appendix 9.A reinterprets the two-gap model of chapter 8 in terms of the real exchange rate, and shows that policies aimed at expansion cause appreciation (rather than the other way 'round) when the nontraded goods balance is treated as a restriction that binds. The practical problem of course is that resultant deterioration in the trade account may render expansionary policy infeasible in a very short time.

7.1 Devaluation in the Short Run

To set up an apposite exchange rate model, we have to describe how semi-industrialized countries are open to trade. As discussed in Shapiro and Taylor (1990) and Taylor (l990a), the process of industrialization by import substitution replaces foreign supplies of final goods (usually excepting capital goods) by domestically produced commodities. However, production itself remains dependent on imported intermediates—components to be assembled, energy, and sophisticated inputs more generally. The export basket shifts away from primary products with externally determined world prices to include "industrial" goods with demand sensitive to local costs of production transformed to foreign terms through the exchange rate.

Harking back to chapter 3, note that these means of orienting an economy to the world block a familiar channel via which reductions in the money wage can reduce real labor costs. In a fully open economy price arbitrage for traded goods might be expected to stabilize the national price level, so money wage cuts cheapen the real wage as well. By curtailing the importance of commodities subject to "the law of one price," import substitution makes this linkage weak. For purposes of price determination, most goods are effectively nontraded and subject to markup or internally oriented flex-price rules.

Under such circumstances money wage increases have two main effects. They drive up prices, cutting export sales and aggregate demand. But they also reduce the share of intermediate imports in variable cost. With a lower foreign saving ratio to output, demand will rise. If the latter effect is stronger, higher money wages can *raise* employment in stagnationist fashion. The exchange rate affects macro equilibrium antisymmetrically to the money wage (i.e., its effects have the same magnitudes but opposite signs). If wage increases are expansionary, devaluation will make output fall.

To see when this outcome takes place, we need a formal model. Table 7.1 sets out equations extending those of table 3.1 to an open semi-industrialized economy. Variable cost now includes imported intermediates, making it convenient to treat output X as value added plus such

Table 7.1
Open economy macroeconomic relationships

(1.1)	$P = (wb + ea)/(1 - \pi)$
(1.2)	$\phi = ea/(wb + ea)$, $\quad q = e/P = \phi(1 - \pi)/a$
(1.3)	$\omega = (1 - \phi)(1 - \pi)/b$
(1.4)	$u = X/K$
(1.5)	$r = \pi u$
(1.6)	$g^i = g^i(\pi, u)$
(1.7)	$g^s = \{s_\pi \pi + [s_w(1 - \phi) + \phi](1 - \pi)\}u$
(1.8)	$\varepsilon = E/K = \varepsilon(q)$
(1.9)	$g^i + \varepsilon - g^s = 0$
(1.10)	$MV = PX$ or $\omega = wKu/MV$

imports (i.e., X is bigger than real GDP). The import/output ratio is a, while the domestic import price is proportional to the nominal exchange rate e. The final goods price from a markup is given by (1.1).

Equation (1.2) defines the share ϕ of imports in variable cost. The analysis that follows hinges on responses of ϕ to changes in e and w; we also at times use the real exchange rate q as an indicator of the effects of money wage changes and nominal devaluation on income distribution. For a given profit share π in total output PX, (1.3) shows that the real wage ω is a declining function of ϕ (or q). Equations (1.4) through (1.6) carry over from (1.3)–(1.5) in table 3.1.

In (1.7) national saving per unit of capital g^s rises along with ϕ—a higher import cost acts as a vehicle for foreign saving. Exports ε per unit of capital appear in (1.8). Their volume is an increasing function of the real exchange rate for the reasons discussed above. In (1.9) exports raise aggregate demand while imports reduce it by supplementing total saving in (1.7). Monetary balance is defined by (1.10).

Various questions can be addressed with this model. We begin with the most obvious one: How do changes in the nominal wage and exchange rate affect output when it is free to adjust?

If the markup stays constant, it is easy to show that devaluation—an increase in the nominal exchange rate e—reduces output in the table 7.1 model when the inequality

$$\eta\left(\frac{E}{X}\right) < (1 - s_w)qa \tag{1}$$

holds, where η is the elasticity of export volume with respect to the real exchange rate in (1.8). The import coefficient a may be high in semi-industrialized economies, well over 0.25. With an initial trade deficit, E/X will be less than qa, and the elasticity η will not usually exceed one. The implication is that contractionary devaluation ($du/de < 0$) is by no means an unlikely event, at least in the short to medium run before export responses build up. The WIDER studies cited in preceding chapters and Taylor (1988a) provide confirmatory evidence along these lines.[2]

Remarkably the condition for an expansionary money wage increase is exactly the same as the one for contractionary devaluation. A higher w expands output in stagnationist fashion when condition (1) applies, for the reasons discussed above. Formally in (1.7) a higher w reduces the foreign saving coefficient ϕ with $d\phi/dw = -(1 - \phi)(w/\phi)$. Workers' saving goes up by $s_w(d\phi/dw)$. With $s_w < 1$ we get forced saving in reverse, with the income distribution shifting from the trade deficit toward workers. Overall demand rises if exports from (1.8) do not fall very much in response to increased domestic costs because the elasticity η is low.

7.2   Implications of Contractionary Devaluation

Economies in which devaluation is contractionary are harder to manage than those in which its effect on output goes the other way. We illustrate this observation three ways in this section, considering possible stop-go export and output cycles in response to real exchange rate changes, and then the implications for fiscal and monetary management of contractionary as compared to expansionary devaluation. All these exercises presuppose that capital movements adjust endogenously to shifts in the balance of trade; autonomous capital flows are taken up in the following section.

Cycles in which output rises in response to an export push, followed by wage increases that cut back on exports and ultimately demand and real wages themselves, are by no means unknown in the developing world. Endogenous policy fluctuations involving (possibly inopportune) exchange rate adjustments can be superimposed on these events. Following Larrain and Sachs (1986) and Taylor (1989a), it is easy to model interactions over time between exports and the real wage or exchange rate.

For formal analysis equation (1.8) for exports has to be dynamized. A simple differential equation takes the form:

$$\dot{\varepsilon} = \psi[\varepsilon^*(q) - \varepsilon], \tag{2}$$

in which there is lagged adjustment of actual exports ε to a target level

$\varepsilon^*(q)$ consistent with the current value of the real exchange rate. Because of preexisting contracts, the need to search for new markets, and so on, exports do not instantly respond to price signals. Rather, their dollar value ε/e is likely to follow a J-curve after a nominal devaluation, first dropping off as e jumps up and then gradually rising according to (2) over time.

For money wage dynamics it is simplest to adopt the Phillips curve relationship (1.12) from table 3.1:

$$\hat{w} = h(bu - \bar{\lambda}).$$

According to this equation higher capacity utilization u will bid up money wages and reduce ϕ from equation (1.2) in table 7.1. The real exchange rate q also jumps down in value (or "appreciates" in the usual confusing terminology), leading export expansion to slow. Real exchange rate dynamics are given by

$$\hat{q} = (1 - \phi)[\hat{e} - h(bu - \bar{\lambda})], \tag{3}$$

where $\hat{e}$ is an exogenous growth rate of the nominal exchange rate.

Around a steady state in which $\dot{\varepsilon} = \hat{q} = 0$ with positive ε and q, the signs of the Jacobian of (2) and (3) are as follows:

	ε	q
$\dot{\varepsilon}$	$-$	$+$
$\hat{q}$	$-$	$+$

The real exchange rate shows potentially unstable behavior, since a higher q reduces output (the real wage and aggregate demand fall), making $\hat{w} < 0$ and therefore $q > 0$ as a result.

The cross-diagonal terms can stabilize the system, especially if the response of ε^* to the real exchange rate is large. If this is the case the slope of the J-curve schedule along which $\dot{\varepsilon} = 0$ will be relatively shallow, as in figure 7.1. The Phillips curve locus corresponds to $\hat{q} = 0$.

Starting from an initial equilibrium position, a maxi-devaluation followed by an exchange rate freeze displaces the real exchange rate upward. The system may then return to equilibrium with cyclical fluctuations of the real exchange rate and exports (as well as output and inflation), or else diverge along the outer spiral path. Depending on the strength of nonlinear damping forces, a limit cycle may also materialize around an unstable equilibrium where the curves cross, representing enduring stop-go export fluctuations in the present model.

As noted in chapter 4, a policy alternative to a maxi-devaluation is a crawling peg in which the nominal exchange rate is continually readjusted in response to inflation, to hold the real rate stable or modify it gradually over time. The effect in figure 7.1 would be to shift the Phillips curve to the right, leading to a long-term export gain but a lower real wage.[3] If productivity were to rise in response to faster export growth (along the lines of Kaldor's technical progress function discussed in section 2.3), then the economy could jump to a faster long-term growth path. Amsden (1989) suggests that the South Korean export miracle has followed such dynamics, even permitting real wages to rise over time. Of course, they haven't grown as rapidly as productivity, meaning that unit labor costs have declined and exports have risen even more! The real exchange rate has been quite stable—a crawling peg—but maxi-devaluations and other moves to "get the prices right" have had little to do with Korea's success.[4]

The next topic involves dropping export dynamics in favor of fiscal complications. If t is the trade balance (per unit of capital stock), we can expect a response function of the form

$$t = t(\gamma, e) \tag{4}$$

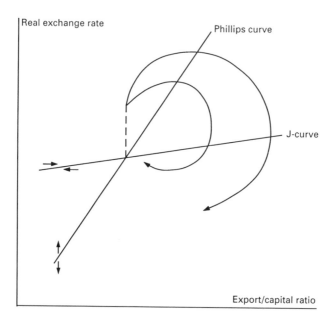

Figure 7.1
Real exchange rate and export dynamics

to apply, where γ stands as usual for fiscal dissaving. The likely signs of the partials are $\partial t/\partial\gamma < 0$ and $\partial t/\partial e > 0$, as both reduced spending and devaluation improve trade performance.

The output/capital ratio will respond as

$$u = u(\gamma, e), \tag{5}$$

with $\partial u/\partial\gamma > 0$ while $\partial u/\partial e$ can take either sign, depending on whether devaluation is expansionary or contractionary.

Policy trade-offs in this simple model are illustrated in figure 7.2. In the upper diagram, the $u = \bar{u}$ and $t = \bar{t}$ loci correspond to constant values of capacity utilization and the trade balance, assuming that devaluation is expansionary so that the $u = \bar{u}$ schedule has a negative slope. The dashed line represents an improved trade balance. If it is to occur with a stable level of activity, then currency devaluation should be combined with fiscal

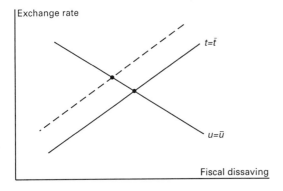

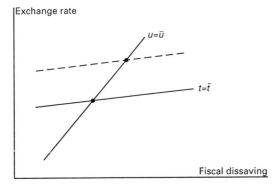

Figure 7.2
Trade-offs between fiscal expansion and devaluation

restraint. This is the usual recipe in IMF-style balance of payments stabilization programs.

The contractionary devaluation case appears in the lower diagram. Now fiscal *expansion* is required to hold output constant as devaluation improves the balance of trade. Applying the orthodox package in this case leaves the door wide open for output collapse and the usual accusations of mainstream macroeconomic "overkill." On the other hand, stepping up the fiscal deficit when the trade gap is wide looks *prima facie* like a risky move. As usual, policy design in a stagnationist economy is not an easy task.

The positive output response to a higher money wage that goes hand in hand with contractionary devaluation also poses a dilemma between internal and external balance targets in monetarist stabilization packages aimed at improving the current account, as Jose Maria Fanelli (in correspondence) points out. Suppose that nominal wages fall with tight money, to maintain the quantity theory with predetermined M and V—a sufficiently prolonged and draconinan monetary policy might bear this assumption out. Combining (1.3) and (1.10) then gives

$$\frac{(1 - \phi)(1 - \pi)}{b} = \frac{wKu}{MV},\tag{6}$$

from which it is easy to show that capacity utilization u has elasticities of unity and $-(1 - \phi)$ with respect to changes in M and w, respectively. Equation (6) gives the downward sloping "equation of exchange" schedules in figure 7.3.

A "monetarist stagnationist" might also believe that a higher money wage stimulates output, as in the output response curve in the upper diagram of figure 7.3. Then monetary contraction (the dashed line) makes both u and w fall, while there is real devaluation. The balance of payments improves from both lower intermediate imports and enhanced exports, at the cost of reduced employment and a more regressive income distribution (assuming a constant markup rate and profit share π). In a stagnationist economy the diagram again illustrates the overkill of which the IMF and other stabilizers are often accused. Fiscal expansion would ameliorate the effects of tight money on aggregate demand but at the cost of a still lower money (but not real) wage. Needless to say, combined fiscal and monetary contractions are the course most commonly pursued—the employment target is sacrificed to the current account.

If money wage cuts raise output (with a fairly weak response to preserve macro stability), the less unpleasant outcomes of the lower diagram occur. Tight money still makes the real wage fall from (1.3) since a lower w raises

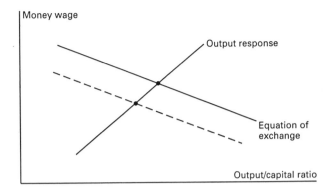

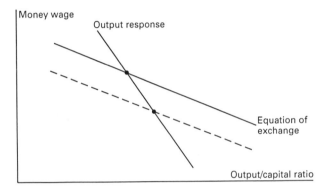

Figure 7.3
Effects of tight money that passes through into lower money wages in situations where a
money wage increase stimulates (*upper diagram*) and reduces (*lower diagram*) aggregate
demand

ϕ, but at least output and employment rise. The point keeps reappearing that an economy that contracts with devaluation and expands in response to money wage increases is harder to direct than one in which the responses run the other way. The lessons of chapters 3 and 4 about the difficulties of managing a wage-led system carry over to the open economy case.

7.3 Capital Market Complications

Entire textbooks are written about devaluation, the trade balance, and capital flows.[5] That is not our intention here. We concentrate on one issue of great policy relevance: destabilizing foreign asset speculation in the wake of overvaluation, following Frenkel (1983). Two topics are addressed: the real and asset market effects of slowing exchange rate devaluation when there is ongoing inflation in an "active" crawling peg aimed at reducing the rate of price increase, and how these effects may cumulate over time to upset this "orthodox shock" stabilization strategy. The focus is on foreign assets held by the private sector, while chapter 8 takes up further complications caused by large stocks of public external and internal debt. In many countries the state's liabilities are the mirror image of private foreign asset stocks built up in the final phases of financial crises of the sort examined here.[6]

Table 7.2 sets out the financial structure for a three-asset model like the one in section 6.1. Instead of "gold," wealth-holders now own foreign assets with a domestic value of eY in addition to loans to firms and

Table 7.2
Financial structure

Banking system	
Base money H	D Deposits
Bank loans L_b	
Foreign reserves eR	
Firms	
Capital stock PK	L_b Loans from banks
	L_p Loans from the public
The public	
Bank deposits D	W Wealth
Loans to firms L_p	
Foreign assets eY	

deposits. The banking system also has foreign reserves in the amount eR. Total public wealth is

$$W = PK + e(Y + R) + H = PK + eJ + H,$$

where J stands for total foreign assets of the nation. The total J *cannot* change in the short run, since foreign asset stocks only accumulate or decumulate on a flow basis through the current account of the balance of payments. If the public reduces its foreign holdings then bank reserves must jump upward, and vice versa.

Asset market equilibrium is determined when two of the public's three excess demand functions equal zero:

$$\delta\left(i, \hat{P}, \frac{\sigma}{e}, u\right)[V + A + 1] - \xi\left[1 + A - \left(\frac{eY}{H}\right)\right] = 0 \tag{7}$$

and

$$\chi\left(i, \hat{P}, \frac{\sigma}{e}, u\right)[V + A + 1] - \frac{eY}{H} = 0 \tag{8}$$

In these expressions $\xi = D/(H + eR)$ is the credit multiplier controlled by the monetary authorities, $V = PK/H$ is the velocity of the domestic component H of base money (coming from fiscal deficit spending) with respect to capital stock, and $A = eJ/H$ is the ratio of total foreign asset value to the monetized fiscal debt.

In the asset demand functions δ and χ, the usual arguments appear along with σ which stands for the expected return to holding foreign assets. We can set $\sigma = j + \hat{e} + \rho$, where j is the foreign real interest rate, $\hat{e}$ is the expected ($=$ actual) rate of exchange rate devaluation, and ρ is a confidence-based expected extra return from holding Y. The nominal interest rate i is the variable that adjusts to satisfy (7), while Y itself shifts in (8) when the exchange rate is pegged—in financial markets we have a preview of the fix-price/flex-price commodity market models worked out in chapter 9. Inflation $\hat{P}$ is assumed to come from costs according to dynamic equations like those in chapter 5, and u is determined by aggregate demand.

As recounted by Díaz-Alejandro (1981) and Frenkel, the stabilization strategy in vogue in South America's Southern Cone in the late 1970s was based on freezing (or drastically reducing the rate of depreciation of) the nominal exchange rate. Through the law of one price in commodity markets and also via "rational" expectations, this policy move was supposed to slow inflation drastically. Inflation turned out to have cost-based, structural

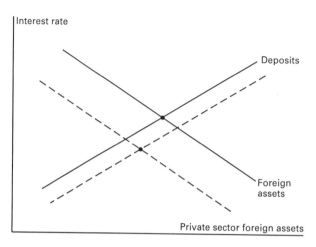

Figure 7.4
Asset market responses to a slower pace of nominal devaluation

causes, and the policy failed to hit its major target. It also strongly desta-
bilized the real sides of the economies (Argentina, Chile, and Uruguay)
in which it was tried. It is interesting to use the model of this section to
spell out the reasons why.

Figure 7.4 illustrates equilibrium in asset markets, with the "deposits"
schedule corresponding to equation (7), and the "foreign assets" schedule
to (8). The shifts in the curves result from credibly reducing $\hat{e}$,[7] so the
return σ to holding foreign assets falls.

The deposits locus in the diagram slopes upward since an increase in Y
must reflect itself into reduced bank reserves in the short run. Deposit
supply $\xi(H + eR)$ contracts, leading the interest rate to rise. In the market
for foreign assets, a higher interest rate reduces demand and Y declines,
explaining the negative slope of that schedule.

When $\hat{e}$ is decreased, two main reactions transpire. Desired asset portfolios shift toward the domestic market, and the interest rate declines (as
might also be expected from the tendency of i to line itself up with the
foreign asset return $\sigma = j + \hat{e} + \rho$). In the diagram the deposits curve
shifts downward. Moreover foreign holdings are also cut back, so that
since $R + Y = J =$ constant in the short run, the money supply goes up.
Therefore the interest rate is also reduced by a leftward shift of the foreign
assets schedule.

The implication is that in the short run, slowing $\hat{e}$ is likely to stimulate
the domestic economy by relaxing credit tightness. Moreover, since $\hat{P} =$

$(1 - \phi)\hat{w} + \phi\hat{e} + \eta i$, ongoing wage increases plus a relatively weak Cavallo-Patman effect mean that inflation will not drop off as rapidly as the exchange rate, (i. e., there will also be real appreciation). If depreciation is contractionary, then appreciation must work the other way. Besides the interest rate impact, aggregate demand will also rise due to forced dissaving from income redistribution in favor of nationals from abroad.

This short-run response can set off dynamic instability, via the lower σ leading to its own further decline. In other words, reducing the return to foreign assets stimulates the economy, but then the improved domestic situation may reduce the expected return further still. A positive feedback of local euphoria into itself is the classic signal for financial fragility, as the discussions in chapters 5 and 6 have pointed out.

A model is easy to set up in terms of the expected extra return to holding foreign assets ρ (which directly pushes up the overall return σ) and the state variable $A = eJ/H$. The evolution of σ over time is discussed informally below. The equation for $\hat{A}$ is

$$\hat{A} = \hat{e} + \left(\frac{t}{J}\right) + j - \gamma V, \tag{9}$$

where t is the trade balance relative to the value of the capital stock. The steady state solution at $\hat{A} = 0$ and $A > 0$ is

$$J = \frac{t}{\gamma V - \hat{e} - j}, \tag{10}$$

showing that sustainable foreign assets rise with the trade balance, the pace of devaluation, and the foreign interest rate, and decline with the growth rate of fiscal debt, $\hat{H} = \gamma V$.

Formally speaking, we should work with three state variables: σ, A, and V. As usual, velocity stabilizes the system (possibly in chaotic fashion), and the gist of the story is preserved if it is told in terms of σ and A. Changes in these state variables affect their rates of increase as follows:

$\partial\dot{\sigma}/\partial\sigma > 0$: The initial downward jump in σ ($=j + \rho + \hat{e}$) from slowing the crawl increases bank reserves R and stimulates domestic activity. The expected incremental return ρ declines, as national financial assets look increasingly attractive. The process reverses when the trade balance declines, leading to reserve loss, higher internal interest rates, and lower activity.

$\partial\dot{\sigma}/\partial A < 0$: Higher foreign assets from any source make their expected return decline.

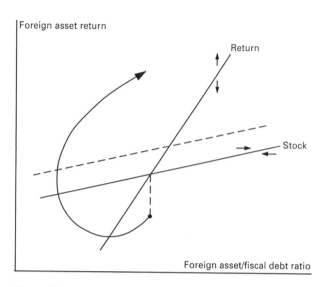

Figure 7.5
Potentially unstable dynamics of the return to foreign assets

$\partial \hat{A}/\partial \sigma > 0$: An increase in σ pulls the public toward foreign holdings, reversing the adjustment in figure 7.4. Interest rates increase, activity decreases, and the trade surplus t goes up. From (9), $\hat{A}$ rises.

$\partial \hat{A}/\partial A < 0$: Higher foreign assets mean more reserves R and monetary expansion. The resulting increase in economic activity reduces the trade surplus and $\hat{A}$.

The phase diagram for A and σ appears in figure 7.5. Slowing a crawling peg makes σ jump down from an initial steady state; from (10) the steady state value of J (and therefore A) declines, as shown by the dashed line. After the policy change, foreign assets begin to fall immediately since greater economic activity makes the trade surplus decrease. Nonetheless, because of the portfolio switch discussed in connection with figure 7.4, bank reserves R go up as private foreign holdings Y jump down—the authorities see no need to be apprehensive and continue to let the currency grow stronger.

For a time the return to foreign assets keeps falling, even though the trade surplus is declining and the exchange rate is becoming increasingly overvalued. At some point the widening trade deficit becomes handwriting on the wall as the trajectory crosses the "return" schedule along which $\dot{\sigma} = 0$, and σ begins to rise. Capital flight in the form of portfolio switches toward foreign assets ensues, leading to output contraction and excess demand inflation (see chapter 8) as the foreign exchange constraint commences to bind. The likely outcome is a period of stagnation before foreign asset stocks start to rebuild as contraction produces a trade surplus; lagged export responses as in figure 7.1 can complicate this process. In practice, the agony may be cut short by a maxi-devaluation before the trajectory reaches the "stock" schedule above which A starts to rise. The maxi amply rewards the speculators, and with good luck, assets held abroad may begin to flow home. With bad luck, "hysteresis" in the form of declining confidence in the national project on the part of the bourgeoisie may hold national asset stakes down in the very long run. As of 1990 repatriation was possibly beginning in Mexico and was still out of the question in Argentina even though capital had been flying out of both countries for more than ten years.

7.4 Political Economy

The sad story just recounted repeats itself with some frequency in the developing world. There is no sure way to avoid its recurrence so long as there are attractive asset markets abroad. However, controls on capital movements can temper destabilizing flows, while a sensible crawling peg policy helps keep foreign and domestic asset returns (not to mention cash flows of exporters and import substituters) stable relative to each other over time. Steady asset market signals reduce the likelihood of the unstable dynamics of figure 7.5. Opening capital markets and dramatically altering asset returns—the recipe applied by Southern Cone monetarists in the 1970s—may make foreign resource speculation almost a sure thing. In their own ways both regressive income redistribution which makes speculation attractive in the absence of domestic economic activity and excessive redistribution and fiscal expansion which leads toward socially disruptive forced saving—inflation tax macroeconomic regimes can lead to the same result.

Figure 7.5 also illustrates the perils of overvaluation. The fact that exchange depreciation can be contractionary and inflationary in the short run (as well as contributing to fluctuations like those in figure 7.1) means that appreciation looks extremely attractive. But it is a long step down a primrose path, since the trade balance will inevitably deteriorate, making the foreign resource gap bind. Besides unstable foreign asset speculation, we will see in chapter 8 that the outcomes could include secular stagflation of the most unpleasant kind.

Getting the real exchange back to a "reasonable" level after it becomes overvalued is an extremely difficult process, precisely because of the adverse real aspects of devaluation discussed in sections 7.1 and 7.2. For the reasons sketched in chapter 4, a prolonged period of real depreciation via a peg crawling a bit more rapidly than inflation is probably less painful than a series of maxi-devaluations aimed at shocking the exchange rate enough to get it "right." The maxis will almost certainly provoke enough inflation and stop-go growth to render their beneficial effects virtually nil.

Finally, the level of the exchange rate can complicate programs aimed directly at stabilizing inflation. There are basically four sorts of policy tools that can usefully be applied (usually combined in one package or another): (1) price freezes and deindexation (i.e., a heterodox shock), (2) manipulation of relative prices (e.g., real wage reduction or appreciation of the exchange rate), (3) import liberalization, or spending foreign exchange to reduce excess demand for flex-price commodities in critical markets, and (4) fiscal and monetary austerity.

If the exchange rate is out of line, then so will be the frozen price structure after a heterodox shock, making the program's viabilility that much less likely. Quite clearly, appreciation as an anti-inflation move from an initially overvalued position does not make a lot of sense, while import liberalization will be more costly in terms of foreign exchange if domestic foreign goods prices are relatively low. An exchange rate that is overvalued forces the authorities back to austerity as their principal anti-inflationary tool, with all its political and social costs, as well as the possibility that it can prolong recession into a very long run.

The moral perhaps is that if the real exchange rate is roughly "right" (as it was in the Korean case), then policies should be orchestrated to keep it where it is. Letting it become badly overvalued is the worst policy mistake that the authorities in a small, open economy can make.

8

Gap Disequilibria: Inflation, Investment, Saving, and Foreign Exchange

Structuralist literature has always emphasized how—depending on institutional and historical circumstances—different factors can limit feasible changes in growth and income distribution in a developing economy. In the analysis of growth, this notion is often formalized in terms of a binding constraint on capital accumulation: The difference between the capital stock growth rate feasible under the binding constraint and under less stringent restrictions can be called a "gap." Since model constraints are usually set up in terms of national income and product accounting identities that have to be satisfied ex post, the presence of a gap signals macroeconomic disequilibrium. How it can be removed is an important aspect of gap diagnosis. Numerous possibilities are explored for an open developing economy in this chapter.

The gap tradition was launched by Chenery and Bruno (1962). They unveiled the two-gap model based on internal and external balance, or saving and foreign resource constraints. The model shows that potential growth of an economy can be limited by either its saving or trade performance, while some mode of macro adjustment must equalize ex post the gaps between investment and saving, and between imports and exports.

A few years after the Chenery-Bruno paper appeared, Cauas (1973) pointed out that there is an ex ante gap between the inflation rate coming from the side of costs and the rate that ensures macro balance via the inflation tax and forced saving. This discrepancy made applied financial programming in Chile (where Cauas was vice president of the Central Bank) less harmonious than the typical IMF exercises. Unsurprisingly, the inflation gap has subsequently been recognized elsewhere in Latin American (e.g., Fanelli, Frenkel, and Winograd 1987).

Finally, fiscal limitations can open a gap between desired and feasible growth rates through the public sector accounts. On the one hand, there is much recent discussion about how private investment is strongly crowded in by public capital formation through complementarities between the sorts of projects that the two sectors undertake. But, on the other hand, public investment has been drastically cut after the debt crisis in many developing countries because foreign obligations are owed by the government, which has to channel its own resources to honor them. Growth has slowed dramatically as a consequence, as discussed empirically in the context of models like the present one by Bacha (1990) and Taylor (1990c).

In this chapter all four gaps—saving, foreign exchange, inflation, and investment—are put into one framework to discuss modes of macroeconomic response to external shocks and the forces affecting medium run growth. We begin in section 8.1 by deriving the saving and foreign gaps from representative flows of funds along the lines of section 4.2. How capital flight, the inflation tax, forced saving, and other factors affect adjustment is the question addressed. Section 8.2 adds an investment function permitting both crowding-in and crowding-out of private by public capital formation.

Section 8.3 shows how these three relationships interact pairwise: The emphasis is on the multiplicity of policy actions a developing economy may take, each with its good and bad features. Section 8.4 gives a graphical resolution of the three gaps under one well-defined set of adjustment rules, and section 8.5 introduces inflationary disequilibrium illustrated by the effects of heterodox shocks. Section 8.6 gives an initial discussion of medium term projections using gap models, and an analysis of the trade-offs between faster inflation and cutting public investment as devices for holding down growth to satisfy limits on inflows of foreign exchange.

Sections 8.7 and 8.8 close this chapter's discussion by showing how the ratios of domestic and foreign debt to the capital stock can become unbounded if the growth performance of the economy is not strong. Such internal and external "debt traps" are serious threats to economic stability in the majority of developing countries in today's world. Finally, appendix 9.A illustrates how the two-gap model can be interpreted in terms of the fix-price/flex-price formulations presented in the next chapter.

8.1   Saving and Foreign Exchange Gaps as Flows of Funds

Apart from the foreign exchange constraint, we assume for the most part that output X (measured gross of intermediate imports) can vary freely in the short run; a capacity restriction is introduced briefly in section 8.5. As usual, the level of activity is indicated by the output/capital ratio, $u = X/K$. Following the specification in chapter 7, labor and intermediate imports are the variable production inputs, with fixed input-output coefficients b and a, respectively. Variable cost per unit output is therefore $wb + ea$, where w and e stand for the nominal wage and exchange rates, and the import price is normalized at unity. The output price is set by a markup factor $1/(1 - \pi)$ over variable cost,

$$P = \frac{wb + ea}{1 - \pi}.$$

(1)

An important aspect of developing countries' lack of economic independence is that the import substitution process rarely extends to capital goods. Poor economies—especially small ones with limited markets—do not acquire technology to produce most "equipment," which accounts for roughly half of total investment demand (the balance being "plant," which can often be produced at home). For formal modeling we assume that the capital stock is made up in proportions θ and $1 - \theta$ of nationally produced and imported goods, respectively; the import share $1 - \theta$ might be 30–50 percent or even more. The cost of a unit of investment is $P_k = \theta P + (1 - \theta)e$. In what follows we do not explicitly consider devaluation, so it is simplest to set $e = P_k = P$.

Following the analysis in section 4.2, saving and foreign exchange gap equations can be derived from flows of funds augmented by hypotheses about uses and sources of national saving. We work with four flows—for private savers and investors, the financial system, the government, and the foreign sector—and assume that private saving is channeled to higher bank deposits, increases in the stock of narrow money, and asset-holdings abroad through capital flight.[1] The level of nominal saving is assumed to depend on income and the rate of inflation, in line with the discussion in chapter 4.

The monetary side of the economy is treated as a pure credit banking system of the sort described by Wicksell (1935) and in effect used by the IMF in its exercises in "financial programming" (Taylor 1988a). Let A_p be bank assets (credits, loans) advanced to the private sector, A_g be advances to the government, and eR be the value of foreign reserves. Bank liabilities are deposits D and narrow money M. The banking system balance sheet is

$$A_p + A_g + eR = D + M,$$

which we will analyze in flow terms,

$$\dot{A}_p + \dot{A}_g + e\dot{R} = \dot{D} + \dot{M},$$ (2)

where a "dot" over a variable denotes its time derivative, $\dot{x} = dx/dt$.

If there is no depreciation, then $g = I/K$ is the growth rate of capital stock. Real investment I in turn is the sum $I_p + I_g$ of private and public capital formation. Let $I_g = \kappa K$ be the government's investment decision—its own capital formation is set as a share κ of the total capital stock. The value of private investment is $(g - \kappa)PK$, and we assume that banks issue new loans $\dot{A}_p$ to finance the increase in private capital,

$$\frac{\dot{A}_p}{PK} = g - \kappa.$$ (3)

The overall investment function determining g is presented as a reduced form (depending on credit availability among other factors) in section 8.2. For the moment (3) is best interpreted as an accounting "identity."[2]

Let real government current spending $G = \gamma K$. As usual, we treat γ as a proxy for the noninvestment fiscal deficit or government dissaving to avoid carrying along symbols representing taxes. The government also borrows abroad. Its outstanding stock of loans is F upon which it pays an interest rate j. Let $\xi = eF/PK$ be the debt/capital ratio and T be the net transfer of new money from abroad relative to capital stock: $T = (e\dot{F} - jeF)/PK = (\hat{F} - j)\xi$, where a "hat" over a variable signifies its growth rate ($\hat{x} = \dot{x}/x$). There is a net inflow of foreign resources if the debt growth rate $\hat{F}$ exceeds the interest rate j, a condition violated in much of the Third World in the late 1980s. The government turns to the banking system to finance the part of its spending it cannot cover with foreign loans,

$$\frac{\dot{A}_g}{PK} = \kappa + \gamma - T.$$ (4)

Domestic borrowing can be a substantial share of GDP when T is less than zero. As we have already observed, debtor country governments owe large foreign obligations (typically having taken over private loans in internal financial "reforms" in the early 1980s) but do not own the resources to generate foreign exchange to pay; the outcome is a severe fiscal crunch.

Finally on the bank asset side, the increase in reserves is

$$\frac{e\dot{R}}{PK} = T + \varepsilon - au - (1 - \theta)g - Q,$$

where $\varepsilon = E/K$ is the ratio of exports (net of competitive imports) to capital stock, imports go only for intermediates au and capital goods $(1 - \theta)g$, and

Q stands for net acquisition of foreign assets (relative to the capital stock) by the private sector.

To describe the saving gap, we have to add hypotheses about sources of deposits and narrow money. Following Ros (1989), we assume that saving desired by nationals in the absence of price inflation is directed either to foreign asset accumulation or else to increased bank deposits:

$$Q + \frac{\dot{D}}{PK} = [\pi s_\pi + (1 - \pi)(1 - \phi)s_w]u = s(\pi, \phi)u,$$

where s_π and s_w are the saving rates from profit and wage income flows respectively. As in chapter 7, $\phi = ea/(ea + wb)$ is the share of intermediate imports in variable cost, so that $(1 - \pi)(1 - \phi)u$ is the ratio of the wage bill to the capital stock. Boiling all the dynamics of section 7.3 down into one parameter, we assume that a share λ of saving flows abroad ($Q = \lambda su$), so the above equation becomes[3]

$$\frac{\dot{D}}{PK} = (1 - \lambda)su.$$

Putting (2) through (6) together shows that the increase in the supply (or "emission") of narrow money is

$$\frac{\dot{M}}{PK} = g + \gamma - (1 - \lambda)su + [\varepsilon - au - (1 - \theta)g - Q]$$

$$= g + \gamma - (1 - \lambda)su + \left[\frac{\dot{R}}{PK} - T\right] \tag{7}$$

where the terms in brackets represent the balance of payments (net of capital flight) on current and capital account in the first and second lines, respectively.

What can be said about the growth rate of money demand, say, $\hat{\mu}$? Although it gives the analysis a monetarist cast, it is instructive to follow the model of section 4.2 and set up a cumulative process inflation by postulating that a quantity equation links the two assets in the system, $\mu V = PK$, and that V is constant. Hence $\hat{\mu} = \hat{P} + g$, or

$$\frac{\dot{\mu}}{PK} = \left(\frac{1}{V}\right)(\hat{P} + g). \tag{8}$$

Money demand rises in proportion to the inflation rate $\hat{P}$ and the growth rate of the capital stock (or capacity) g. Recall from chapter 4 that the first component is often called the "inflation tax"—we will observe its taxlike effects on aggregate demand shortly. Higher money demand due to capacity growth is "seigniorage"; so to speak, it is the money that the banking system gets to create without inflationary complications.

Our first macro equilibrium condition is that excess supply growth of money (or excess demand for goods) should be zero. Setting $(\dot{M} - \dot{\mu})/PK = 0$ gives a slightly modified version of the usual investment-saving balance:

$$\left[1 - \left(\frac{1}{V}\right)\right]g + \gamma + \frac{e\dot{R}}{PK} - T - (1 - \lambda)su - \left(\frac{1}{V}\right)\hat{P} = 0. \tag{S}$$

This equation says that the difference between demand injections and leakages must be zero. Injections include investment net of seigniorage, government spending (or dissaving), and the increase in reserves representing a reduction in the trade deficit. Leakages include net foreign resource inflows (or "foreign saving"), the share of zero-inflation private saving directed toward bank deposits, and the inflation tax.

The final term shows that effective demand declines as inflation runs faster—this is the taxlike aspect of $(1/V)\hat{P}$. As we have seen, the demand reduction can be interpreted in various ways. One is that the public is forced below its desired consumption schedule by preemption of output by the government and investors; they have a prior claim on output, financed by money emission. A second is that $(M/P)\hat{P}$ represents the instantaneous loss in the value of real money balances caused by a price increase $\dot{P}$. The public is supposed to raise its saving in this amount to reconstitute its wealth—a rational act. Finally, faster inflation means that people need a bigger money stock for transactions purposes. With no easily liquifiable assets at hand, the only way they can build it up is to save more.[4] On all three counts, consumption declines from its zero-inflation level $[1 - s - (e/P)a]u$.

The other independent restriction that comes from the flows of funds is a restatement of (5):

$$\varepsilon + T - (1 - \theta)g - (a + \lambda s)u - e\dot{R}/PK = 0, \tag{F}$$

stating that sources less uses of foreign exchange must equal zero. The capital flight term λsu increases the foreign exchange loss associated with higher capacity utilization beyond the leakage au implicit in the economy's dependence on imported intermediates to support the production process.

Equations (S) and (F) are the saving and foreign resource gaps respectively. As discussed in appendix 9.A, they can be treated as independent constraints on macro performance under reasonable assumptions (e.g., the structure of the flows of funds and quantity equations presented here). We will see how they interact in section 8.3, but before that it is useful to list other macro responses that one might want to build into the model:

Olivera-Tanzi Effect

Especially when the tax system is not indexed to inflation, its efficiency drops as $\hat{P}$ goes up. As pointed out in chapter 2, the usual explanation is that due to lags in tax collection, real receipts progressively decline as inflation runs faster; for the algebra see Olivera (1967) or Tanzi (1977). In our framework this linkage could be captured by making γ an increasing function of $\hat{P}$.

Forced Saving

Forced saving raises its head-in gap models in which output is limited by foreign exchange. Any demand increase will make prices rise, but some may not be fully responsive. If, for example, money wage rates lag general inflation, the real wage will fall and the markup factor $1/(1 - \pi)$ and profit share π will increase. With $s_\pi > s_w$ in (6), the overall saving rate $s(\pi, \phi)$ will go up along with $\hat{P}$, reducing aggregate demand back toward the constrained level of supply. The effect is practically important—real wages have fallen by 50 to 90 percent in some African and Latin American economies under inflation with severe external restrictions during the 1980s.

Fiscal Adventurism

When inflation accelerates, the government may seek to offset the ill effects of forced saving on workers' real incomes by higher spending or transfer programs such as food subsidies. With output bounded by available foreign exchange, the attempt will not work: As shown in chapters 2 and 3, the paradox of thrift applies. Often, governments do not (or choose not to) acknowledge this problem. They make γ into an increasing function of $\hat{P}$ from the expenditure as opposed to the Olivera-Tanzi taxation side.

Variable Velocity

As we have observed, the stylized fact is that V is an increasing function of $\hat{P}$. The rationale is that the public economizes on its use of money, the more rapidly its value is being eroded by inflation. From equation (S), the demand-reducing effect of an increase in $\hat{P}$ weakens as V rises when inflation runs faster. Ultimately $d(\hat{P}/V)/dP$ can become negative, as the elasticity of V with respect to $\hat{P}$ exceeds unity and the economy crosses to the "wrong" side of the inflation tax's Laffer curve. In what follows we assume that this eventuality does not arise.

Export Responsiveness

Especially in semi-industrialized economies, an inverse relationship between capacity utilization and exports is often noted (Taylor 1988a, 1990c). The usual explanation is that as domestic demand declines, potential exporters in the manufacturing sector become more aggressive in seeking markets abroad. Such a response is less likely in a primary-product exporting country. Reduced internal demand will not release large quantities of copper or bananas for potential buyers overseas.

8.2   Investment Crowding-out and Crowding-in

Relative to capital stock, we assume that private investment demand is given by the function

$$\frac{I_p}{K} = g_0 + \alpha u + \beta \left(\frac{I_g}{K} \right) + \psi \left[\left(\frac{\dot{D}}{PK} \right) - \left(\frac{\dot{A}_g}{PK} \right) \right]. \tag{9}$$

The term αu is an instantaneous accelerator—an output-investment linkage is common in developing country econometrics. Including lags would complicate the algebra but not add much economics. Since we are not explicitly modeling income redistribution in this chapter, we do not include a separate effect on investment of the profit rate in (9).

   The term in I_g/K shows that public investment crowds in private capital formation because of complementarities and other external effects. Demonstrating the importance of crowding-in became a thriving cottage industry in the late 1980s, and it makes sense to incorporate the possibility in any growth model.[5]

   The last term in (9) introduces financial crowding-out as a potential counterpoise to direct crowding-in. We assume along conventional lines that investment is cut back when the government puts pressure on financial markets. Specifically, I_p falls when new government borrowing $\dot{A}_g/PK$ grows with respect to the deposit increase $\dot{D}/PK$. The rationale could be that banks raise interest rates and tighten credit limits when more of their deposit base is absorbed by the government. This simple flow specification is dimensionally equivalent to the quantity theory of money demand (8) and saves the use of asset stock or state variables.

Plugging (4) and (6) into (9) and simplifying gives

$$-g + g_0 + [\alpha + \psi(1 - \lambda)s]u + (1 + \beta - \psi)\kappa - \psi\gamma + \psi T = 0. \qquad \text{(I)}$$

This relationship shows that the capital stock growth rate g increases endogenously in response to greater capacity utilization u due to the accelerator and also because higher private saving creates deposits which banks use to finance investments. Government investment κ has an overall crowding-in effect if $1 + \beta > \psi$. This condition will be satisfied if $\beta \geq 0$ and $\psi \leq 1$, as is likely. Finally, an increase in net foreign transfers T or a reduction in government dissaving γ cuts back on public borrowing from the banks, again permitting private investment to rise.

8.3   Interactions between the Gaps by Pairs

The gap equations (S), (F), and (I) are easy to solve simultaneously under plausible assumptions about endogenous and exogenous variables, but the reduced form obscures the complexity of macroeconomic adjustment in the Third World. Indeed, illustrating the manifold constraints that developing economies face was Chenery and Bruno's original goal. They switched axes in a number of two-dimensional constraint diagrams to hammer the point home. We will do the same in this section, as we follow Bacha (1990) and Eyzaguirre (1989) in discussing possible channels via which disequilibrium "gaps between the gaps" are removed pair-by-pair, before giving a full solution based on specific adjustment rules.

Saving and Foreign Exchange

Figure 8.1 is the traditional two-gap diagram, with foreign transfers on the horizontal axis and the capital stock growth rate that they permit measured vertically. The foreign exchange constraint FF has a slope exceeding 45 degrees because the import content of investment is less than 100 percent: A one-unit increase in the trade deficit lets investment rise by an amount $1/(1 - \theta) > 1$. The slope of the saving gap SS also is greater than 45 degrees because of seigniorage but less than the slope of FF with plausible parameters.

Suppose that transfers are cut from T_0 to T_1; alternatively, there could be an increase in the rate of capital flight λ. After either shock, investment is limited to a lower value by its import content than by potential saving. How does the economy adjust?

Several responses can occur. First, capacity use u is likely to fall, as scarce foreign exchange is shared among intermediate and capital goods importers by market and nonmarket devices. The intermediate import flow au will decline. Next, saving from both transfers T and income su will fall, creating excess commodity demand at the initial investment level. The natural response is for inflation $\hat{P}$ to speed up, to generate extra saving via the inflation tax and forced saving. Finally, as we have noted, in the medium run in semi-industrialized economies at least, low domestic demand means that exports ε tend to rise.

A likely transition path is from A toward B then C. The upward shift of FF comes from reduced intermediate imports and (with a lag) higher exports. The saving constraint shifts downward as u declines, partly offset by a higher $\hat{P}$. There will be greater output loss and faster inflation, the less responsive are exporters to opportunities abroad. Countries like South Korea and Brazil represent favorable cases in which FF shifts strongly upward as exports rise. Alternatively, foreign exchange may be saved by

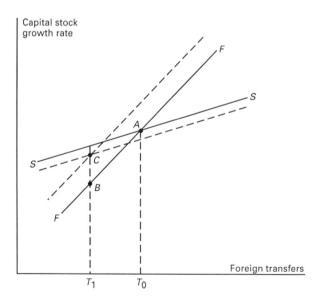

Figure 8.1
Saving and foreign exchange gaps

effective import quotas as in Kenya and Colombia in the early 1980s—
Ocampo (1987) and Rattsø (1990a) set up instructive models. The medium-
run problem with quotas is that it is often easier to raise exports ε from a
low level than to force the import coefficient a down toward zero.

Saving and Investment

Figure 8.2 shows that the saving limit on growth SS is an increasing
function of the inflation rate, while investment demand II does not depend
on $\hat{P}$.[6] A smaller foreign transfer means that both curves shift downward,
due to reduced saving for SS, and to restricted bank finance for private
investment along II as the government replaces foreign by domestic loans.
If financial crowding-out of domestic investment is relatively weak ($\psi \leq 1$),
inflation will rise from A to B as illustrated in the diagram.

Various responses can occur. The healthiest perhaps is a reduction in γ
due to government spending cuts and higher taxes. Both schedules return
toward their original positions, alleviating tendencies toward inflation. But
there is still a foreign exchange disequilibrium to be resolved by the
mechanisms discussed above. Fiscally based adjustment of this sort seems
politically more feasible in Asia than elsewhere in the world.

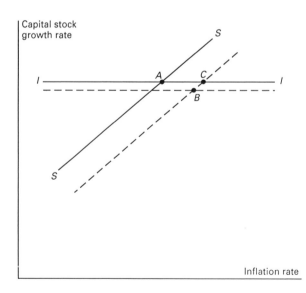

Figure 8.2
Saving and investment constraints

A second option is to increase public investment κ, shifting the II locus back to its initial position. Inflation rises from B to C. This move represents adjustment a la Brazil, at least through the mid-1980s.

The poorest choice is to increase γ to support employment and try to offset real wage losses via transfer programs. This shift will be exaggerated if Olivera-Tanzi effects are strong. In addition public investment may be maintained, on long-term planning grounds. SS shifts further downward and II moves up, pushing inflation higher. Chile and Peru more or less followed this path in the early 1970s and late 1980s, respectively.

Finally, quantitative restrictions can drive intermediate imports down, reducing capacity use and employment but perhaps allowing public investment targets to be met—an African scenario.

Figure 8.3, with the foreign transfer replacing inflation on the abscissa, illustrates adjustment when foreign resources go up or capital flight diminishes. There is an excess of nationally usable saving over investment ex ante, creating tendencies for both u and $\hat{P}$ to decline. The obvious offsetting maneuvers are to increase public investment κ (shifting II upward) and to pursue price and incomes policies leading inflation to fall more than output as SS shifts downward.

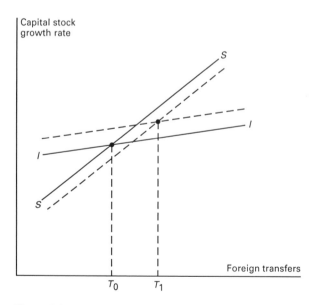

Figure 8.3
Saving and investment constraints

Investment and Foreign Exchange

The foreign exchange FF and investment II schedules appear in figure 8.4. FF has the steeper slope because the import share of investment is well less than one. A transfer decrease from T_0 to T_1 means that growth is constrained by FF. An immediate response might be to run down foreign reserves, shifting FF temporarily upward. But in a longer run, public investment is likely to be cut, quotas imposed on capital goods imports, and so on, to make II move down to a new equilibrium at B.

What happens if extra resources become available at T_2? Now investment is held down along II by insufficient financial crowding-in. Again, various adjustments are possible. The authorities may opt to cut net exports and shift FF down by liberalization of import quotas and tariff reduction—a policy line often recommended by the World Bank and IMF. Domestic producers of traded goods will object, and depending on the balance of political forces, liberalization may be curtailed. If not, deindustrialization is a likely outcome, such as in Chile and Sri Lanka in the late 1970s.

The central bank may "sterilize" part of the extra transfer by wiping up arrears, buying back external debt, and so forth. Such policies also often provoke domestic resistance—why not use the dollars at home? The part

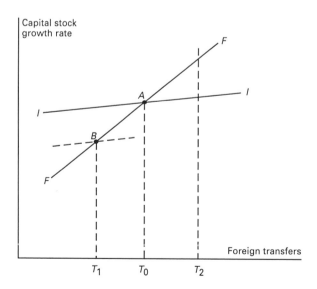

Figure 8.4
Investment and foreign exchange constraints

of the inflow that does not go to extra imports or sterilization will have to be accumulated as reserves. The resulting money supply expansion can lead to faster inflation, increased capacity utilization, or both. Policies have to be designed to enhance output as opposed to price increases.

Finally, public investment κ can be raised to shift the II locus upward, absorbing part of the extra foreign exchange in capacity growth.

8.4   A Three-Gap Resolution

The preceding discussion suggests that there is no dearth of mechanisms by which the gaps can be resolved. The policy challenge is to select a relatively comfortable adjustment path. For analytical purposes a related question is how to set up a plausible set of adjustment rules to close the model fully.

In this section we present an example based upon the recursive structure of equations (S), (F), and (I). Suppose that the growth rate g is the adjusting variable in (I). Capacity use u varies in (F), with intermediate imports (and capital flight) absorbing the foreign exchange left over after investment needs are met. In effect, output is constrained by available yen or dollars. To attain overall macro balance in (S), saving has to be brought into line with fiscal and investment demand. A changing inflation rate $\hat{P}$ is the vehicle, acting through forced saving and the inflation tax. Routh-Hurwitz criteria applied to the three-equation model easily show that this adjustment process is locally stable.

Figure 8.5 in the (u, g) plane illustrates how the macro response to a reduced foreign transfer takes place. The solid lines refer to an initial equilibrium position. The foreign exchange locus FF has a negative slope, reflecting the competition between investment and current economic activity for scarce foreign exchange that is frequently brought out in economic analyses for Africa (e.g., Green and Kadhani 1986; Ndulu 1986). The investment schedule II has a shallow positive slope, depending on the strength of accelerator and financial crowding-in effects.

The SS schedule is one of a family of inflation contour lines (or iso-$\hat{P}$ loci), of the sort introduced in section 5.3. It shows combinations of capacity utilization u and the capital stock growth rate g that hold the inflation rate constant in equation (S). Since an increase in g or a reduction in u signals incipient excess commodity demand, curves in the family to the left of SS correspond to faster inflation rates. Standard macro stability arguments of the sort developed in chapters 2 and 3 ensure that SS will be steeper than II.

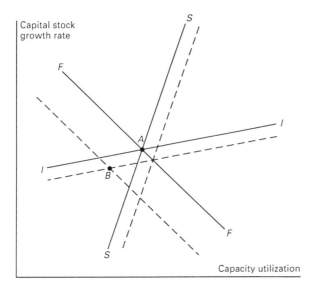

Figure 8.5
Joint solution of investment, saving, and foreign exchange constraints

A reduced transfer means that the investment locus must shift downward and the foreign exchange constraint to the left. Capital stock growth unambiguously falls. Capacity utilization will also decline unless financial crowding-out of investment demand is very strong, releasing enough foreign exchange to permit production to be maintained. Since for given u and g, a reduced transfer means that $\hat{P}$ rises in (S) to replace lost saving, the whole family of isoinflation curves shifts to the right. The new real equilibrium at B lies to the left and the shifted inflation contour to the right of the initial point A, so inflation accelerates.

What are possible policy responses? Stepping up public investment moves the II curve back toward its original position, restoring capital stock growth at the cost of greater stagflation. An export increase (or effective import substitution) shifts FF to the right, raising u and g while decelerating $\hat{P}$. Cutting government dissaving makes the investment-curve move upward by reducing crowding-out, and slides the inflation contour lines back toward the left. The net result of a lower γ is that output is still held down by scarce foreign resources, but growth recovers and inflation slows down. Blending these policies could bring the economy from point B back toward A, but designing and managing such a comprehensive program would not be an easy task.

8.5   The Inflation Gap

Although it is beloved by monetarists, the inflation theory that we have
been using so far is a bit farfetched. To maintain financial equilibrium,
inflation is supposed to adjust instantly to drive excess commodity demand
(or excess money supply in flow terms) to zero via the inflation tax
supplemented by forced saving. The big problem with this approach was
pointed out in chapter 4: At any time, observed inflation $\hat{P}_c$ will be determined from the side of costs, for example, from a growth rate version of
the price equation (1),

$$-\hat{P}_c + (1 - \phi)\hat{w} + \phi\hat{e} + \frac{\dot{\pi}}{1 - \pi} = 0. \tag{10}$$

Unless wage inflation, exchange rate inflation, or movements in the profit
share quickly adjust to changes in excess commodity demand, the inflation
equilibrium condition

$$\hat{P} - \hat{P}_c = 0 \tag{P}$$

will be violated. Monetarists implicitly assume that $\hat{w}$, $\hat{e}$, and/or $\dot{\pi}$ jumps
to allow (P) to be satisfied, but they rarely explore the implications for income distribution and effective demand. The contrasting structuralist view
is that class conflict and propagation mechanisms such as contract indexation often make $\hat{P}_c$ the driving force behind inflation, and that $\hat{P}$ (through
endogenous fiscal and monetary policy) has to adjust.

Figure 8.6 shows what happens when the observed inflation rate $\hat{P}_c$ is
suddenly reduced from a preexisting equilibrium, say, by price controls and
deindexation in a heterodox shock anti-inflation program of the sort analyzed in chapters 4 and 5. The previous discussions concentrated on internal repercussions of the shock; here we consider its balance of payments
implications.

To reach saving-investment equilibrium after $\hat{P}_c$ is cut, u and g have to
lie along the dashed $S'S'$ line in figure 8.6, whereas enough money is still
being created to be consistent with an inflation rate corresponding to SS
Experience suggests that consumption demand will rise in response to the
reduced inflation tax, so that investment will be limited by scarce foreign
exchange. With II lying above FF along $S'S'$, there is incipient excess
commodity demand unless the investment curve shifts downward or there
are greater capital inflows, increased exports, or reserve losses and/or a
run-up in arrears to move FF up. Demand pressure will be more severe
insofar as the increase in u lifts output close to installed capacity.

Unfortunately, foreign exchange generation by exports or capital inflows may not be on the cards. Foreign sales are not likely to rise when consumer demand is booming, especially in a semi-industrialized economy. To analyze changes in net capital flows, we have to ask how private sector demand for foreign assets will change under the anti-inflationary shock.

We can begin by noting that when $\hat{P}_c$ falls, V will decline as money becomes less costly to hold. If the economy is on the "right" side of the Laffer curve, there will be an *in*elastic response of velocity to inflation. In equation (8) V falls less than $\hat{P}$ so that money demand growth will decrease: $\dot{M}/PK > \dot{\mu}/PK$ after the shock. Initially wealth-holders have to accept the excess money that is being created. But a natural response on their part is to search for alternative assets, so λ will rise. There will be pressure on the black market exchange rate, perhaps forcing devaluation and renewed cost pressure. At the same time, all the solid curves in figure 8.6 will shift unfavorably, as in figure 8.5. In the medium term, foreign exchange reserves will decline, but the consequent reduction in money supply growth may come too late to offset macroeconomic deterioration.[7]

The moral seems to be that cost-oriented anti-inflation programs are best accompanied by increased transfers from abroad to move FF up, cuts in fiscal dissaving to shift the $S'S'$ locus toward the left, or public investment restraint to shift II down. It is noteworthy that the price-freeze packages that have succeeded at least for a time—in Mexico and Israel especially— have been characterized by high T's and low γ's and κ's in terms of the notation adopted here.

The opposite case of $\hat{P}_c > \hat{P}$ occurs when cost pressure increases, say, from devaluation. The economy tends toward the intersection of a leftward-shifted SS schedule with II. There is an excess supply of foreign exchange as both g and u decline. It can be absorbed by the policies discussed above, but initally we observe the stagflationary effects of devaluation stressed in the models of chapter 7.

In closing, it bears emphasis that our discussion of figure 8.6 hinges on the narrow, quantity theory view of financial adjustment built into equations (7) and (8). As illustrated in chapters 5 and 6, a more realistic approach is to treat $V = PK/M$ as a (usually) stable state variable, evolving according to the laws that govern $\hat{P}$ (responding to class conflict or demand pressures, as befits the economy at hand), g, and $\dot{M}$. When one works with such a model, it is clear that there will be economic forces (such as interest rate increases and better tax collection) shifting SS and $S'S'$ toward one another after a heterodox shock. Political factors can offset (or exacerbate)

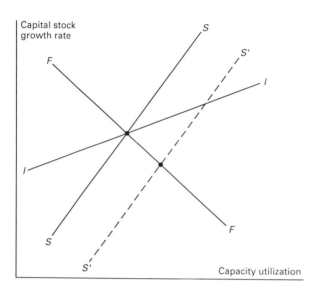

Figure 8.6
The inflation gap superimposed on investment, saving, and foreign exchange constraints

tendencies toward capital flight. In applied anti-inflation programs, policy formation has to take such possibilities into account.

8.6   Growth Projections

Although Chenery and Bruno concentrated on adjustment problems, subsequently the two-gap model has mostly been used to make conditional forecasts of medium-term growth. In early applications equations (S) and (F) were used separately, with a constant "technically given" output/capital ratio u and omitting inflation taxes and reserve changes. One or the other equation would give a lower g for a given T, and the corresponding constraint was said to be binding. Although they were recognized, macro adjustment issues of the type discussed here were usually not incorporated into growth projections.

Bacha (1984) suggested a more sophisticated procedure based on solving (S) and (F) simultaneously for g and u (given $\hat{P}$) and also setting T equal to $(\hat{F} - j)\xi$ so that both new money inflows and interest payments could be taken into account. The discussion here would suggest using (S), (F), (I), and (P) together to make projections, with a mix of quantity theory and cost-based inflation processes appropriate to the economy at hand.

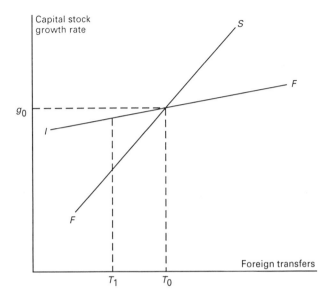

Figure 8.7
Relationships between the foreign exchange/saving and investment/foreign exchange constraints

Figure 8.7 illustrates potential policy issues, in a diagram based on semi-reduced forms from the model on the familiar foreign transfer versus growth rate plane.[8]

The schedule labeled FS results from eliminating capacity utilization u between the saving and foreign exchange constraints (F) and (S), for a given rate of inflation. Its slope exceeds unity, because the import content of investment is less than 100 percent. Faster inflation (a bigger inflation tax) means that less foreign saving is required to support a given rate of growth, so FS shifts leftward as $\hat{P}$ rises.

The IF curve comes from eliminating u between (I) and (F). Overall macro stability requires that it be less steep than FS, and a reduction in public capital formation κ shifts IF downward. The intersection of the curves defines a growth/capital inflow equilibrium at (T_0, g_0). How will the economy adjust if the required inflow is not forthcoming?

The possibilities that are easy to analyze in the diagram are faster inflation and cuts in public investment (both can be complemented by reduced fiscal dissaving). Inflation permits T_0 to fall to T_1 with the growth rate determined along IF as FS moves to the left, while cutting public capital formation means that *IF* shifts downward along the steeper *FS*. There is a lower cost in terms of growth from the inflationary as opposed to the investment-cutting solution, which perhaps shows that Brazil's strategy discussed in section 8.3 may not have been pure folly after all. However, at the same time, higher demand inflation worsens the income distribution via forced saving and feeds back into more and faster contract indexation, and so forth, which can make trending prices much more difficult to tackle from the $\hat{P}_c$ side. The policy question is multifaceted: How much fiscal restraint in terms of current spending or taxation is required to support a healthy level of public investment (with private investment crowding-in) as well as a politically acceptable inflation rate under likely prospects for capital inflows and success in promoting exports and holding imports down?

8.7   An Internal Debt Trap

After pausing for breath in wake of the last question, we can also bring two other topics into view, *viz* is economic growth even feasible given the ominous increases in both internal and external public debt that are being observed in developing economies around the world? We tackle the internal and external debt traps in this and the next section, respectively.

Discussion of public debt accumulation follows Domar (1944, 1950) in inquiring about the evolution of a state variable of the form $\zeta = Z/PK$, where Z is the outstanding stock of nonmonetized government debt. A debt trap may be at hand if the differential equation for $\dot{\zeta}$ is not stable.

To address this possibility, we must change hypotheses and assume that in the country we are analyzing, there is indeed an active market for (typically) short-term government obligations resembling U.S. Treasury bills (e.g., we are talking about India, Zimbabwe, Brazil, and at most a few other developing economies). Fiscal deficits in the rest of the Third World typically have to be monetized, meaning that a foreign resource constraint reflects directly into emission and possible (hyper)inflation, as we have seen.

Since the private sector is purchasing government obligations, its flow of funds (exclusive of the inflation tax and seigniorage) takes the form

$$su + i\zeta = \frac{\dot{D}}{PK} + Q + \hat{Z}\zeta, \tag{11}$$

where i is the interest rate on public debt and the corresponding income flow $i\zeta$ is assumed (without much loss of generality) to be wholly saved. The increase in debt relative to capital stock is $\hat{Z}\zeta = \dot{Z}/PK$.

Following Arida (1986), we assume that the government has to peg its interest rate by a rule such as $i = j + \Delta + \hat{P}$, where j is the international interest rate (as before) and Δ is a premium designed to get the public to hold the state's liabilities. In the discussion that follows, Δ is treated as a policy variable, manipulated to increase the share v of non-monetized savings flows su directed to $\dot{Z}/PK$ and to reduce the share λ going to capital flight. Finally, it is reasonable to include a term $-\theta(j + \Delta)$ in the private investment function (9) and the investment gap (I), to capture the adverse effect of a real interest rate increase on investment demand.

The government accounting balance (4) can be restated as

$$\frac{\dot{A}_g}{PK} + (\hat{Z} - i)\zeta + (\hat{F} - j)\xi = \kappa + \gamma. \tag{12}$$

Two points are worth making about this expression. First, with large net foreign payment obligations, $(j - \hat{F})\xi \gg 0$, net internal sources of finance must also be large, $\dot{A}_g/PK + (\hat{Z} - i)\zeta \gg 0$. As we have already noted, the external debt burden maps into high internal debt, in either monetized (A_g) or nonmonetized (Z) form.

The second observation is that with double- or triple-digit inflation, the government's nominal interest payments $(j + \Delta + \hat{P})Z$ will be very high, perhaps 10 percent of GDP or more. Since sensible asset-holders should save at least the inflationary component $\hat{P}Z$ to avoid running down their real wealth, the demand injection will not be large.[9] Setting up inflation-proof fiscal accounting to recognize this fact has been a bone of contention between the IMF and the country authorities benefiting from its counsel to avoid expansion of aggregate demand (Taylor 1988a). The analytical issues are reviewed by Ros (1987).

When equations (2), (3), (12), (5), and (11) are consolidated to give the increase in money supply $\dot{M}/PK$, the terms in ζ cancel between (11) and (12), so (7) remains unchanged in a model including government debt (under our assumption that all public interest payments are saved). There is no direct effect of ζ on short-term equilibrium as illustrated in figure 8.5. It is easy to show that an increase in the interest premium Δ will reduce g and $\hat{P}$, while permitting u to rise along the binding foreign exchange constraint.

Differential equations giving the changes in ζ and ξ over time take the form

$$\dot{\zeta} = vsu + (j + \Delta - g)\zeta \tag{13}$$

and

$$\dot{\xi} = \xi(\hat{F} - g). \tag{14}$$

The equation for $\dot{\xi}$ is independent of ζ. From figure 8.5 an increase in the net transfer $T = (\hat{F} - j)\xi$ increases the growth rate. Hence, if $\hat{F} > j$, we have $\partial \dot{\xi}/\partial \xi < 0$ in (14). To pursue the discussion of a potential internal debt trap, we assume that this condition is satisfied, although in fact it is violated in many countries in the 1990s world.

For $\partial \dot{\zeta}/\partial \zeta$ in (13) to be negative, the condition $g > j + \Delta$ must apply; that is, the real interest rate that the state has to pay to get the public to hold its obligations cannot exceed the rate of growth. This condition is reminiscent of Domar's. In the slow-growing corners of the Third World (Sub-Saharan Africa, Latin America), it is not satisfied. An internal debt trap looms when the rate of capital stock growth is less than the real interest rate on government debt. Unfavorable external conditions which mandate slow growth and force the internal interest rate to be high to offset dim expectations make the trap speedier to close.

If the system (13)–(14) is in fact stable, the steady state conditions are that the national growth rate is equal to the growth rate of foreign debt, $g = \hat{F}$ from (14), and that ζ takes the value

$$\zeta = \frac{vsu}{g - (j + \Delta)}. \tag{15}$$

Evidently, external debt growth must be high, $\hat{F} > j + \Delta$, for ζ to take a positive value in steady state. Even if it does, the level may be unreasonably large, such as 2.5 times real GDP in a recent calculation for India (Taylor 1988b).

Finally, note that a model with predetermined $\hat{F}$ has certain undesirable features. For example, higher public investment κ cannot raise the steady state rate of growth. However, by totally differentiating (13)–(14), it is easy to show that an increase in κ does reduce both ξ and ζ in a new steady state by causing a transitory growth rate excursion. From (15) a smaller steady state ζ must be associated with *lower* long-run capacity utilization u; that is, higher public investment crowds out private capital formation by making the level of economic activity decline. This effect could be offset by a higher interest premium Δ to reduce the denominator and raise v and u in (15), even though such a move would offset the short-run growth increase from raising κ. An economy facing a strictly predetermined growth rate of foreign debt is not easy to run at all.

8.8   An External Debt Trap

The crowding-out effects just recounted are caused (as usual) by a binding restriction on supply, in this case from scarce foreign exchange. To add perspective on growth prospects, it is useful to study the case in which the economy can borrow what it needs to satisfy its own internal dynamics of accumulation. The obvious question to ask is whether in such a situation the ratio of external debt to capital threatens to become unbounded.[10] We set out a provisional answer here.

By the rules of closure analysis, if we let $\hat{F}$ be determined endogenously in the short run, a new restriction has to be added to the model. The simplest choice in the present context is to use constant capacity $u = \bar{u}$, even though in practice the authorities in charge of a depressed economy who get new access to foreign exchange might opt for phased increases in both u and g. If we stick with constant capacity, then the foreign balance (F) transforms into a differential equation giving the change in ξ:

$$\dot{\xi} = -\varepsilon + (a + \lambda s)\bar{u} + (1 - \theta)g + (j - g)\xi. \tag{16}$$

The short-run system (ignoring cost inflation) is made up of (S) and (I), with $\hat{P}$ and g as the accommodating variables. It is still independent of ζ, and it is easy to show that an increase in ξ increases the growth rate g, so long as the current net transfer from abroad is positive. Depending on what happens to aggregate demand, $\hat{P}$ can shift either way.

An external debt trap, or $\partial\dot{\xi}/\partial\xi > 0$ in (16), is more likely when θ is small and/or g is not much greater than j—a small θ is more likely to be observed in a small, open developing economy that lacks sufficient internal market size to pursue import substitution of capital goods. In the (unlikely?) event that the trap is not a threat, the steady state value of ξ is

$$\xi = \frac{-\varepsilon + (a + \lambda s)\bar{u} + (1 - \theta)g}{g - j}, \tag{17}$$

and the steady state value of ζ comes from (15), with $u = \bar{u}$.

With the possibility of running up external debt freely, an increase in public investment κ in this model can speed up the rate of growth. If intermediate imports plus capital flight exceed exports, then from (17) faster growth reduces the debt ratio ξ in the long run. This favorable development can occur even though from (16) $\dot{\xi}$ can easily rise initially after κ is raised. From (15) faster growth is also likely to make the internal debt ratio fall

The problem is of course that there are many possible slips 'twixt the higher public investment cup and the sustainably faster growth rate lip—not least the risk that foreign creditors will cut off access to funds. The problems of how to manage an exchange-constrained economy are not fundamentally different from the ones visible in the early 1960s, but the fiscal/external debt crises in most countries of the Third World make them even more urgent now than they were when Chenery and Bruno began to analyze disequilibrium growth adjustment and gaps.

Varying Terms of Trade, Distribution, and Growth

The agrarian question has long been at issue in economic debate. It involves all the macroeconomic forces discussed heretofore: class differences in economic power, saving and consumption behavior; modes of macroeconomic adjustment; and cumulative processes of growth. In intersectoral matters, these factors concatenate to link "agriculture" and "industry"—two institutionally and technologically distinct economic spheres. In this chapter we first take up interactions between agriculture and industry in a specific framework and then go on to address cognate issues: the relationships between sectors producing traded and nontraded goods, and between nations of the world grouped into economic blocs called the "North" and "South," respectively, exporting into quantity- and price-clearing markets.

In our first model agriculture is assumed to have supply fixed in the short run and a market-clearing price while industry has its output determined by demand with a markup pricing rule. These hypotheses are extreme but fit the stylized facts about the two sectors—low short-run supply elasticities and fluctuating prices, on the one hand, and demand determination of output, on the other. We use the model to explore three aspects of the agrarian question.

The first is Engel's law: If income per head increases, then resources should shift from agriculture toward industry due to changes in demand composition. Second, Engel effects mean that policies aimed at increasing agricultural output and income can backfire by reducing the sector's terms of trade in the face of lagging demand. And finally, agricultural income per head may influence population growth in the sector, feeding back into per capita income change economywide.

To formalize these possibilities, we begin in section 9.1 with a two-sector fix-price/flex-price model in which Engel's law applies; that is, the consumption budget share of agricultural products declines as per capita income goes up. Along the lines of the Ricardo-Malthus debate discussed in chapter 1, extra demand for agricultural products (e.g., from exports) is shown to reduce industrial output when Engel effects are strong. The terms of trade shift against industry, cutting real income generated by that sector and thereby its own demand since Engel's law implies that purchases of goods from agriculture will not fall by very much.

If there is higher autonomous demand for industrial products (e.g., investment may rise), there will also be a terms of trade shift toward agriculture, as extra saving comes in part from higher industrial output and in part from increased farm income that the higher agricultural price creates. The real wage falls, meaning that forced saving also comes onto the scene.

To analyze growth, we assume in section 9.2 that investment in agriculture responds to the terms of trade, and in industry to the level of activity. We explore the implications of an "agriculture-first" strategy in which autonomous investment in the sector is increased (e.g., by public intervention). The three issues raised above directly apply.

First, higher real per capita income economywide (the fruit of past accumulation or slower population growth) raises industrial output and reduces the agricultural price because of Engel's law. Second, faster growth of capital stock in agriculture than industry reduces the former sector's price since it increases supply. Despite higher output, real income originating in agriculture also may decline when income and price elasticities of demand for its products are low. Finally, we assume that higher real income in agriculture slows the rate of population growth, in line with historical generalizations about the demographic transition (Birdsall 1988).

How will the agriculture-first strategy affect long-run equilibrium, compared across steady states in which all income levels are constant and both sectors grow at the same rate? The answer depends on whether enhanced supply growth in agriculture makes the sector's income fall or rise. If the latter, then population growth slows and economywide per capita income goes up in the new steady state. There may even be an increase in the share of capital stock located in industry, even though the strategy is directed toward making the other sector's capacity increase.

In the case where increased agricultural supply reduces farmers' income, these outcomes can reverse—population growth does not slow, overall real income may decline, and there can be deindustrialization. The moral is that when a sector faces inelastic demand, attempts to raise its supply can easily prove self-defeating, as we will also see in discussing the fate of a primary-product exporting South in sections 9.5 and 9.6. Alternatively, an agricultural investment push combined with rural income redistribution may pave the way for a transition from a low-level macro equilibrium to a more industrialized economy, as we illustrate in closing section 9.2.

Before taking up global macroeconomics, we turn our attention in sections 9.3 and 9.4 to a model with two sectors producing traded and nontraded goods. We concentrate on intermediate inputs, whose nontradability stems either from the nature of the goods and services involved (energy, internal communication and transport, etc.) or from quotas on imported intermediates. The price of the intermediate is flexible, while the final goods industry that uses it has markup pricing based on variable wage and input costs.

In one exercise the effects of a foreign exchange bonanza are considered, for example, resulting from greater volume or a higher price of a primary export product (or else from extra foreign aid). There is a spillover increase of demand for national goods, leading to pressure on intermediate supply and a rising price. The resulting real appreciation of the exchange rate can lead to reduced exports of the final good and deindustrialization more generally. As these effects build up over time, the economy is said to be suffering from Dutch disease. When the bonanza ends, recovery can be a prolonged and unpleasant process.

The other main topic in section 9.3 is import quotas. They contribute to income flows by generating rents from importing intermediates cheap (up to the quota level) and selling them dear in the internal market. Relaxing the quota and letting in more imports is shown to *reduce* activity in both final goods and domestic intermediate production, when supply response to a changing price in the latter sector is strong. Such potential deindustrialization (which can cumulate over time) is a valid argument against the liberalization programs often recommened by the institutions of Bretton Woods. Similarly, the anti-inflationary impact of devaluation under quotas (it wipes out cost-supporting rents) is shown to go hand-in-hand with output contraction as well. Finally, section 9.4 shows that if quota rights become assets (after all, they generate income flows), then by reducing the return to rights, liberalization can drive up interest rates and have contractionary effects through that channel.

In section 9.5 the product with a flexible price is exported by the South in the world market, while the North's product has mark up pricing. Global macro equilibrium is considered, in which the sum of investment minus saving in each region must be zero. Evidently, from the two pairs of saving and investment flows, one item cannot be independently determined. It is natural to take the South's investment level as endogenous, illustrating one form of dependency to which the region is subject. Another is the South's reliance on imported capital goods, already discussed in chapter 8 and carried over into the present discussion.

Southern or primary exports are typically assumed to face price- and income-inelastic demands in world markets, like agriculture in sections 9.1 and 9.2. This aspect of dependency shows up in falling profit rates and saving in the South when the global macro system is hit by adverse shocks, such as an oil crisis.

Despite these dependency burdens the South grew relatively strongly in the 1970s, though not thereafter. The explanation lies in the direction of global financial flows (i.e., "recycling" of oil rents in the 1970's followed by the debt crisis in the following decade, at least for most Latin and African economies). Section 9.6 develops these linkages in a simple flow model of global finance, which shows how Northern fiscal and monetary policy decisions strongly affect the poorer region's economic fate.

Two final issues, discussed in appendix 9.A, are how to interpret the two-gap model of chapter 8 in fix-price/flex-price terms, and the role of devaluation when the foreign exchange constraint is tight. The conclusions are that the gap model focuses on disequilibria more fundamental that those resulting from "mere" overvaluation, and that when scarce foreign exchange represents a strictly binding limitation on economic activity, then devaluation may prove expansionary in the short run.

9.1   Agriculture and Industry

Output in agriculture is assumed to be fixed in the short run, determined by its capital stock via a technically fixed output/capital ratio κ,

$$X_a = \kappa K_a,$$

while its price P_a varies to equate demand with available supply. Short-run agricultural supply responsiveness could be incorporated by making κ an increasing function of P_a, but for simplicity we eschew this extension (in practice, it is tantamount to postulating a higher value of the demand elasticity ν introduced below).

The nonagricultural sector (or industry) has markup pricing,

$$P_n = \frac{wb}{1 - \pi},$$

and its output X_n adjusts to meet demand.

The value of overall consumption demand D can be written as

$$D = (1 - s_a)P_aX_a + (1 - s_n)\pi P_nX_n + (1 - \pi)P_nX_n$$

$$= \gamma_aP_aX_a + \gamma_nP_nX_n, \tag{1}$$

where we assume that industrial workers do not save and that there is no class differentiation in agriculture.[1]

For agriculture the important stylized fact about consumer demand is Engel's law: The income elasticity of demand for food products is less than one. To emphasize low elasticities and save notation, we assume that all classes have the same pattern of consumption demand (implications of class differences in consumer behavior are taken up in chapter 10). If N stands for total population and $Y = D/N$, then the values of consumption of the two sectors' products can be written as

$$P_aC_a = \phi(Y, z)D$$

and

$$P_nC_n = [1 - \phi(Y, z)]D,$$

where $z = P_a/P_n$ is the relative agricultural price, or the terms of trade. The agricultural budget share ϕ depends on total per capita consumption and relative prices, as usually assumed. Indeed, we have the partial derivatives

$$\phi_Y = \frac{(\eta - 1)\phi}{Y} < 0$$

and

$$\phi_z = \frac{(1 - v)\phi}{z} > 0,$$

where η and v, are respectively the income and own-price elasticities of demand for food (v is treated as having a positive sign). Engel's law states that η is less than one and v is usually "small." The implications are that as Y rises, the food budget share falls, whereas an increase in z raises the budget share since quantity consumption does not decline very much in response to a higher price. Agriculture, as always, is characterized by low elasticities of demand and supply.

Excess demand functions for the two sectors can be written as

$$C_a + E - X_a = 0 \tag{2}$$

and

$$C_n + I_a + I_n - X_n = 0, \tag{3}$$

where E stands for exogenous agricultural exports, and I_a and I_n are the levels of investment undertaken in the two sectors (only the industrial sector produces capital goods). The variables that adjust to bring equilibrium in the two sectors are P_a or the terms of trade z,[2] and X_n or the industrial output/capital ratio $u = X_n/K_n$.

As a prelude to growth analysis in section 9.2, it is convenient to restate the model in terms of ratio variables. We already have defined $z = P_a/P_n$, $Y = D/N$, and $u = X_n/K_n$. Additionally let $\varepsilon = E/K_a$, $\lambda = K_a/K_n$, and $k = P_n K_n/N$. Then, using (1), the value of total consumer spending can be written as

$$D = (\gamma_a \kappa \lambda z + \gamma_n u) P_n K_n = \delta P_n K_n, \tag{4}$$

while consumption per capita is

$$Y = \frac{D}{N} = \delta k. \tag{5}$$

Normalized by $P_n K_n$, the sectoral excess demand functions (2) and (3) become

$$\phi(\delta k, z)\delta + (\varepsilon - \kappa)z\lambda = 0 \tag{6}$$

and

$$[1 - \phi(\delta k, z)]\delta + g_a \lambda + g_n - u = 0, \tag{7}$$

where $g_a = I_a/K_a$ and $g_n = I_n/K_n$ are the growth rates of capital stock in the two sectors, and δ is defined in (4).

For short-run analysis we treat ε, g_a, g_n, λ, and k as predetermined; the endogenous variables are z and u. In (6) a higher u increases δ, and therefore demand for agricultural goods since some part of greater industrial income will be directed toward food. In a stable system an increase in z means that excess demand falls off. Hence the "agriculture" locus along which (6) is satisfied has a positive slope in the diagrams of figure 9.1.[3]

Excess demand for industrial goods in (7) is an inverse function of u. However, it can either rise or fall with z. Better agricultural terms of trade will stimulate the other sector when the propensity to consume industrial goods from agricultural income and the price elasticity v are both high. Otherwise, increased agricultural prices cut industry's output by reducing

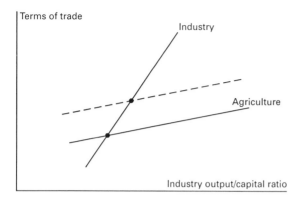

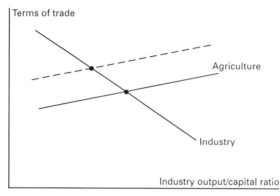

Figure 9.1
Response of the agriculture/industry economy to increased agricultural exports

real wages. Forced saving does *not* strongly influence food consumption when the relevant elasticities are small. It spills over into lower industrial demand.[4]

Figure 9.1 illustrates how the two-sector economy responds to an exogenous increase in agricultural exports ε. In the upper diagram higher terms of trade stimulate industry, so the locus along which (7) holds has a positive slope (steeper than the agriculture schedule for overall stability). For given values of u, the higher ε bids up the terms of trade along the dashed schedule, and in the new equilibrium industrial production goes up. This result corresponds to Malthus's arguments against repeal of the Corn Laws recounted in chapter 1—agriculture accounts for the bulk of industrial demand at the margin so that both sectors benefit when food prices rise.

The lower diagram illustrates the opposite (or "Ricardian") case in which higher agricultural exports are stagflationary. Conflict between the sectors is more apparent here; it would be correspondingly harder to put together a coalition supporting increased agricultural exports or reduced imports via tightened Corn Laws.

In both diagrams it is easy to see that an upward shift in the industry schedule would lead to increases in z and u. The interpretation is that forced saving (via higher terms of trade) and greater industrial income combine to provide the saving counterpart to increased investment demand. Lessons about historical experiences such as the Soviet industrialization push under Stalin have already been drawn in chapter 1.

9.2 Agriculture First

We assume that once capital is placed in either sector it cannot be relocated. Then a strategy aimed at increasing agricultural supply must concentrate on raising that sector's real investment. An obvious question to ask of the model is whether long-run national income per capita will rise. An answer must start from sectoral investment functions, which can be written as

$$g_a = \bar{g}_a + \alpha_a z$$

and

$$g_n = \bar{g}_n + \alpha_n u.$$

Capital formation responds to higher profitability as reflected by agriculture's terms of trade or industry's output. An agriculture first strategy would be embodied in policies aimed at increasing autonomous agricultural investment $\bar{g}_a$.

The two state variables in the dynamic system are $\lambda = K_a/K_n$ and $k = P_n K_n/N$; both are constant in a steady state in which $g_a = g_n = N$. We begin by asking how the economy responds in the short run to changes in λ and k, bringing in population dynamics below. For simplicity agricultural exports ε are set to zero.

When they include the investment functions just stated, equations (6) and (7) for zero excess sectoral demands in the short run can be written in differential form as

$$
\begin{bmatrix}
\kappa\lambda(\gamma_a\phi\eta - v) & \gamma_n\phi\eta \\
\lambda\alpha_a + \kappa\lambda[v + \gamma_a(1 - \phi\eta) - 1] & \alpha_n + \gamma_n(1 - \phi\eta) - 1
\end{bmatrix}
\begin{bmatrix}
dz \\
du
\end{bmatrix}
$$

$$
= \begin{bmatrix} (1 - \phi\eta\gamma_a)\kappa z \\ -(1 - \phi\eta)\gamma_a\kappa z - g_a \end{bmatrix} d\lambda + \begin{bmatrix} \delta(1 - \eta)\phi/k \\ -\delta(1 - \eta)\phi/k \end{bmatrix} dk + \begin{bmatrix} 0 \\ -\lambda \end{bmatrix} d\bar{g}_a
$$

$$
+ \begin{bmatrix} 0 \\ -1 \end{bmatrix} d\bar{g}_n. \tag{8}
$$

For a given capital composition λ, overall income per person will increase with k, or $P_n K_n/N$. The first thing to observe in (8) is that a change in k will not affect z and u when η, the income elasticity of demand for agricultural products, is one. Next, note that with plausible parameter values, the elements on the main diagonal of the matrix in the first line of (8) are negative. The implication is that when $\eta < 1$, the impact effect of an increase in k on one variable while the other is held constant is to reduce z and raise u, as might be expected from Engel's law. Also on impact, a shift in the capital stock composition toward agriculture ($d\lambda > 0$) reduces the terms of trade and raises industrial output. Finally, the immediate effect of higher autonomous investment $\bar{g}_a$ or $\bar{g}_n$ is to make u rise.

To see whether these effects persist in a new macroeconomic equilibrium, we have to solve (8) for dz and du. The manipulations are tedious but give the following conclusions:

1. The determinant of the matrix in (8) is $\Delta = \gamma_n \phi \eta \lambda [\kappa(1 - \gamma_a) - \alpha_a] - \kappa\lambda(1 - \gamma_n - \alpha_n)(\gamma_a \phi \eta - v)$. For stability Δ should be positive. This condition is most naturally satisfied if $\gamma_a \phi \eta - v < 0$, so that price adjustment in the market for agricultural goods is stable (cf. note 3), as well as if $\kappa(1 - \gamma_a) - \alpha_a > 0$ and $1 - \gamma_n - \alpha_n > 0$. The latter two inequalities mean that sectoral marginal saving rates $\kappa(1 - \gamma_a)$ and $1 - \gamma_n)$ must exceed the corresponding marginal propensities to invest. As we have seen repeatedly, stability requirements of this sort are normal in investment-driven models. With $\Delta > 0$ and the entries on the main diagonal both negative (so that the trace of the matrix is less than zero), it is easy to see that the total derivatives $du/d\bar{g}_i$ and $dz/d\bar{g}_i$ ($i = a$ or n) are all positive.

2. For the total derivatives with respect to k to satisfy the conditions $dz/dk < 0$ and $du/dk > 0$, we require $\eta < 1$ and also the inequalities on marginal saving and investment rates just discussed.

3. Although it is not strictly necessary, the condition $\kappa z(1 - \gamma_a) > g_a$ helps ensure that the total derivatives of z and u with respect to λ satisfy the conditions $dz/d\lambda < 0$ and $du/d\lambda > 0$.[5] This inequality means that in agriculture there is an excess of total saving $\kappa z(1 - \gamma_a)$ over investment g_a; that is, there is a "resource transfer" from agriculture to industry. For most

economies—especially agroexporters where commodity flows are easily taxed—the stylized fact is that this condition is satisfied even though the overall transfer may be a small share of GDP (Quisumbing and Taylor 1989).

4. A convenient measure of income distribution in the economy is $z\lambda = (P_a/P_n)(K_a/K_n)$—agricultural spending power rises relatively when $z\lambda$ goes up. We have seen that an increase in λ makes z fall; hence the sign of the derivative $d(z\lambda)/dz$ is not clear. Relative income $z\lambda$ will decrease when the inequality $\kappa z(1 - \gamma_n - \alpha_n)(1 - v) > \gamma_n \phi \eta \overline{g}_a$ applies. High elasticity values η and v are needed if agricultural income is to be favored by reallocation of capital stock toward the sector. An increase is $z\lambda$ is also more likely when industry's saving rate is low and its investment accelerator coefficient high.

5. The equations can be extended to include the effects of income re-distribution within the urban sector (obvious additions to the model are nonzero saving from wage income and a profit-rate term in the investment function for g_n). Although the formal algebraic expressions contain no dearth of terms, the main conclusion from section 3.1 carries over to the two-sector model: Progressive redistribution outside agriculture will in-crease industrial output and also the terms of trade when the difference in savings propensities from profit and wage incomes is large and the effect of a higher profit share on investment is weak. Wage-led output expansion and inflation can easily arise in the present specification.

6. Finally, as noted above, the model can be expanded to deal with policy wedges between prices. For example, the government may separate P_a and a consumer price $P_c = (1 - \xi)P_a$, where ξ is a subsidy rate. What happens if ξ is increased, in an attempt to cheapen food? Arguments like those developed in chapters 2 and 3 show that the paradox of thrift applies: Unless food imports are brought in, stocks are run down, or agricultural supply is highly price-elastic, P_a will rise *more* than in proportion, making P_c rise in response to the subsidy attempt. The IMF is typically strongly opposed to food subsidies, perhaps because of their implicit dependence on food imports.

With these observations in hand, we can turn to dynamics. An important stylized fact, both historically in now rich economies and in developing countries since World War II, is that population growth slows as per capita income goes up in a process called the "demographic transition" (first death rates drop and then birth rates follow with a lag). In our simple model the most reasonable way to reflect such population changes is to assume that agriculture dominates natality—rural family sizes tend to decrease as the sector's relative income $z\lambda$ rises. We will in fact assume that this transition is reversible if agricultural income rises and subsequently falls. Such simple dynamics does violence to historical changes in family structures but may be justified if we interpret the model as referring mainly to secular trends.

In formal terms, we set $\hat{N} = \hat{N}_0 - \beta z\lambda$. Then normalizing $P_n = 1$ for simplicity, we get the differential equation

$$\hat{k} = g_n - \hat{N} = \bar{g}_n + \alpha_n u - \hat{N}_0 + \beta z\lambda \tag{9}$$

for the growth in industrial capital per head (and, for given λ, real income per capita). By slowing population growth, a higher $z\lambda$ makes k grow faster.

The equation for the growth rate of $\lambda = K_a/K_n$ is

$$\hat{\lambda} = g_a - g_n = \bar{g}_a + \alpha_a z - \bar{g}_n - a_n u. \tag{10}$$

Together these equations determine transitions of the economy between steady states in which $g_a = g_n = \hat{N}$. We want to compare a "new" steady state differing from an "old" one due to a higher value of $\bar{g}_a$, the outcome of an incentive strategy aimed at stimulating agriculture.[6]

Using the results we have just derived, the signs of responses of the growth rates $\hat{k}$ and $\hat{\lambda}$ to changes in the state variables and $\bar{g}_a$ go as follows:

	k	λ	$\bar{g}_a$
$\hat{k}$	$-$	$\pm$	$+$
$\hat{\lambda}$	$-$	$-$	$+$

where "small" value of the investment parameter α_n ensures that $\partial\hat{k}/\partial k < 0$ and also $\partial\hat{\lambda}/\partial\bar{g}_a \gg \partial\hat{k}/\partial\bar{g}_a$. The ambiguous sign of $\partial\hat{k}/\partial\lambda$ arises because $z\lambda$, and thereby population growth can move either way when λ goes up.

The dynamics are shown in figure 9.2. The upper diagram illustrates the case in which a higher λ increases $z\lambda$ and slows population growth, making $\hat{k}$ rise—the "income growth" schedule along which $\hat{k} = 0$ has a positive slope. Since $\hat{\lambda}$ responds negatively to both k and λ, the "allocation" locus along which $\hat{\lambda} = 0$ slopes negatively.

An increase in $\bar{g}_a$ shifts the curves to the dashed positions when α_n is "small." In the new steady state, both k and λ rise—the economy is richer, population growth is slower, and there is reallocation of the capital stock toward agriculture.[7]

The lower diagram illustrates the (perhaps more) plausible situation in which low elasticities make agricultural income decline when capital shifts

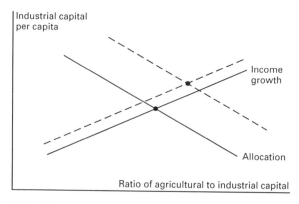

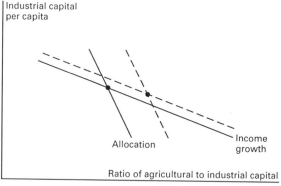

Figure 9.2
Shifts between steady states when relative agricultural income rises (*upper diagram*) and falls (*lower diagram*) when capital shifts toward the sector

toward the sector and its supply rises. Now economywide income per head falls, there is deindustrialization, and population grows faster. The implication is that an agriculture-first strategy can backfire, if historically and institutionally determined demand and supply conditions are not right. Which case applies is a weighty question for poor economies with large agricultural sectors all around the developing world. It bears importantly, for example, on practical proposals for development strategies such as those of Chakravarty (1987) and Caballero and Rao (1990).

Indeed, the present model can be used to illustrate Caballero and Rao's argument for combining an agriculture first investment strategy with policies such as land reform and rural income redistribution as a basis for agricultural development. The initial conditions are illustrated in the upper section of figure 9.3. We assume that when the economy is highly agri-

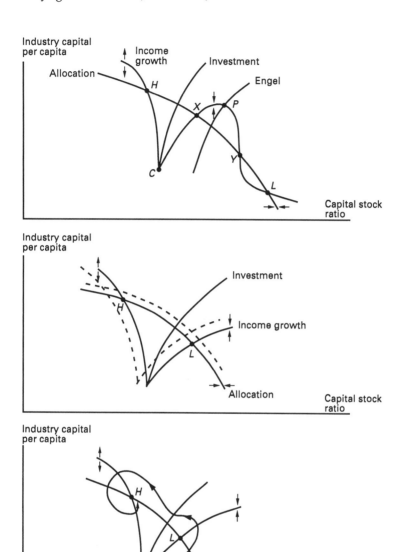

Figure 9.3
An agricultural transformation

cultural and poor (with a high value of λ and a low k), it behaves as in the lower diagram of figure 9.2. An increase in λ reduces the terms of trade and speeds population growth enough to make $\hat{k}_\lambda$ ($=\partial\hat{k}/\partial\lambda$) negative. For somewhat higher values of k and λ, this sign may reverse, to the left of the "Engel" locus showing combinations of k and λ for which $\hat{k}_\lambda = 0$. At a still lower value, the positive effect of k on u may become strong enough to make $\hat{k}_k > 0$ via the nonagricultural investment demand function for combinations of the state variables to the left of the "investment" curve along which $\hat{k}_k = 0$.

These sign changes give rise to a complicated "income growth" locus along which $\hat{k} = 0$. There is an inflection point at the peak P where $\hat{k}_\lambda = 0$, and a cusp at C where $\hat{k}_k$ vanishes. The "low-" and "high-level" equilibria at L and H are stable, while X and Y are both unstable. Caballero and Rao suggest policies via which a transition from L toward H can be set underway.

The solid lines in the middle diagram show that happens when rural income redistribution helps raise demand for food. An increase in output due to a higher λ depresses the term of trade less sharply, permitting $z\lambda$ to increase and population growth to slow. The "Engel" sign shift of $\hat{k}_\lambda$ is eliminated from the picture, leaving two stable equilibria at H and L with the investment schedule in between. An agricultural investment push shifts the schedules to the dashed positions.

The lower diagram illustrates a possible dynamic path after the curves have shifted. It starts to spiral toward a low-level equilibrium at L, but if the investment push is strong enough, the trajectory may cross the investment locus and divert toward the high-level equilibrium at H. A combination of redistributive policy and directed investment can lead the economy though an agrarian transformation from a low-level trap to high one with a relatively small agricultural sector and lower terms of trade but enhanced prosperity overall.

Finally, it bears noting that per capita income is constant at both H and L because the present model does not include productivity growth or economies of scale, as discussed in chapter 10. But even if technical progress occurs, Houthakker (1976) observed in a somewhat simpler model that the ambiguous results that we have developed continue to apply (as the reader may wish to verify with the present version). A sector or an economy producing for a price-clearing market with low elasticities of demand and supply enjoys no guarantee for rapid income growth.

9.3   Traded and Nontraded Goods

Fix-price/flex-price models of the sort discussed in sections 9.1 and 9.2 apply to many economic issues besides the agrarian question. An obvious example is an economy with distinct sectors producing traded and nontraded goods. In this section we use a formulation devised by Boutros-Ghali (1981) and Barbone (1985) to illustrate real and price effects of foreign trade bonanzas and changes in an import quota regime, while section 9.4 takes up financial market implications of the quotas and appendix 9.A presents an interpretation of the two-gap model in fix/flex price terms.[8]

Many essential intermediate inputs such as transport services, energy, and communication are nontraded in most circumstances. In economies pursuing industrialization via import substitution, traded intermediates are likely to come into the country subject to quantitative restrictions, which often take the form of quotas on import supply. Both sorts of nontradability can be captured if we assume demand for intermediates can be satisfied either by domestic products M or quota-limited imports $\overline{M}$. There may be a rising supply curve for M:

$$M = M\left(\frac{P_m}{w}\right),\tag{11}$$

where P_m is the flexible price of the intermediate sector and w is the money wage. Imported intermediate supply is simply $\overline{M}$, determined by the quota. Such imports have a border price equal to the exchange rate e, assuming that their dollar c.i.f. price is normalized to unity. After they are landed, the imports can be sold in the national market at price P_m, giving a "rent" $(P_m - e)\overline{M}$ to those fortunate (or powerful) enough to hold quota rights.[9]

Regardless of source the intermediates are used to produce final goods in an industry where output X_n is determined by demand and the price P_n is given by the markup rule

$$P_n = \frac{wb + P_m a}{1 - \pi},\tag{12}$$

where b is the labor/output ratio and a is the input-output coefficient for the intermediate.

Let $\alpha = wb/(wb + P_m a)$ and $\beta = wL_m/P_m M$, where L_m is employment in the intermediate sector. It is simplest to hold the wage share β constant in the discussion that follows. The obvious micro "foundation" (for those who take such matters seriously) is to postulate that the intermediate sector is competitive with a production function of the form $M = (L_m)^\beta$; the supply function (11) becomes $M = [\beta(P_m/w)]^{\beta/(1-\beta)}$. If there is no saving from wage income, the value of total consumer spending D on final goods is given by

$$D = [\alpha(1 - \pi) + (1 - s)\pi]P_n X_n + [\beta + (1 - s)(1 - \beta)]P_m M$$

$$+ (1 - s)(P_m - e)\overline{M} + \gamma_h eH$$

$$= \gamma_n P_n X_n + \gamma_m P_m M + \gamma_\mu(P_m - e)\overline{M} + \gamma_h eH,$$

where s is the saving rate from profit and rental income and $\gamma_h eH$ is the share of primary export income eH directed toward purchases of domestic goods. Implicitly we assume that these exports are produced in a separate sector, with some of the income so generated finding a market at home.[10] As in equation (1) the subscripted γ's stand for consumption propensities from values of final output (or γ_μ for rents), and vary across income flows.

Let $E = E(e/P_n)$ stand for exports of final goods. They are sold into a noncompetitive world market, so that export volume rises as the foreign f.o.b. price P_n/e of "our" products declines. Under these hypotheses the market balance equation for final goods can be written as

$$D + P_n E - P_n X_n = 0. \tag{14}$$

Adopting our usual trick of normalizing balance equations by $P_n K_n$, the value of the capital stock in the final goods sector, we can define quantity ratio variables as $u = X_n/K_n$, $m = M/K_n$, $\bar{m} = \overline{M}/K_n$, $\varepsilon = E/K_n$, and $h = H/K_n$ and price relatives as $v = P_m/P_n$ and $q = e/P_n$ (where v is analogous to the terms-of-trade variable z of sections 9.1 and 9.2 and q to the real exchange rate of the same symbol used in chapter 7). With all this notation we can combine (13) and (14) to write the excess demand function for final goods as

$$(\gamma_n - 1)u + (\gamma_m m + \gamma_\mu \bar{m})v + (\gamma_h h - \gamma_\mu \bar{m})q + \varepsilon = 0. \tag{15}$$

Excess demand for intermediates, in turn, is given by[11]

$$au - m - \bar{m} = 0. \tag{16}$$

Equations (15) and (16) form a two-by-two system in the relative price of intermediate inputs v and the level of activity in the final goods sector u. The next step is to explore how these variables respond to changes in the level of imports permitted by the quota, devaluation, and external conditions as reflected in the volume (or, for our purposes equivalently, the exogenous price) of primary exports h.

Let $m' = dm/dv$, $\varepsilon' = d\varepsilon/dq$, and $\bar{\alpha} = (1 - \alpha)/\alpha$. Using this notation, we can write (15) and (16) in differential form as[12]

$$
\begin{bmatrix} \gamma_n - 1 & (\gamma_m - 1)m + (\gamma_\mu - 1)\bar{m} + v\gamma_m m' + (q/\bar{\alpha}v)[\gamma_\mu \bar{m} - \gamma_h h - \varepsilon'] \\ a & -m' \end{bmatrix} \begin{bmatrix} du \\ dv \end{bmatrix}
$$

$$
= \begin{bmatrix} -\gamma_m(v - q) \\ 1 \end{bmatrix} d\bar{m} + \begin{bmatrix} -\gamma_h q \\ 0 \end{bmatrix} dh + \begin{bmatrix} (q/e)[\gamma_\mu \bar{m} - \gamma_h - \varepsilon'] \\ 0 \end{bmatrix} de \qquad (17)
$$

As in the model of sections 9.1 and 9.2, income effects can make demand for the good with markup pricing respond to changes in the flexible price with either sign: The entry in the northeast corner of the matrix in (17) for $\partial u/\partial v$ has no shortage of terms. It will be negative or positive depending on propensities to consume as well as on whether final goods exports and the intermediate supply function react weakly or strongly to a change in v. We concentrate on the supply response in the discussion that follows.

Figure 9.4 shows stable model adjustments to an increase in the quantity of imports allowed under the quota when m' is small (upper diagram) or large (lower diagram). In both cases one can show by solving (17) explicitly that the relative price of intermediates falls when more such goods are permitted to enter the system. The implication from (12) is that final goods become cheaper, stimulating their domestic and foreign demand. But on the other hand, the price cut from more imports means that incomes generated by quota rents and the national intermediate goods industry decline. A weak supply response m' can help stabilize the intermediate sector's income, supporting demand enough to make final goods output rise. This case is illustrated in the upper diagram; its favorable outcome is more likely insofar as the export derivative $d\varepsilon/dv = q\varepsilon'/\bar{\alpha}v$ is large.

The lower diagram is analogous to Malthus's argument against repeal of the Corn Laws. Here a large m' means that when v is reduced, output and income from the domestic intermediate industry shrink enough to make demand for final goods decrease as well. Weak final goods export responsiveness to a change in v makes the lower picture's configuration more likely.

Since quota liberalization is often urged upon developing countries by the International Monetary Fund and (especially) the World Bank, the shifts of the curves in figure 9.4 are of practical interest. With a strong intermediate supply response, liberalization leads to a loss in industrial output. Through accelerator-driven investment demand and/or a Kaldorian techni-

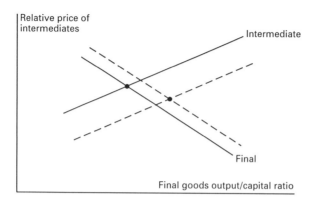

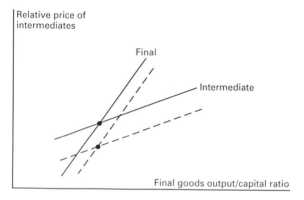

Figure 9.4
Responses of an economy with an intermediate goods sector when the quantity of
intermediate imports allowed to enter under a quota is increased

cal progress function, this short-run adjustment could cumulate into a
reduced rate of output growth and industrialization over time. Tighter
quotas (or, more generally, lack of access to imports) could lead to an
industrial spurt of the sort that Furtado (1971) chronicles in Brazil in the
1930s when the collapse of world trade cut off that country's import access.
At times import-substituting industrialization *can* work.

The diagrams also show that in both cases tighter quotas as illustrated
by shifts from the dashed to solid lines make the relative price of intermediates rise (with a reduction in final goods output when the domestic
intermediate supply response is weak). Generalized inflation can easily
result along chapter 4 lines as higher intermediate input prices are passed
along to final goods. If quotas are tightened as a consequence of scarce

foreign exchange, we get another inflationary impact of external strangulation to add to the one discussed in chapter 8.

Inflation can also result from too much foreign exchange, when primary exports h increase and shift the final goods loci to the right. This is the Dutch disease case, which also leads to a reduction in the real exchange rate $q = e/P_n$ unless the authorities undertake nominal devaluation (unlikely when there is ample foreign exchange). With price-responsive final goods exports, ε declines due to real appreciation, reducing the economy's "external diversification" as well. Adding an investment function to the present model, Boutros-Ghali (1981) shows that slower growth can result; lack of cumulating technical progress can lead to the same result, *vide* Krugman (1987) and chapter 10.

Finally, nominal devaluation has interesting effects. From (17) it is associated with a reduction in final goods output when the export response to price changes is weak [in analogy to condition (1) in chapter 7]. The final goods loci shift leftward in figure 9.4, reducing the price of intermediates and thereby P_n as well. Following Krueger (1974), orthodox economists such as IMF mission chiefs in Africa often assert that when quotas are rampant devaluation will not be inflationary since it wipes out rents. In the present model this pleasant outcome only occurs when domestic output is wiped out as well: You can't savor the anti-inflationary frosting without tasting the contractionary cake.

9.4 Quota Rents as Assets

Still more effects of quota liberalization take place in financial markets, as Barbone (1985) points out. Since import rights generate income flows summing to $(v - q)\bar{m}$ in total, control over a share of the national quota amounts to an asset. In practice there may be markets for rights, and they can also be used as loan collaterals, and so forth. For simplicity we assume an explicit market here, in which quota rights R sell for a market-clearing price P_r, along the same lines as "gold" in chapter 6. The return to holding a right is given by $(v - q)/P_r$.

In addition to deposits and loans to firms, quota rights act as a third asset in a variant of the models of chapters 6 and 7 (where "gold" and foreign exchange were the extra assets, respectively). We need two excess demand functions, for deposits and rights:

$$\delta\left[i, \frac{v - q}{P_r}, u\right](P_n K_n + H + P_r R) - \xi H = 0 \tag{18}$$

and

$$\zeta\left[i, \frac{v-q}{P_r}, u\right](P_n K_n + H + P_r R) - P_I R = 0. \tag{19}$$

In these equations i is the interest rate on loans to firms, H is base money, and ζ is the deposit/base money multiplier. The interest rate i and the asset price P_r are the adjusting variables in (18) and (19). Comparative statics of these excess demand equations are easy to describe.

Liberalization leads to a lower import price v. Deposit demand in (18) shifts upward, as the return $(v - q)/P_r$ to holding rights falls; the interest rate therefore tends to rise. At the same time the demand for quota rights falls off, and P_r drops in response to the lower return. The outcomes are a lower P_r and under appropriate circumstances a higher interest rate i.

These financial adjustments have real consequences. We have already seen in connection with (17) that liberalization in the form of a higher $\bar{m}$ may be associated with less industrial output along with lower prices for intermediate and final goods. These price changes reduce the return to holding quota rights and can bid up the interest rate, further cutting demand. On both the financial and real sides of the economy, relaxing quotas can prove problematic in the short run. Regardless of its advertised efficiency benefits, a liberalization exercise can prove self-defeating by liquidating wealth and inducing recession before favorable results appear. Indeed, long-run effects of liberalization can also be counterproductive, as we will see in chapter 10.

9.5 Trade Relationships between the North and South

In this section, we quickly sketch a simple North–South trade model developed in more detail elsewhere (Taylor 1983). The regions are assumed to be completely specialized in production of an industrial good with markup pricing (the North) and a primary good with a price-clearing market (the South). A third region—"OPEC"–controls the price of a commodity used as an intermediate input by the North. The model aims to capture stylized global macroeconomic relationships, especially the forms of dependence of the South. It is extended to include global financial flows in the following section, to provide a broad rationale for the comparative growth performance of the two regions during the decades following 1970.

The North is treated in Kaleckian terms. Its pricing rule is

$$P_n = \frac{w_n b_n + vm}{1 - \pi},$$ (20)

where w_n and b_n as usual stand for the money wage and labor/output ratio, while v is the price of the OPEC export ("oil") and m is its input-output coefficient.

Let ϕ be the share of oil in total import cost: $\phi = vm/(w_n b_n + vm)$. If s_n is the saving rate from Northern profit income, s_o the rate from OPEC's income (the balance is spent on consumption of Northern goods), and all Northern wage income is consumed, then macroeconomic balance can be written as

$$P_n(G + I_n + Z) - [\pi s_n + (1 - \pi)\phi s_o]P_n X_n = 0,$$

where G is government dissaving, I_n is investment, and Z is the region's real trade surplus with the South.

Scaling variables by the North's capital stock, we have $\gamma = G/K_n$, $g_n = I_n/K_n$, and $z = Z/K_n$. The profit rate is $r_n = \pi(X_n/K_n) = \pi u$, and we can write the investment function as

$$g_n = g_0 + hr_n.$$

In normalized form, the Northern aggregate excess demand function becomes

$$\gamma + g_0 + hr_n + z - \left[s_n + \frac{(1 - \pi)\phi s_o}{\pi} \right] r_n = 0,$$ (21)

where we treat r_n as the index of economic activity. Solving this equation together with the investment function gives the North's growth rate g^N as

$$g^N = \frac{[s_n + (1 - \pi)s_o \phi]g_0 + h(z + \gamma)}{\Delta},$$ (22)

where $\Delta = s_n + (1 - \pi)\phi s_o/\pi - h > 0$ is the standard stability condition that demand leakages exceed injections at the margin. For a given trade surplus z, (22) fixes the North's growth rate *independent* of any effect from the South. The growth rate g^N increases with z, such as when foreign aid from North to South goes up. The policy relevance of this "global Keynesian" linkage is stressed in some passages of the well-known report of the Brandt (1980) Commission.

The northeast quadrant of figure 9.5 shows how g^N follows from the intersection of the investment and saving functions.[13] The rest of the diagram depicts Southern accommodation to macroeconomic conditions in

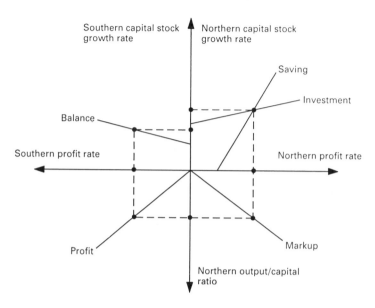

Figure 9.5
Global price and quantity equilibrium

the North. As noted in the introduction to this chapter, global equilibrium requires that

$$(I_n - S_n) + (I_s - S_s) = 0,$$

where I_i and S_i are, respectively, regional investment and saving functions. We have already specified I_n and S_n; we now turn to S_s, leaving investment in the South to be endogenously determined as a condition for world balance.

Since the South exports primary products, we can assume that it faces income- and price-inelastic demand in a price-clearing market. The share of Northern value-added directed toward consumption is $\rho = (1 - s_n)\pi + (1 - \phi)(1 - \pi)$. A convenient way to model demand inelasticities is to assume that Northern consumers behave according to the following relationships:

Value of demand for Northern commodity = $(1 - \beta)\rho P_n X_n - \theta P_s$

Value of demand for Southern commodity $= \beta\rho P_n X_n + \theta P_s$

Total consumption demand $= \rho P_n X_n$

where P_s is the world market price of the South's commodity.

These equations are a simple variant of the linear expenditure system.[14] As with any linear function, demand for the South's commodity will be income *in*elastic when its equation has a positive intercept (i.e., we assume $\theta > 0$).

On the supply side we assume as in section 9.1 that output of the primary commodity is determined by available capital stock,

$$X_s = \kappa K_s,$$

and moreover that all the South's capital is produced in the North.[15] We also follow the classical economists and Lewis (1954) in presuming a labor surplus: The South's wage rate w_s, is fixed in terms of its own commodity. Then the South's profit rate is defined by the relationships

$$r_s = \frac{P_s X_s - P_s w_s b_s X_s}{P_n K_s} = \frac{P_s(1 - w_s b_s)}{P_n}, \tag{23}$$

where b_s is the labor/output ratio. Profits are the difference between output and wage costs, assuming that workers produce the good that they consume. For $r_s > 0$, we need $w_s b_s < 1$ so that a surplus exists in the Ricardian profit equation (23).

The demand-supply balance for the South's commodity is

$$\beta \rho P_n X_n + \theta P_s + P_s(w_s b_s - 1)\kappa K_s = 0,$$

assuming (again to simplify) that the South's profit income recipients do not consume their own region's goods and that wage income recipients neither save nor consume Northern goods. It is easy to solve this equation for the Southern commodity's price as

$$P_s = \frac{\beta \rho P_n X_n}{(1 - w_s b_s)\kappa K_s - \theta}, \tag{24}$$

and substitution into (23) gives the profit rate as

$$r_s = \frac{(1 - w_s b_s)\kappa K_s}{(1 - w_s b_s)\kappa K_s - \theta} \beta \rho u \lambda, \tag{25}$$

where $\lambda = K_n / K_s$ is a convenient indicator of the size of the North's economy relative to the South's.

Equation (24) shows that the price of the Southern good depends directly on Northern economic activity; (25) restates this observation for the profit rate. In the southeast quadrant of figure 9.5, the "markup" schedule represents the identity $r_n = \pi u$. The "profit" schedule in the southwest corresponds to (25), showing that r_s is determined directly from the North's macroeconomic equilibrium.

A few comparative static exercises are of interest at this point. First, higher labor productivity in the South is represented by a *lower* value of b_s. From (24) a productivity increase would lead P_s to fall, if under surplus labor conditions there was not a compensating increase in the real wage. Further, from (25), Southern profits would also decline when $\theta > 0$ and demand for the South's product is income inelastic. Such results are common in developing country analyses of their foreign trade position and emphasize the difficulties of selling into a competitive world market. The gains from productivity improvements redound to consumers abroad.

Second, note from (21) and (22) that an "oil shock" in the form of a higher value of v would raise ϕ and rotate the Northern saving schedule counterclockwise, reducing aggregate demand and g^N. The consumption share ρ would also decline, shifting the South's profit curve (southwest quadrant) to the right. In effect the South would be doubly hit by an overall decline in Northern activity and a reduction in demand for its products.

Finally, a Northern productivity increase or lower b_n would raise ϕ, with the same effects. However, historically in advanced capitalist economies, wages have tended to rise with productivity (a topic addressed further in chapter 10), providing an offset. If w_n does rise as b_n falls, then Southern profits (and as we will see, the rate of growth) are hurt only by local and not distant technical advance.

Turning to growth, we can write the South's saving-investment balance in the form

$$s_s(1 - w_s b_s)P_s X_s + s_z P_n Z - P_n I_s = 0,$$

where s_s is the saving rate from Southern profit income and s_z the rate from capital inflows.[16] Since X_s and Z are predetermined in this equation and P_s follows from (24), I_n is the endogenous variable. The same is true of the South's capital stock growth rate, g^S, when Southern macroeconomic balance is normalized by the value of the South's capital stock $P_s K_s$:

$$s_s r_s + s_z z \lambda - g^S = 0. \tag{26}$$

The "Balance" schedule in the northwest quadrant of figure 9.5 represents (26). It shows how the South's growth rate follows from factors outside direct control of the region. From the comparative static exercises outlined above, we can conclude that: g^S falls in response to Southern labor productivity increases (when $\theta > 0$) and events such as an oil shock, while it is unchanged by Northern productivity gains so long as the real wage increases in tandem. More aid to the South raises g^S directly and also by increasing the North's activity level and the South's flow of profits from (25).

To extend these results to the long run, we can consider steady states in which $\hat{\lambda} = g^N - g^S = 0$. Such an equilibrium is easily seen to be stable, since from (22) g^N is independent of λ, while from (25) a higher λ increases r_s and thereby g^S from (26).[17] In figure 9.5, g^S is less than g^N, so $\hat{\lambda} > 0$. As a consequence the profit schedule in the southwest quadrant rotates clockwise over time, while the intercept of the balance schedule in the Northwest slides up. Both changes ultimately lead g^S to rise to g^N. When that happens, the South's long-run profit rate becomes

$$r_s^* = \frac{[s_n + (1 - \pi)\phi s_0/\pi]r_n^* - (1 + \lambda s_z)z - \gamma}{s_s}. \tag{27}$$

Since the North's saving rate from profits is likely to exceed the South's, we have $r_s^* > r_n^*$ (for relatively low values of capital flows z and Northern government dissaving γ). This prediction is in line with the stylized facts.

9.6   Endogenous Capital Flows

The North–South model captures stylized aspects of trade and growth in rich and poor countries, and can easily be extended to deal with another region made up of Southern newly industrialized countries (NICs) which has learned to sell goods with elastic demand in the North and also has its own, independent investment function. Total capital flows Z go to both parts of the South, with poorer countries taking what is left after the NIC region finances its investment with its own saving plus a share of Z. The NICs of 1990 mostly comprise East Asian economies but in the 1970s included Latin and West Asian representatives as well.

Indeed, the experience of the 1970s constitutes a much more serious objection than the existence of NICs to the model as just described. In that decade of oil shocks, the South grew faster than the North, directly contrary to what figure 9.5 has to say. And in the more stable 1980s, the South (Asian NIC's and large, closed China and India aside) grew more slowly. To rationalize these observations, we have to build endogenous financial flows into the system, or discuss why z (and therefore g^S) was relatively high in the 1970s but declined thereafter. Following Lal and van Wijnbergen (1985) and Vos (1989), this section takes up that task.

Most discussion of global macroeconomics is based on flow instead of stock descriptions of financial markets, and we observe that convention here. Following chapters 4 and 8, flows of funds in the Northern-based international banking system can be described as follows:

$$\dot{A}_n + \dot{A}_s + \dot{A}_g - \dot{D} - iA_s = 0, \tag{28}$$

where $\dot{A}_n$ is the increase in bank credit to nongovernment borrowers in the North, $\dot{A}_s$ is the increase in credit to the South, $\dot{A}_g$ is new lending to governments in the North, $\dot{D}$ is the increment in deposits in the banking system, and iA_s stands for interest payments from South to North at the "world" interest rate i (interest payments within the North are netted out for simplicity).

The deposit increase is given by a function such as

$$\dot{D} = \delta(i)[s_n + (1 - \pi)\phi s_0]r_n P_n K_n + \xi s_s r_s P_n K_s, \tag{29}$$

where ξ stands for the portion of Southern saving placed in Northern banks (i.e., there is capital flight as discussed in chapter 8). As the bank interest rate increases, a higher proportion $\delta(i)$ of saving from the North and OPEC finds its way into deposits.

The growth of credit to the South can plausibly be expected to follow a rule such as

$$\dot{A}_s = \sigma(i)A_s, \tag{30}$$

where σ is an *inverse* function of i, so that the South can borrow less as interest rates go up. The function σ will also shift over time along the lines of chapters 6 and 7 in response to numerous indicators of confidence, such as the South's existing debt burden, export and output growth, and political circumstances.

Since $P_n Z$ is the South's trade deficit in terms of foreign currency, the region's overall balance of payments (ignoring reserve changes) becomes

$$P_n Z = \sigma A_s - iA_s - \xi s_s r_s P_n K_s,$$

or normalized by $P_n K_s$,

$$\lambda z = [\sigma(i) - i]q - \xi s_s r_s,$$

where $q = A_s/P_n K_s$ is the ratio of the South's foreign debt to its capital stock.[18]

Following (26), the equation for the South's capital stock growth rate is

$$s_s r_s + s_z[(\sigma - i)q - \xi s_s r_s] - g^S = 0$$

or

$$(1 - s_z\xi)s_sr_s + [\sigma(i) - i]s_zq - g^S = 0. \qquad (31)$$

Southern growth is penalized insofar as the real interest rate i on its external debt exceeds the debt's growth rate σ—a Domar-type condition of the sort discussed in chapter 8. A reduced national saving effort as capital flows come in ($s_s < 1$) and capital flight ($\xi > 0$) reduce g^S as well.

With the interest rate in the picture, the North's investment function should be written as

$$g_n = g_0 + hr_n - ki. \qquad (32)$$

Ignoring new equity placements as well as retained earnings of firms, we assume that investment is financed by new bank loans,

$$\dot{A}_n = g_nP_nK_n, \qquad (33)$$

while new credit to the government is

$$\dot{A}_g = \mu P_nK_n, \qquad (34)$$

where μ is the share of public dissaving that is "monetized" or financed through banks.

Equations (28) through (34) provide enough information to set up a simple IS/LM style model in r_n and i to determine global equilibrium. The first step is an equation for excess demand in the North,

$$\gamma + (g_0 + hr_n - ki) + \frac{[\sigma(i) - i]q}{\lambda}$$

$$- \left[s_n + \frac{(1-\pi)\phi s_0}{\pi}\right]r_n - \left(\frac{\beta\rho\xi s_s}{\pi}\right)r_n = 0. \qquad (35)$$

This expression amplifies (21) by including interest rate effects in the determination of the Northern investment level and its trade surplus with the South. The final term shows that capital flight is a source of saving for the North.[19] For short-run stability, marginal leakages should exceed injections as functions of r_n, implying that world excess demand falls when the Northern profit rate goes up. It also decreases with the interest rate, so we get a downward-sloping IS schedule in figure 9.6.

Plugging (29), (30), (33), and (34) into (28) and normalizing by P_nK_n shows that the excess demand function for bank credit takes the form

$$\mu + (g_0 + hr_n - ki) + \frac{[\sigma(i) - i]q}{\lambda}$$

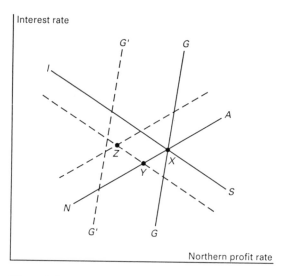

Figure 9.6
Real and financial world equilibrium in the 1970s

$$- \delta(i)\left[s_n + \frac{(1 - \pi)\phi s_0}{\pi} \right] r_n - \left(\frac{\beta \rho \xi s_s}{\pi} \right) r_n = 0.$$

We could use this expression together with (35) to determine world macro balance. But it is simpler to subtract it from (35) to get excess demand for nonmonetary assets:

$$(\gamma - \mu) - [1 - \delta(i)]\left[s_n + \frac{(1 - \pi)\phi s_0}{\pi} \right] r_n = 0. \tag{36}$$

Here an increase in the interest rate pulls funds toward banks, so excess demand for other assets goes up. Higher profits increase savings flows toward all assets, so (36) responds negatively to r_n. The outcome is a positively sloped NA curve in figure 9.6.

To explore the implications of shifts in the IS and NA loci for growth in the South, we can use level curves giving values of r and i that trade off to hold g^S constant. Inserting (25) into (31) and differentiating totally gives

$$\left. \frac{di}{dr} \right|_{g^S = \text{const.}} = \frac{(1 - s_z \xi) s_s \beta \rho \lambda / \pi}{(1 - \sigma') s_z q}, \tag{37}$$

where $\sigma' < 0$ is the derivative of a with respect to i.

The GG schedule in figure 9.6 is a level curve representing (37). It will be steeper insofar as r_n has a strong positive effect on Southern saving and growth (in the numerator) and the South's debt burden q is low (denominator). Points to the right of GG represent higher values of r_n and lower i, hence faster Southern growth. From (32) isogrowth loci for the North are also sloped positively like GG.

An immediate question to ask of the model is about the effects of an upward shift in the $\sigma(i)$ function, for example, from more foreign aid. The IS curve shifts upward (not shown) but from (36) the NA locus is unaffected. Hence both the Northern profit and interest rates rise. If the GG schedule is steeper than NA, growth in the South speeds up. But for a sufficiently shallow GG, g^S could decline. The "story" involves financial crowding-out: More borrowing on international financial markets to pay for foreign aid raises the interest rate enough to make g^S (and also conceivably g^N) fall off. Global Keynesianism need not be observed if credit markets are tight.[20]

The shifted lines in figure 9.6 illustrate developments actually observed in the 1970s. For the North the story of that decade (at least after the first oil shock) is a downward shift in the IS curve from initial equilibrium at X. For a steep GG a new temporary equilibrium at Y would lead to slower growth in the South along the lines discussed in section 9.5. Tight money aimed at slowing cost-push inflation from the oil price increases raised the NA schedule; at point Z the South's growth prospects look even worse. But the oil shock was also accompanied by "recycling" of OPEC's new bank deposits to the South, so in (31) lower values of ρ and r_s were offset by a big upward jump in financial transfers σ. The GG schedule shifted to $G'G'$, and (at least in the middle-income countries that got access to commercial bank credit) Southern growth sped up.

One outcome of this process was that the debt burden q rose, making the GG curve rotate clockwise. The 1980s picture thus looks more like figure 9.7. Still tighter money (the "Volcker shock" of the early 1980s) and loose fiscal policy (the Reagan tax cut and defense spending increase) shifted Northern equilibrium from X to Y—high interest and profit rates together. With a shallow GG schedule, Southern growth was crowded out. Given the South's outstanding debt burden, higher Northern activity cannot do much to benefit the region's growth. Barring structural changes in its export mix and own-saving generation, lower interest rates and/or increased transfers (assuming that they themselves do not put great pressure on capital markets) seem essential for the South to resume rapid growth. Even more helpful would be debt forgiveness or repudiation,

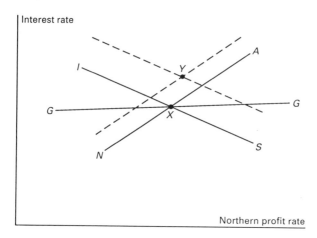

Figure 9.7
Real and financial world equilibrium in the 1980s

which would make the GG level curves steeper and permit buoyant Northern growth to trickle down more effectively to less fortunate corners of the world.

Appendix 9.A   Gap Disequilibria and the Real Exchange Rate

The approach developed in this chapter can be extended in several directions. One of the more interesting is a revisionist critique of the two-gap model, which purports to show that gap problems result fundamentally from misalignment of the real exchange rate, interpreted as the relative price of nontraded to traded goods (Findlay 1973; van Wijnbergen 1986). The model we develop to refute the critics also extends naturally to illustrate macro balance problems from which small, primary-exporting economies (many in Sub-Saharan Africa) suffer, following recent structuralist analyses by Gibson (1985), Ndulu (1986), Fitzgerald (1989), and Rattsø (1990a).

The real exchange rate can be defined as $\rho = P_n/P_e$, where P_n is the price of nontraded goods and P_e the internal price of a (net) export sector—think of agricultural commodities that can either be traded or consumed at home. Marketing boards exist in almost all primary exporting countries to smooth violent product price fluctuations of the type discussed below. But if they don't intervene too heavy-handedly, over time the trade arbitrage relationship $P_e = eP_e^*$, where e is the nominal exchange rate and P_e^* the world price of traded goods, will hold approximately. Note also that ρ is the inverse of the real rate q considered in chapter 7 and sections 9.3 and 9.4 (i.e., an increase in ρ represents real appreciation). In other notational conventions, let u stand for the output/capital ratio in the nontraded sector, g the growth rate of its capital stock, and ε the export/capital ratio.

With this notation, Walras's law (the sum of excess demands in the economy should be zero) can be written as

$$P_e[au + (1 - \theta)g - \varepsilon - T] + \{\gamma_n[(1 - a)P_n u + P_e \varepsilon] + P_n \theta g - P_n u\}$$

$$+ \text{ Excess demand in other markets} = 0 \qquad (38)$$

Here a is the input-output coefficient for intermediate imports into the nontraded sector (we do not consider an intermediate import-substituting industry, as in section 9.3), θ is the share of capital goods produced nationally, T is a transfer from abroad (in dollar terms) that the economy receives, and γ_n is the share of disposable income generated in both the nontraded and export sectors spent on consumption of nontraded goods. For the moment we do not consider domestic consumption of the export commodity.

The "other markets" in (38) will typically be financial, such as for money (perhaps with a quantity equation and an inflation tax, as in chapter 8) or for loans with a market-clearing interest rate. Along with u and ρ, the financial variables will adjust to the trade constraint which can be written in the form

$$P_e[au + (1 - \theta)g - \varepsilon] - P_e T = 0. \qquad (39)$$

This equation signifies that T is predetermined and represents the *only* foreign inflow that the economy receives. When (39) applies as a binding restriction, then (38) can be rewritten as

$$\{\gamma_n[(1 - a)P_n u + P_e \varepsilon] + P_n \theta g - P_n u\} + \text{ Excess demand in other markets}$$

$$= 0.$$

If we assume that other markets clear, then from (39) this equation implies the relationship

$$(1 - \gamma_n)[(1 - a)P_n u + P_e \varepsilon] + P_e T - P_n g = 0,$$

or

$$(1 - \gamma_n)[(1 - a)u + \left(\frac{1}{\rho}\right)[(1 - \gamma_n)\varepsilon + T] - g = 0, \qquad (40)$$

which represents the investment-saving balance in terms of nontraded prices.

Equations (39) and (40) are just the foreign exchange and savings constraints built into the two-gap model. So long as there are other markets in the economy these two equations are independent. Of course the functions in them should respond to financial variables (e.g., the interest rate or the inflation tax as in chapter 8), but there is no question that they are separate relationships.

Critics have simplified the gap model by assuming that *only* markets in traded and nontraded goods exist. This means that the "excess demand in other markets" formula should be dropped from the equations, and that if the nontraded market clears then so will the market for traded goods, and vice versa. The two gap equations are no longer different restrictions.

The revisionist literature basically asserts that the real exchange rate can adjust to drive excess demand in the market for nontraded goods to zero, assuring overall macro balance from Walras's law. To check this possibility out, we have to consider likely effects of an increase in ρ on the sector's market-clearing condition

$$[\gamma_n(1 - a) - 1]u + \theta g + \left(\frac{1}{\rho}\right)\gamma_n\varepsilon = 0. \tag{41}$$

When ρ increases, we would expect the following changes:

1. Nontraded supply u will presumably rise.

2. If there is substitution in consumer demand, γ_n will decrease. So may $(1 - a)$, or the share of intermediate inputs produced nationally. The outcome will be a reduction in consumption of nontraded commodities from income generated by production of the same goods.

3. Exports ε may decline.

4. The share of national goods in investment θ may fall.

5. As ρ rises, the value of exports in terms of nontraded goods will be smaller.

All these effects go together as shown in figure 9.8 to give market equilibrium. But the point to be stressed is that γ_n, a, and θ are not likely to be very sensitive to changes in ρ. Also resource reallocation between traded and nontraded sectors may not be easy, so u and ε will be price insensitive as well. Hence both the supply and demand schedules in figure 9.8 will be inelastic or *steep*. An adverse external shock in the form of a

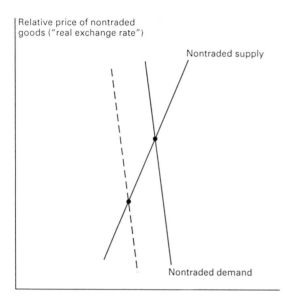

Figure 9.8
Equilibrium in the market for nontraded goods

downward shift in ε or P_e (the dashed line) will require a large reduction in ρ to restore equilibrium. But given a massive devaluation's other adverse economywide effects, it may be infeasible to depreciate enough to regain nontraded balance in the short to medium run. For this reason price adjustments are not likely to be a solution to the two-gap riddle, even in the restricted form of equation (41). One is naturally driven back to a fix-price, output-adjusting analysis based on (39) and (40), holding ρ constant in the latter equation since its effects on the included variables and parameters are likely to be small.[21]

The difficulties of exchange rate adjustment can be further illustrated if we allow domestic consumption of the exportable. Export and nontraded market balances can then be written as

$$(1 - \gamma_e)z - \gamma_e(1 - a)\rho u - \varepsilon = 0 \qquad (42)$$

and

$$[\gamma_n(1 - a) - 1]u + \theta g + \left(\frac{1}{\rho}\right)\gamma_n z = 0, \qquad (43)$$

where γ_e is the propensity to consume exportables from disposable income and z is exportable supply. To permit saving in the system, the restriction $\gamma_e + \gamma_n < 1$ has to apply.

The key trade-off here is between domestic consumption of exportables and their sale abroad to finance intermediate and capital goods imports. Closure of the model is fairly simple, in that (43) can be solved to determine ρ (subject to the *caveats* just raised), with exports following from (42). Suppose that national demand increases, say, from a higher investment rate g. This shock corresponds to a shift from the dashed to the solid line in figure 9.8, leading to real appreciation caus*ed* by expansion (instead of caus*ing* it, as in chapter 7). But then in (42) presumably z will fall and γ_e will rise, making exports ε decline.

The problem of course is that after this maneuver the trade constraint will bite, making the initial expansion infeasible. Indeed, one can easily extend the model to show that if (39) truly binds, then a reduction in ρ will bring more free foreign exchange into the system by at least marginally increasing exports and reducing import requirements, permitting output to expand. Whether this closure in which devaluation is expansionary because supply is limited by a binding foreign exchange contraint or a demand-determined scenario applies more realistically is a question that can only be answered in the context of the institutions and situation of the economy at hand. The authors cited at the beginning of this appendix suggest that the forex-constrained closure is appropriate in many small, primary-exporting economies, especially after the dramatic adverse external shocks that they have suffered since the mid-1970s (Taylor 1990c).

10 Decreasing Costs, Productivity Increases, Demand Composition, Commercial Policy, and Growth

In this chapter we take up four key factors affecting the growth rate of potential output as determined by the capital stock—the possibility that technologies with decreasing costs (or economies of scale) may permit output expansion to accelerate, the response of the growth rate to productivity gains induced along Kaldorian lines by higher unit labor costs or capacity utilization, cumulative processes induced by changes in sectoral demand patterns due to income redistribution or secular demand trends, and the impact of changes in commercial policy in a multisectoral system.

Largely using fix-price, output-adjusting specifications for simplicity, sections 10.1 through 10.4 take up these growth linkages in turn. In the first exercise the growth model has just one sector, but two possible production technologies—without and with economies of scale. At an initial equilibrium the increasing returns to scale (IRS) technique generates a lower potential profit rate than its constant returns (CRS) alternative— hence it is not adopted. The CRS-equilibrium is locally stable, and a non-marginal change is required to push the economy into IRS circular flow: Such multiple equilibria are characteristic of increasing returns. In the example developed here, progressive income redistribution or an investment push can provoke a transition, but other possibilities arise as well. One is the "buy/make/sell" decision regarding tradable goods in an open economy, which is analyzed briefly.

Scale economies are often hard to distinguish in practice from endogenous productivity growth. In section 10.2 we concentrate on labor productivity increases that reduce unit labor costs. How productivity change is absorbed is a deep macroeconomic question. As Dutt (1986) observes, "The issue is ... both important and complicated ... and has received attention from economists no less than Smith, Ricardo, and Marx.... While Smith, the early Ricardo, and neoclassical economists have eulogized the effects of technological change, Malthus, the later Ricardo (on machinery), Marx, the Luddites, and most labor unions have generally held a contrary opinion." One interpretation of these positions is that the proproductivity growth camp believe that output is profit led (reduced labor unit costs raise aggregate demand, e.g., from exports or an investment push), whereas the anti-productivity group view the macro system as wage led. How these linkages work out-is the central theme of the discussion here.

In the model of section 10.3, we first ask whether income redistribution via a tax-*cum*-transfer from profit income toward workers will raise the post-transfer labor income share, after sectoral outputs adjust in a demand-driven model set up to emphasize compositional effects (markups are assumed equal in both sectors and savings rates of the two classes are the same, but their consumption baskets differ). The intervention will not markedly raise the labor share if it creates many jobs (a result reminiscent of the paradox of thrift in chapter 2). But job creation is strong precisely under a condition required for the transfer to increase the steady state rate of growth. The moral is that redistributional policies are at least a two-edged sword—a conclusion that would only be strengthened in the presence of economies of scale or induced technical advance.

The model of section 10.4 deals with trade policy: In particular, will reduction of trade barriers as advocated by mainstream economists lead to faster output growth? A three-sector setup including home goods, an industry substituting intermediate imports, and an export is used to explore this question. The answer is that there is no particular growth benefit to be expected from noninterventionist trade policy; indeed, properly designed interventions can shift profitability patterns to make growth speed up. The practical issue that emerges is how to identify candidate "leading sectors" when their potential success depends in part on nonlocal factors with characteristics that cannot be inferred from recent historical experience.

10.1 Decreasing Costs

The root of economic progress has long been thought to be grounded in increasing returns or decreasing average cost, as the title to Young's (1928) famous article pointed out.[1] As observed in chapter 1, scale economies were central to the first wave of modern discussion of economic development after World War II: Additional profits from decreasing costs could potentially finance the investment required for Rosenstein-Rodan's (1961) "Big Push." They also figure in Keynesian analysis of stabilization issues.

For example, Kaldor (1982) argues that decreasing costs may offset inflationary pressure from expansionist macro policy.

An essential characteristic of increasing returns and/or indivisibilities in the production process is that they permit multiple equilibria—economic decisions taken on the basis of only "local" considerations around a preexisting equilibrium may not guide the economy toward a globally maximized output level or rate of growth.[2] We take up this conundrum here, asking how income redistribution or an investment push can lead to a shift from a slower to a more rapidly expanding configuration of circular flow. The emphasis is on once-for-all shifts toward an IRS technology, a decision especially relevant in a small economy. In a big or rich country, the question is more typically whether to build IRS factory number $N + 1$ when N plants already exist (where N may be a "large" number, like ten). The perturbations caused by shifts among nonconvex production technologies are likely to be much less dramatic in this case, as Farrell (1959) was perhaps the first to point out.

Figure 10.1 illustrates two convenient ways to parameterize declining average costs as the scale of production (measured by output X) goes up. One possibility is to assume that total costs increase according to a "factor rule" function such as

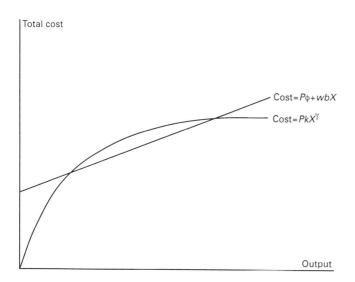

Figure 10.1
Approximations to total cost under increasing returns

Cost $= PkX^\gamma$,

where $\gamma < 1$ (in practice engineers often use $\gamma = 0.6$ or 0.7 as a scaling factor) and P is the price level. Alternatively, one can use a "fixed charge" formulation in which there is a sunk cost involved in just operating the technology. If the fixed charge takes the form of a quantity of output ϕ, then

$$\text{Cost} = P\phi + wbX, \tag{1}$$

where w is the money wage and b the labor/output ratio.

The diagram shows that within a range, the two approximations are close. We adopt the fixed charge version here, although results like those that follow can also be derived from a six- or seven-tenths factor rule and also when the fixed charge is in terms of labor instead of goods.

We assume that with their existing capital stock, firms can utilize either a CRS or IRS technology, depending on which gives the higher rate of profit.[3] If technology number one is CRS, its pricing rule is just

$$P = \frac{wb_1}{1 - \pi},$$

while if firms take a markup on variable cost under IRS technique number two (the usual supposition), then following (1) but with the fixed charge scaled in terms of capital (note 3), the cost breakdown is

$$PX = P\phi K + \frac{wb_2 X}{1 - \pi}.$$

From this equation the average price level under IRS is

$$P = \frac{wb_2}{(1 - \pi)[1 - (\phi/u)]},$$

which evidently declines as $u = X/K$ rises.

We want to ask how capacity utilization u and the profit rate $r = (X - \omega bX - \phi)/K$ (where $\omega = w/P$ is the real wage) respond to switches between techniques. For any (ϕ, b_i) combination characterizing a technology, capacity utilization (net of the fixed charge) and the profit rate in a demand-driven macro model are given by the expressions

$$u - \phi = \frac{g_0 + [(s_\pi - s_w)\omega b_i + \beta]\phi}{\xi_i} \tag{3}$$

and

$$r = \frac{1 - \omega b_i)g_0 + (\beta - s_w \omega b_i)\phi}{\xi_i}, \tag{4}$$

where

$$\xi_i = s_\pi - (s_\pi - s_w)\omega b_i - \beta.$$

These equations incorporate an accelerator investment function,

$$\text{Investment} = (g_0 + \beta u)K, \tag{5}$$

and presuppose savings rates s_π and s_w from profit and wage income flows. In line with the analysis in chapter 3, both the accelerator term β and the differential savings rates $(s_\pi > s_w)$ lead to a consumption-led macro system in which real wage increases raise both capacity utilization and the rate of potential output growth.

Suppose that the economy is utilizing technology one with utilization u_1. For the alternative equilibrium with $\phi > 0$ to be feasible, we clearly need $b_2 < b_1$. To first-order approximations from (3) and (4), the changes in u and r that would result from adopting the IRS technique are

$$\Delta u = \frac{-\omega u_1 (s_\pi - s_w)(b_1 - b_2) + s_\pi \phi}{\xi_1}$$

and

$$\Delta r = \frac{-\omega u_1 (\beta - s_w)(b_1 - b_2) + (\beta - s_w \omega b_1)\phi}{\xi_1}.$$

Several points stand out in these formulas. First, so long as $s_\pi > s_w$, output would decrease insofar as $b_2 < b_1$. Production jobs disappear in a shift from the CRS to IRS technique; aggregate demand could drop if the fixed charge ϕ is small. Second, the change in the profit rate depends on the accelerator coefficient. A small β means that r would fall if ϕ is large in comparison to $b_1 - b_2$; this observation is reversed for $\beta > s_w$.

For $\Delta r < 0$ the condition

$$\frac{\omega u_1 (b_1 - b_2)}{\phi} > \frac{\beta - s_w \omega b_1}{\beta - s_w}$$

is required. For $\Delta u > 0$ the condition is

$$\frac{\omega u_1 (b_1 - b_2)}{\phi} < \frac{s_\pi}{s_\pi - s_w}.$$

Both inequalities can hold when the stability condition $\xi_1 > 0$ applies. In other words, it is possible that switching to IRS would reduce real profits (which of course is why the switch is not made) but also raise output.

If the IRS technique is less profitable at the output/capital ratio u_1, the following inequality applies to the potential profit rates r_i at the initial real wage ω_1:

$$r_2 = u_1 - \omega_1 b_2 u_1 - \phi < r_1 = u_1 - \omega_1 b_1 u_1.$$

Rearranging, we have

$$r_2 - r_1 = \omega_1 u_1 (b_1 - b_2) - \phi < 0.$$

The potential IRS profit flow will increase if either the real wage or output goes up. Indeed, for r_2 to rise above r^1, we need

$$\omega \Delta u + u \Delta \omega \geqslant \frac{\phi}{b_1 - b_2}.$$

The required real wage increase could be arranged by a reduction in the markup rate π.[4] Taking into account the effect of $\Delta\omega$ on Δu, the required wage change is given by

$$\Delta\omega \geqslant \frac{\phi \xi_1}{(b_1 - b_2) u_1 (s_\pi - \beta)}. \tag{6}$$

The output increment could come from a jump in autonomous investment g_0, satisfying

$$\Delta g_0 \geqslant \frac{\phi \xi_1}{b_1 - b_2}. \tag{7}$$

Both (6) and (7) can hold with plausible values for the parameters.

Figure 10.2 illustrates the transition between techniques when (6) is satisfied, presupposing the real wage adjustment process introduced as equation (2.9) in table 4.2:

$$\hat{\omega} = h(\omega, u), \tag{8}$$

with $\partial h/\partial\omega < 0$ and $\partial h/\partial u > 0$. The "real wage" locus plots the condition $\hat{\omega} = 0$. The CRS and IRS schedules correspond to the "output response" curves of figure 4.7, under constant and increasing returns, respectively. As the schedules are drawn, aggregate demand goes up in response to an increase in ω in a wage-led macro system.

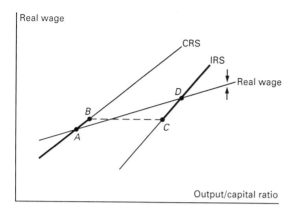

Figure 10.2
Change from a CRS to an IRS technique in response to a real wage increase

Point A in figure 10.2 is the initial equilibrium, stable for a range of values of ω, as indicated by the thickened line. If the real wage jumps to B, profitability of the IRS technique rises enough to cause a switch to a new short-run equilibrium at C, at a higher output level. The real wage starts to go up in response, leading to a final IRS equilibrium at D. With the accelerator investment function (5), capital stock (and potential output) growth will accelerate in the medium run.

Figure 10.3 tells the story for an increase in autonomous investment, or a Big Push. The CRS and IRS schedules are drawn after the increase in g_0, which immediately leads output to jump from point A to B. Since ω lies below the real wage schedule, it rises over time to C where (6) is satisfied. The IRS technology kicks in and output jumps upward to D. Another round of wage increases leads to final equilibrium at E. Alternatively, there could be a direct switch to the IRS technique if Δg_0 satisfies (7).

In any real economy transitions toward increasing returns technologies are more complex than shifting curves in diagrams, but the pictures do reflect historical changes. Young and Rosenstein-Rodan saw a Big Push as a dynamic process unfolding over many sectors, some providing cheaper intermediate inputs for user industries, and others responding to shifts in the level and composition of aggregate demand. Following Westphal and Cramer (1984) some part of their vision is illustrated (in partial equilibrium) in figure 10.4 for the "buy/make/sell" decision in an economy open to foreign trade.

The c.i.f. price of imports in the diagram is P_m while P_e is the f.o.b. price at which exports can be sold. The domestic supply curve for low

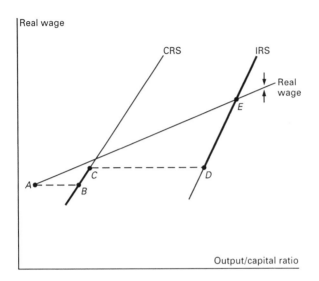

Figure 10.3
Change from a CRS to an IRS technique in response to higher investment demand

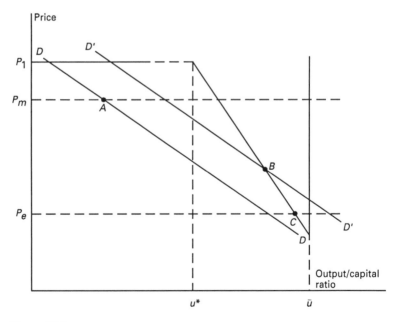

Figure 10.4
The buy/make/sell choice in partial equilibrium

levels of the output/capital ratio (or capacity use) u is flat as in (2)—the price sticks at P_1 with a CRS technology. When u rises to u^*, an IRS technique becomes profitable (perhaps with a jump in u as techniques shift), and the output price declines as in equation (2).

For low levels of domestic demand along curve DD, the import price lies below potential domestic cost, and the good in question is not produced at all. Point A represents market equilibrium, with imports coming in to satisfy local needs at price P_m. A big enough income redistribution, investment push, or some other factor can shift the demand curve outward to $D'D'$. IRS production becomes profitable, and equilibrium jumps to point B—instead of being bought, the good is made. Exports in volume are the "sell" option (another nonmarginal change), with production at point C, near full capacity use at $\bar{u}$. Capital accumulation might permit still further cost reduction, in effect shifting point C to the left.

Intersectoral linkages could further complicate matters, for capital goods or widely used intermediates such as metal products or chemicals. The Big Push in practice may look like a sequence of uncoordinated Big Hops, Skips, and Jumps as different industries cross the IRS threshhold. But after all, that is what the balanced/unbalanced growth debate was all about.[5]

10.2 Productivity Growth

The labor productivity increases that occur as per capita income grows complement economies of scale. In this section we hark back to Kaldor's "technical progress function" (chapter 2) to ask how a rising output/labor ratio is accommodated in wage- and profit-led macroeconomic systems.

We assume a CRS production technology, with markup pricing. If ε is the export/capital ratio, the investment function is (5), and saving comes only from profit income at rate s, then the demand-determined output/capital ratio is given by

$$u = \frac{g_0 + \varepsilon}{s(1 - \omega b) - \beta},\qquad(9)$$

where ω is the real wage and b the labor/output ratio. It is convenient to define $\lambda = \omega b$ as labor cost per unit output, and assume that $\varepsilon = \varepsilon(\lambda)$. Exports decline as supply costs rise, so $d\varepsilon/d\lambda < 0$. The profit share π is inversely related to unit labor cost: $\pi = 1 - \lambda$.

A labor productivity increase is a reduction in b. We assume that productivity increases over time as a function of unit labor costs and output,

$$\hat{b} = -\phi(\lambda, u) < 0. \tag{10}$$

Typically one would suppose that $\partial\phi/\partial\lambda > 0$; in other words, more expensive labor spurs the search for productivity gains. However, if technical advance is specially stimulated by international competition (as proponents of export-led growth assert), then by reducing ε, a higher λ could make productivity growth slow. Higher capacity utilization coupled with greater investment from (5) should aid productivity as in Kaldor's formulation discussed in chapter 2: $\partial\phi/\partial u > 0$.

With productivity rising, unit labor costs become the natural object of distributional conflict. Equation (8) for real wage growth is replaced by

$$\hat{\lambda} = \hat{\omega} + \hat{b} = h(\lambda, u) - \xi\phi(\lambda, u) = h(\lambda, u) + \xi\hat{b}. \tag{11}$$

In these expressions ξ is the share of productivity growth that is passed through to lower unit cost in the short run; alternatively, (11) can be written as

$$\hat{\omega} = h(\lambda, u) + (1 - \xi)\phi(\lambda, u),$$

so that a share $1 - \xi$ of higher productivity feeds into real wages. In Korean experience, for example, ξ takes a value around one-half.

A steady state for (11) is defined by $\hat{\lambda} = 0$, so $\hat{\omega} = -\hat{b}$ and there is a constant profit share. Changing levels of u and λ allow the steady state to be obtained via the adjustment process illustrated in figure 10.5. A wage-led scenario is illustrated in the lower diagram. Exports are not strongly responsive to λ, so from (9), $du/d\lambda > 0$ along the "output response" curve. We assume that $h_\lambda - \xi\phi_\lambda < 0$ and $h_u - \xi\phi_u > 0$; that is, induced changes in productivity do not outweigh the distributional effects on real wage changes discussed in chapter 4. The diagram shows a stable equilibrium in which the "cost" schedule along which $\hat{\lambda} = 0$ is less steep than the output response curve.

A burst of technical advance can be represented by an upward shift of the ϕ function, making real unit labor cost decline faster in (11). To bring $\hat{\lambda}$ back up to zero, λ itself would have to fall. The cost schedule shifts downward, and at the new steady state both unit costs and capacity use are lower. From (5) the growth rate would decline. This sort of adjustment is the one that Ricardo writing "On Machinery," Malthus, the Luddites, and Marx deplored. Technical advance cuts labor's real spending power, and in wage-led economy aggregate demand and growth recede.

The upper diagram is based on the hypothesis that $d\varepsilon/d\lambda \ll 0$, or that exports are highly responsive to costs. As a consequence aggregate de-

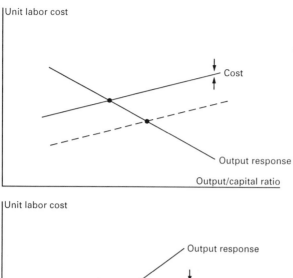

Figure 10.5
Effects of faster labor productivity growth in exhilarationist (*upper diagram*) and
stagnationist (*lower diagram*) macroeconomic systems

mand is an inverse function of λ, in-a profit-led system. Faster productivity
growth leads to a new steady state where u is higher and the capital stock
growth rate speeds up. Such a virtuous shift in circular flow can occur in a
nation at any income level. Blecker (1989) emphasizes the importance of
such responses in the industrialized world, and it is also characteristic of the
newly industrializing countries (NIC). How to find at all income levels the
export mix that converts local rent-seekers into NIC-style entrepreneurs is
a key industrial policy task.

As Dutt (1986) points out, technical change should also be examined
when output is limited by either the available labor supply or capital stock.
Kaldor's model discussed in chapter 2 deals with the labor-constrained case.
Like the neoclassical model, by construction Kaldor's specification contains
a positive effect of productivity gains on output growth—an outcome

which figure 10.5 shows is by no means guaranteed when production follows demand.

When capital constrains output, u is fixed "technically" and λ follows from (9) via forced saving. Hence $\hat{\omega} = -\hat{b}$ to hold $\hat{\lambda} = 0$; that is, faster technical progress just feeds into real wage increases without affecting the rate of output growth. Open unemployment would rise with a larger ϕ in (10), perhaps rendering capital-constrained growth impossible in the socio-political long run.

Two further thoughts should be added in closing. First, we have not considered nominal price changes and inflation. In moderate inflation regimes productivity increases can help stabilize prices from the side of costs—a practically important linkage which is analytically straightforward to pursue.

Second, both Schumpeter (1934) and stagnationists such as Baran and Sweezy (1966) argue for a positive effect of productivity increases on investment, making the upper diagram in figure 10.5 more likely to apply.[6] Institutions matter for these-effects. Baran and Sweezy believe, for example, that monopoly capital might limit adoption of "normal" innovations but cannot thwart "epoch-making" ideas such as the steam engine, railroad, and automobile (and consumer electronics?) which "... shake up the entire pattern of the economy and hence create vast investment outlets in addition to the capital which they directly absorb." As always, real historical events set the flavor of economic growth.

10.3 Demand Composition

Changes in demand composition go as far back in growth analysis as economies of scale and productivity increases, as we saw in chapter 1. Here we develop a simple model to illustrate how attempts at income redistribution can dissipate in a multisectoral context and also how they influence growth.

We consider two sectors: Number one's products are used for consumption and investment while number two just makes consumer goods—it may be interpreted as producing a new commodity, with implications to be taken up below. Once installed in either sector, capital cannot be moved. Both follow the same markup pricing rule,

$$P_i = \frac{wb_i}{1 - \pi}, \qquad i = 1 \text{ or } 2. \tag{12}$$

Their respective profit rates are

$$r_1 = \pi u_1 \quad \text{and} \quad r_2 = \pi \left(\frac{P_2}{P_1}\right) u_2 = \pi \psi u_2, \tag{13}$$

where $u_i = X_i/K_i$ as usual. Since both sectors have the same markup rate, the price P_i of the one with a lower labor/output ratio b_i will also be lower. For each sector, it will also be true that

$$\pi + \left(\frac{w}{P_i}\right) b_i = 1, \qquad i = 1 \text{ or } 2, \tag{14}$$

a relationship that will prove useful in a moment.

To highlight the effects of changes in the composition of the consumption basket, besides the equal sectoral markup rate we assume that the saving rate s is the same from both wage and profit income flows *but* that the marginal propensities to consume the two commodities differ between classes. In symbols the propensities to consume commodity one are α_w from wages and α_π from profits. Sectoral investment functions take the form

$$I_i = (g_0 + \beta_i u_i) K_i,$$

and the accelerator coefficients β_i can differ.

Market balance relationships for the two sectors are

$$(1 - s)[\alpha_w w(b_1 X_1 + b_2 X_2) + \alpha_\pi \pi (P_1 X_1 + P_2 X_2)] + (g_0 + \beta_1 u_1) P_1 K_1$$
$$+ (g_0 + \beta_2 u_2) P_2 K_2 + \theta P_1 (K_1 + K_2) - P_1 X_1 = 0 \tag{15}$$

and

$$(1 - s)[(1 - \alpha_w) w(b_1 X_1 + b_2 X_2) + (1 - \alpha_\pi) \pi (P_1 X_1 + P_2 X_2)]$$
$$- \theta P_1 (K_1 + K_2) - P_2 X_2 = 0. \tag{16}$$

When it is positive, the new term θ represents a secular trend toward consumption of products from sector one. It can show up for several reasons, including the following:

1. There can be Engel effects in demand. As in chapter 9 such changes are usually linked to income levels but as Pasinetti (1981) points out, the more fundamental tendency under capitalism is for demand for specific commodities to grow more rapidly than the rest of the economy for a time, then to saturate and decline. Pasinetti treats these changes as time trends; equations (15) and (16) relate demand shifts to the total capital stock or

"size" of the economy $P_1(K_1 + K_2)$. For $\theta > 0$, when productive wealth increases, then demand for commodity one goes up.

2. Consumer choice can be manipulated by the state or private sector in well-known ways. There are also deeper, more autonomous movements in demand patterns. Efforts at environmental protection will shift demand composition, as will changes in regulation and "intermediate" inputs of government services to production (Kuznets 1971).

3. Polices aimed explicitly at income redistribution affect the overall consumption basket. For example, a lump-sum tax T on capitalists' income which is transferred to wage earners would increase demand for commodity one by $(\alpha_w - \alpha_\pi)(1 - s)T$. If the tax is scaled to wealth, $T = \tau P_1(K_1 + K_2)$, then we have $\theta = (\alpha_w - \alpha_\pi)(1 - s)\tau$. The tax/transfer policy will affect sectoral balance only insofar as *marginal* propensities to consume good one differ between classes—a theorem perhaps first stated for saving behavior by Lubell (1947). Empirical evidence suggests that such differentials are small; that is, transfers on the order of 5 percent of GDP might be required to shift sectoral production level by one percent or so.[7] Hence, to produce big changes in the sectoral composition of output, small consumption shifts must cumulate through differential sectoral investment behavior, technical advance, or economies of scale. We take up the investment story in this section.

To simplify (15) and (16), let $\lambda = K_2/K_1$ and recall from (13) that $\psi = P_2/P_1 = b_2/b_1$. Also let $\mu = \alpha_w(w/P_i)b_i + \alpha_\pi \pi$ (i.e., μ is the marginal propensity to consume commodity one from each sector's real income). By virtue of (14), $1 - \mu$ is each sector's marginal propensity to consume commodity two. Using these definitions and normalizing (15) and (16) by P_1K_1, we get restated sectoral balance relationships of the form

$$\begin{bmatrix} (1 - s)\mu + \beta_1 - 1 & [\mu\psi(1 - s) + \beta_2]\lambda \\ (1 - s)(1 - \mu) & [(1 - s)(1 - \mu) - 1]\psi\lambda \end{bmatrix} \begin{bmatrix} u_1 \\ u_2 \end{bmatrix}$$

$$= \begin{bmatrix} -g_0(1 + \lambda) \\ 0 \end{bmatrix} + \begin{bmatrix} -\theta(1 + \lambda) \\ \theta(1 + \lambda) \end{bmatrix}. \tag{17}$$

The determinant of the matrix in the first line of (17) is

$$\lambda[\psi(s - \beta_1) + (1 - s)(1 - \mu)(\psi\beta_1 - \beta_2)] = \lambda\Gamma. \tag{18}$$

For stability, we assume that $\Gamma > 0$, a condition that will be satisfied unless the accelerator coefficient β_1 exceeds the saving rate s and/or $\beta_2/b_2 \gg \beta_1/b_1$; that is, the accelerator is excessively strong relative to job creation in sector two. Using (18), it is easy to solve (17) for u_1 and u_2 to get

$$u_1 = \frac{1 + \lambda}{\Gamma}\{[1 - (1 - s)(1 - \mu)]\psi g_0 + (\psi s - \beta_2)\theta\} \tag{19}$$

and

$$u_2 = \frac{1 + \lambda}{\lambda\Gamma}[(1 - s)(1 - \mu)g_0 - (s - \beta_1)\theta]. \tag{20}$$

Unless the accelerator coefficients are unstably large, we have $\partial u_1/\partial\theta > 0$ and $\partial u_2/\partial\theta < 0$ so that a change in demand composition increases the activity level in the sector it favors. Also $\partial u_1/\partial\lambda > 0$ and $\partial u_2/\partial\lambda < 0$; that is, for a given pattern of demand a shift in the allocation of capital toward sector two reduces its rate of capacity utilization (and also profitability) and increases the rate in sector one. Taking these commonplace results for granted, a more interesting question is what does the demand shift do to employment and (for a tax/transfer policy) post-transfer income distribution?

Since the profit share π is the same in both sectors, the labor share of income generated from production will not be affected by a change in output composition.[8] However, the level of employment *can* vary. After the tax-*cum*-transfer described above, the labor share in total income is

$$\sigma = \frac{w(b_1X_1 + b_2X_2) + \tau P_1(K_1 + K_2)}{[w/(1 - \pi)](b_1X_1 + b_2X_2)} = (1 - \pi) + \frac{\tau b_1(1 + \lambda)}{b_1u_1 + b_2u_2\lambda}, \tag{21}$$

where $b_1u_1 + b_2u_2\lambda$ (which we can call E) is total employment relative to sector one's capital stock. Equation (21) shows that the post-transfer labor share rises less strongly insofar as employment is elastic to the transfer rate τ. The same consideration applies to real post-transfer income per worker, as can easily be verified.

After substitution from (19) and (20) and simplification, we find that

$$E = \frac{1 + \lambda}{\Gamma}[b_2g_0 + (\beta_1b_2 - \beta_2b_1)\theta].$$

The elasticity of E with respect to τ (e.g., η) becomes

$$\eta = \frac{(\beta_1b_2 - \beta_2b_1)\theta}{b_2g_0 + (\beta_1b_2 - \beta_2b_1)\theta} < 1, \tag{22}$$

where $\theta = (\alpha_w - \alpha_\pi)(1 - s)\tau$.

The implication is that E is less than unit elastic with respect to τ, so an increased transfer will increase the labor share σ. However, the effect will be attenuated the more strongly two conditions hold: (1) $\alpha_w > \alpha_\pi$ and (2) $\beta_1/b_1 > \beta_2/b_2$. That is, wage-earners have a strong consumer preference for sector one's products and, relative to the number of jobs created by more output, that sector has a strong investment accelerator. Under such conditions an income transfer policy will have a substantial leakage via job creation. Higher earnings per employed worker trade off with more jobs.

What about the long-term effects of the transfer (or other forces creating a demand shift toward sector one)? In particular, what will happen to the steady state rate of growth? Figure 10.6 shows dynamic effects of an increase in θ on the long-term growth rate and the ratio of sector two's capital stock to sector one's.

From (19) and (20) we have seen that a higher λ raises u_1 and reduces u_2. With accelerator-based investment functions, the slopes of the g_i schedules in the diagram follow immediately. A steady state at which $\hat{\lambda} = g_2 - g_1 = 0$ is defined by the intersection of the curves. A higher θ shifts the g_2 locus downward (by reducing u_2 in the short run) and the g_1 locus up. Hence at the new steady state λ unambiguously declines but the growth rate can move either way.

To investigate the change in the growth rate, first note that from the steady state condition $g_0 + \beta_1 u_1 = g_0 + \beta_2 u_2$, the long-run value of λ (or λ^*) can be expressed as

$$\lambda^* = \frac{\beta_2[(1-s)(1-\mu)g_0 - (s-\beta_1)\theta]}{\beta_1\{[1-(1-s)(1-\mu)]\psi g_0 + (\psi s - \beta_1)\theta\}}.$$

From this expression it is easy to see that $\partial\lambda^*/\partial\theta < 0$ as in figure 10.6. Substituting back into (19) and (20) and differentiating also shows that the steady state values of u_1 and u_2 (and thereby g_1 and g_2) both increase when the condition $\beta_1/b_1 > \beta_2/b_2$ is satisfied. That is, the tax-cum-transfer policy accelerates the rate of growth only under a key condition for making its distributional leakages and overall employment effects large. Since the employment elasticity η in (22) is independent of λ, this observation applies in both the short and long runs. Finally, steady state profit rates obey the relationship

$$\left(\frac{\beta_1}{b_1}\right)r_1 = \left(\frac{\beta_2}{b_2}\right)r_2.$$

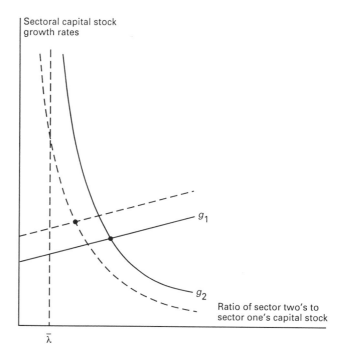

Figure 10.6
Effects of a shift in demand composition toward sector one

We have $r_2 > r_1$ when a demand shift toward sector one increases the steady state rate of growth. Capital becomes relatively scarce in the other sector, bidding up its long-run profit rate.

To close, note that sector two may be producing a new product, disturbing a prior circular flow in which sector one stands for the rest of the economy. Presumably, a lumpy initial investment to produce the new commodity has been made (with the saving counterpart coming from an upward blip in sector one's income and output), giving a sectoral capital stock allocation such as $\bar{\lambda}$ in figure 10.6. The entrepreneur behind the new product would typically expect high profits, and conditions for $r_2 \gg r_1$ when $\bar{\lambda}$ is small can easily be written out for the model, if not the practical world.

From (19) and (20) and the investment functions, g_1 will be relatively low and g_2 will tend toward infinity for a small $\bar{\lambda}$. Consistent with stylized observations and the theory that Pasinetti (1981) sets out, capacity in the new sector will grow more rapidly than in the rest of the economy (i.e., sector one) in the approach to a new steady state. The long-run growth rate will rise or fall according to the conditions we have already discussed. The model's bottom line is that policies aimed at redistribution and demand shifts more generally have complicated effects—on employment, distribution, and growth. The same theme is repeated with class structure variations in section 11.2 and also in another version of the present specification (Taylor 1989b) in which prices are assumed equal in the two sectors so that the one with the lower labor/output ratio b_i has the higher profit share π_i. In addition savings propensities as well as consumer demand patterns are allowed to differ between the classes.

In these circumstances the converse of the well-known Rybczynski (1955) theorem from international economics applies: If profit-recipients preferentially consume the labor-intensive commodity then a tax-*cum*-transfer aimed at shifting income toward labor will *reduce* employment. Moreover, if the accelerator for the sector preferred by capitalists is stronger, the shift in demand composition will reduce the steady state rate of growth. Once again, intersectoral and dynamic trade-offs among transfer policies and other changes in demand composition merit serious consideration.

10.4   Commercial Policy

Our final topic in this chapter is trade policy, in particular, trade liberalization. Mainstream development economists (and development institutions such as the World Bank and International Monetary Fund) arrived at a consensus in the 1980s that liberal commercial policy is a royal road to growth. Shapiro and Taylor (1990) argue that this view misinterprets historical experience with industrial strategy (seen from the perspectives of both historical cases of industrialization in nineteenth century Europe and more recently in South Korea and Brazil, and also in cross-country comparisons), and ignores the insights of early development theory. But it is strongly based on the strand of neoclassical thought that emphasizes "gains from trade" and reflects orthodoxy's intellectual imperialism. The problem is that like any empire, when the mainstream swells over a new area, it submerges quaint cultural survivals with its own way of looking at the world. In the industrialization debate, the insights of Schumpeter, Rosenstein-Rodan, Hirschman, and contemporaries are at grave risk of being drowned.

The question at hand is whether policies aimed at creating "equal incentives" or "level playing fields" will accelerate the rate of growth. An answer in any functioning economy of course would depend on its behavioral linkages and institutions as shaped by historical experience. All we can do here is produce a plausible model in which—depending in part on locally ascertainable circumstances—the results of changes in trade policy can go either way.

The basic specification is similar to the investment-driven multisectoral models of chapter 9 and section 10.3. There are three sectors, labeled X for nontraded or home goods,[9] J for an industry producing intermediate goods which substitute imperfectly for imports, and E for exports. Once installed in a sector, capital cannot be shifted. Its allocation at any point in time is described by the ratios $\lambda_j = K_j/K_x$ and $\lambda_e = K_e/K_x$, where the subscripts denote sectors.

As a large, isolated sector, home goods can be assumed to have markup pricing with a profit share π_x,

$$P_x = \frac{wb_x + P^*a}{1 - \pi_x}. \tag{23}$$

In this equation a is an input-output coefficient for intermediate goods, supplied either by sector J or by imports, and P^* is the price for an aggregate of these two separate commodities, discussed below. For ease in exposition, all capital goods are assumed to be imported, so the profit rate in home goods is

$$r_x = \pi_x \left(\frac{P_x}{e}\right)\left(\frac{X}{K_x}\right) = \pi_x \left(\frac{P_x}{e}\right)u_x, \tag{24}$$

where e is the exchange rate and the import price of capital goods (and all other imports) is normalized to one.

Along lines laid out in computable general equilibrium models (Taylor 1990a), national and imported intermediates are treated as imperfect substitutes in the "production" of an aggregate commodity used as an input by home goods. If the X sector minimizes input costs, it can be viewed as operating along a cost function for the aggregate,

$$P^* = f[P_j, e(1 + \sigma)],$$

where P_j is the price of nationally produced intermediates and $e(1 + \sigma)$ is the price of imports including a tariff at rate σ. If a constant elasticity of substitution (CES) cost function applies,[10] then Shepard's lemma shows that demand for each of the intermediates depends only on its "own" real cost:

$$J = f_j\left(\frac{P_j}{P^*}\right)aX \quad \text{and} \quad M = f_m\left[\frac{e(1+\sigma)}{P^*}\right]aX,$$

where M is the volume of imports and f_j and f_m are the partial derivatives of the function f.

The partials are both decreasing in their arguments, and it is also true that

$$P^* = f_jP_j + f_me(1+\sigma), \tag{25}$$

an expression we use below.

From (25) the impact effect of a higher tariff rate σ is to increase P^*, but less than proportionately. Hence P_j/P^* declines and $e(1+\sigma)/P^*$ rises. Demand for J increases and for M decreases, so there is import substitution in response to the revised tariff. From (23) the price P_x of home goods also goes up.

With a profit share π_j and markup pricing, the profit rate in the J sector is

$$r_j = \frac{\pi_jP_jf_ja}{\pi_xP_x\lambda_j}r_x; \tag{26}$$

that is, r_j is proportional to r_x. Reallocation of capital toward the J sector is represented by a higher λ_j, reducing r_j. As discussed above, a higher tariff rate σ increases f_j and thereby the profit rate (at least in partial equilibrium before r_x adjusts).

Exports are a "primary" commodity as in chapter 9, with output limited by capital stock and price-sensitive world demand. Setting up a model that generates steady states is easier if world demand is scaled to the size of the local economy as measured by the home goods capital stock. The demand function can be written as

$$\frac{E}{K_x} = \varepsilon_0 + \varepsilon_1\left[\frac{e}{P_e(1-\xi)}\right],$$

where ξ is a subsidy rate and P_e is the price that export producers receive. For demand to have a price elasticity greater than one, the usual condition that $\varepsilon_0 < 0$ has to apply.

Export supply is $E = \kappa K_e$, so inverting the demand function gives

$$P_e = \frac{\varepsilon_1 e}{(1-\xi)(\lambda_e\kappa - \varepsilon_0)}. \tag{27}$$

The profit rate in the export sector is

$$r_e = \frac{(P_e - wb_e)\kappa}{eK}. \tag{28}$$

From (27) and (28) an increased export subsidy increases P_e and thereby r_e. Relative movement of capital toward exports (a higher λ_e) has the opposite effect.

Output in the home goods sector is demand determined, with a balance equation that can be written as

$$P_x G + w(b_x X + b_j J + b_e E) + (1 - s)[\pi_x P_x X + \pi_j P_j J + (P_e - wb_e E)]$$

$$- P_x X = 0,$$

where all private consumption demand is satisfied by home goods, G is public consumption, and it is assumed that the saving rates from wage and profit income flows are zero and s, respectively.

Using (23) and (25), this expression can be rewritten as

$$P_x G + [(1 - s)(P_e - wb_e) + wb_e]E$$

$$- [s(\pi_x P_x + \pi_j P_j f_j a) + f_m e(1 + \sigma)a]X = 0. \tag{29}$$

All the price (and price-sensitive) terms in (29) are predetermined in the short run, so it amounts to a standard injections-minus-leakages equation to determine X. The home goods and import substitution profit rates then follow from (24) and (26), while the profit rate in exports comes from (27) and (28).

Comparative statics of the model (23)–(29) are tedious to work out but are quite intuitive:

1. As we have noted, increasing λ_e (or λ_j) reduces the corresponding profit rate r_e (or r_j).

2. We have assumed constant variable cost and excess capacity in the J sector so that the profit share π_j is independent of the sector's demand or level of capacity use. Extending the model to include decreasing returns or forced saving at the sectoral level would make $\partial \pi_j / \partial \lambda_j < 0$ and $\partial r_x / \partial \lambda_j > 0$, as shifting capital toward intermediate production reduces demand pressure and buyer's cost.[11] We consider both $\partial r_x / \partial \lambda_j = 0$ and $\partial r_x / \partial \lambda_j > 0$ in the discussion that follows.

3. As we have noted, an increase in the intermediate import tariff σ makes P_x rise, f_j rise, and f_m fall. With plausible parameters the net effect

from (24) and (29) is likely to be $\partial r_x/\partial \sigma < 0$, as higher input costs reduce home goods profitability. The result $\partial r_j/\partial \sigma > 0$ usually will come out in general equilibrium.

4. In the export sector we have observed that $\partial r_e/\partial \lambda_e < 0$ and $\partial r_e/\partial \xi > 0$. If demand for exports is sufficiently price inelastic ($\varepsilon_0 \gg 0$), then a higher λ_ε may reduce profits from exporting enough to make $\partial r_x/\partial \lambda_e < 0$. A higher export subsidy generates demand and makes home goods profitability rise: $\partial r_x/\partial \xi > 0$.

So far we have sketched effects of policy changes and movements in the state variables λ_i on sectoral profit rates. The approach does not differ in principle from detailed calculation of effective rates of protection or domestic resource costs to find out which sectors are gaining or losing from protection, or (more ambitiously) from solving a static computable general equilibrium model. But how does short-run profitability feed into growth? To answer the question, we have to bring in investment functions, say,

$$g_i = g_0 + \alpha_i r_i, \qquad i = e, x, \text{ or } j. \tag{30}$$

The g_i relationships lead in turn to differential equations for the two state variables,

$$\hat{\lambda}_j = g_j - g_x = \alpha_j r_j - \alpha_x r_x \tag{31}$$

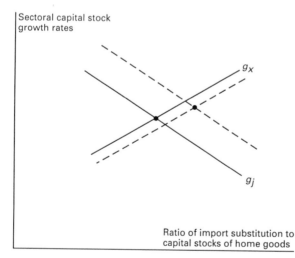

Sectoral capital stock growth rates

g_x

g_j

Ratio of import substitution to capital stocks of home goods

Figure 10.7
Steady state growth for an import substitution and home goods sectors

and

$$\hat{\lambda}_e = g_e - g_x = \alpha_e r_e - \alpha_x r_x. \tag{32}$$

Figure 10.7 shows how a steady state at which $\hat{\lambda}_j = 0$ is attained in (31). From point 2 above, a higher $\lambda_j (= K_j/K_x)$ either increases or leaves unaffected the home goods profit rate r_x. Hence the g_x schedule in the diagram will be horizontal or have a positive slope (as shown). From observation 1, the g_j schedule slopes downward, since $\partial r_j/\partial \lambda_j < 0$. The growth rates equalize at the point where the curves cross.

Now consider an increase in the tariff rate σ. From point 3, r_x falls, shifting the g_x schedule downward. At the same time the import substitution profit rate goes up, shifting the g_j schedule to the right. The shifted curves show that λ_j will be higher in the new steady state—capital is reallocated toward import substitution. And as the dashed schedules are drawn (reflecting relatively large values of $\partial r_j/\partial \sigma$ and/or α_j as well as $\partial r_x/\partial \lambda_j < 0$), the long-term growth rate responds positively to a greater trade distortion.

Similar considerations apply in (32) regarding export subsidies. If ξ is raised, the steady state growth rate will fall if world demand for "our" product is sufficiently price inelastic, but otherwise will go up. If the E sector uses intermediate inputs from the J sector, then trade-offs in adjusting σ and ξ arise. There is no guarantee that equalizing the two rates (or undertaking an overall exchange rate adjustment) will accelerate steady state growth.

The conclusions are that the growth effects of trade policies depend both on the short-term changes in sectoral profit rates that they induce and on how these changes shift sectoral investment demands (perhaps further influenced by public capital formation, as in chapter 8). These linkages are local in nature, and their likely importance can in principle be ascertained from current information. But if increasing returns or induced productivity growth come into play, detailed industrial programming becomes much more difficult.

"Success cases" such as Japan and South Korea show that industrial strategies can work, on the basis of interactive feedback between planners and producers in a sort of guided unbalanced growth. But each success is historically unique, and beyond pointing out that interventionist policy can be productive, formal models are not of great practical use in navigating toward self-sustaining growth. Algebra and computers are no substitute for managed, decentralized decision making which learns from its own triumphs and mistakes.

11

Class Conflict and Growth

How social conficts and compromises affect economic growth is a major theme of this book. We conclude our analysis in this chapter with three last examples.

The first is based on Pasinetti's (1962) growth model, itself a reaction to Kaldor's (1957) model discussed in chapter 2. Pasinetti pointed out that if workers save, then they must accumulate capital. Their saving rate s_w will apply to at least a fraction of profit flows, as opposed to the profit recipients' saving rate s_π. Pasinetti showed that despite this complication, the Cambridge growth equation $g = s_\pi r$ can still hold in steady state.

From the perspective developed in chapter 10, Pasinetti's model is interesting because its equilibrium is not unique. Samuelson and Modigliani (1966) found a "dual" steady state in which rentiers vanish and a Solow-type condition $g = s_w u$ applies—an elementary bifurcation between two potential steady state attractors is the dynamic key. Additional twists to the model depend on the nature of investment demand. If investment is highly sensitive to profit signals, the neoclassical axiom that the rate of profit equals the marginal product of capital may nearly apply. If autonomous investment is large and the profit response weak, neither the Samuelson-Modigliani nor the Pasinetti equilibria may be reached. As Darity (1981) observed, an "anti-dual" solution is economically (but presumably not socially) possible in which the workers' share of both income and capital stock tends toward zero. These and other results are set out in section 11.1.

In section 11.2 a model is developed in which a new sector producing "luxuries" (e.g., as scooters and televisions in India today) can appear. These products are consumed by a new middle class of skilled workers. Their saving also finances the investment required to put luxury goods capacity in place. If investment in turn responds to luxury sales, then a positive feedback loop is in place. Depending on the strength of the investment response, the economy may settle in an equilibrium without luxuries and *embourgeoisement*, or else on another trajectory with faster growth and increased inequality. These possibilities are a more specific version of the results of section 10.3, and also hark back to the multiple possible equilibria under economies of scale in section 10.1. In the present case, however, faster growth is associated with a more regressive income distribution, as predicted by the Latin structuralist authors discussed in chapter 1.

The last example draws on recent Marxist models for rich countries, focusing on the question of why their growth slowed after 20 years of historically unprecedented expansion in the wake of World War II. Different schools relate the boom and subsequent slowdown to effects of changes in the income distribution on either investment incentives or labor militancy. The dynamic implications of these differing interpretations of recent events are set out in section 11.3.

11.1 Pasinetti's Model under Neoclassical and More Congenial Closure Rules

Pasinetti works with two classes—hereditary rentiers and the rest of humanity (or "workers"). The total capital stock is K, and the supply of savings is given by

$$\dot{K} = s_\pi r K_\pi + s_w (X - r K_\pi), \tag{1}$$

where X is output, r is the profit rate, K_π is the capital held by rentiers, and s_π and s_w are rentiers' and workers' saving rates, respectively (with $s_\pi > s_w$). For simplicity the price of output is normalized to one. To ease comparisons between Pasinetti's (1962) and Samuelson and Modigliani's (1966) models, we opt for the latters' neoclassical production function with constant returns to scale and other "nice" properties,

$$X = F(K, L), \tag{2}$$

where L is total employment.

Accumulation of rentiers' capital is given by

$$\dot{K}_\pi = s_\pi r K_\pi, \tag{3}$$

while workers' capital grows as $\dot{K} - \dot{K}_\pi$.

We assume that numbers of both rentiers and workers grow at the same rate g and that all workers are employed. Then (1)–(3) can be put on a per worker basis to give the growth equations

$$\dot{k} = (s_\pi - s_w)rk_\pi + (s_w u - g)k \tag{4}$$

and

$$\dot{k}_\pi = (s_\pi r - g)k_\pi, \tag{5}$$

where capital stocks per worker are $k = K/L$ and $k_\pi = K_\pi/L$, and $u = X/K$. For future reference, let $x_k = \partial X/\partial K$ or the marginal product of capital.

At any time, k and k_π are predetermined in (4) and (5). These equations have three unknowns: the rates of accumulation $\dot{k}$ and $\dot{k}_\pi$ and the profit (or interest) rate r. Another behavioral relationship or closure rule is needed to complete the model. The neoclassical position is that arbitrage makes the profit rate equal the marginal product of capital, or

$$r = x_k. \tag{6}$$

The dynamics of (4)–(6) are easy to depict, as in figure 11.1. From (4) and (6), $\dot{k} = 0$ when the following relationship between k and k_π holds:

$$k_\pi = \frac{(g - s_w u)k}{(s_\pi - s_w)x_k}. \tag{7}$$

From the neoclassical production function, u and x_k are declining functions of k. Hence for k exceeding some value S at which $g = s_w u$, k_π is a positive, increasing function of k, shown by the "total accumulation" locus in figure 11.1. When k_π lies above (below) this curve, then k will be increasing (decreasing), as shown by the small arrows.

The locus along which $\dot{k}_\pi = 0$ has two branches, as can be seen immediately from (5). One has $k_\pi = 0$, along the horizontal axis in figure 11.1. The other branch satisfies the relationships $s_\pi x_k = s_\pi r = g$, shown by the "arbitrage" curve in the lower quadrant. The existence of the two branches means that a pair of growth equilibria can occur.

One shows up when s_π is small, for example, at the point $(g/s_\pi)_0$. We get $s_\pi x_k = g$ when k takes a low value $T_0 < S$. For positive k_π, dynamics of $\dot{k}_\pi$ are shown by the small arrows next to the "rentier accumulation" locus lying to the left. For any initial (k, k_π) point in the upper quadrant, the system will move toward S where k_π is stationary at zero. In this steady state there are no rentiers and from (7) the Solow relationship $g = s_w u$ applies.

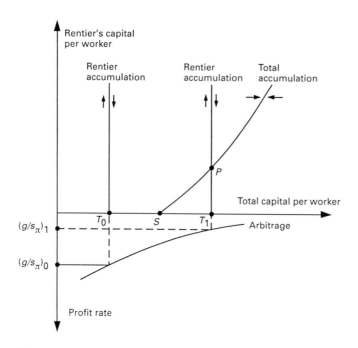

Figure 11.1
Determination of steady state equilibria in the Pasinetti model with a savings-driven neoclassical closure

The other equilibrium takes over when s_π is relatively large, such as at the point $(g/s_\pi)_1$. Now when $s_\pi x_k = g$, k takes the value T_1, exceeding S. The system tends toward the Pasinetti point P with a positive value of k_π; the solution at S is unstable. At P the Cambridge accumulation rule $g = s_\pi r$ applies from (6), independent of the production function. Workers' capital accumulation becomes something of a sideshow, in contrast to the Samuelson-Modigliani "dual" equilibrium at S, where all class distinctions (not least savings rates) cease to matter.[1]

These results show that the nature of long-run equilibrium depends on how vigorously rentiers save. In the patois of catastrophe theory, there is a "transcritical" bifurcation of the stable attractor from S to P as s_π increases. In discrete time there could also be chaotic dynamics of the logistic difference equation form discussed at length by Baumol and Benhabib (1989). These mathematical niceties aside, the model as stated so far is defective in forcing accumulation to be determined by saving supply. To bring in investment demand, we have to drop some relationship. Following Darity

(1981) and ultimately Kaldor (1956), the obvious candidate is the neoclassical marginal productivity relationship (6).

To define an investment function, we can begin by noting that in the Pasinetti setup r measures the cost of capital. It is more an interest than a profit rate (although we omit realistic financial market complications). The expected return to new investment is measured by the marginal product x_k, and a simple investment function along thoroughly orthodox Tobin (1969) lines can be written as

$$\dot{k} = g_0 + \alpha(x_k - r). \tag{8}$$

Investors have in mind some target growth rate g_0 of the per-worker stock of machines but are stimulated to more rapid capital formation when the spread between x_k and r widens. A high value of the response parameter α is analogous to the profit-led version of the model in chapter 3; a small α resembles the wage-led story.

To work out the details of the model incorporating (8) in place of (6), first note that (8) and (4) jointly determine $\dot{k}$ and r from investment-saving equilibrium. The solution for $\dot{k}$ is

$$\dot{k} = \frac{\alpha(s_w u - g)k + (g_0 + \alpha x_k)(s_\pi - s_w)k_\pi}{\alpha + (s_\pi - s_w)k_\pi}, \tag{9}$$

and (5) and (9) describe accumulation in the investment-driven Pasinetti model. As α tends toward infinity, (9) reduces to the saving equation (4); for a low value of α, capital stock growth will be close to g_0.

To study dynamics, we begin by noting from (8) that $\dot{k} = 0$ when $r = (g_0/\alpha) + x_k$ and from (5) that $\dot{k}_\pi = 0$ when $r = (g/s_\pi)$. Putting these conditions together gives the curves in the lower quadrant of figure 11.2. The I_1 schedule corresponds to a low value of g_0/α and I_2 to a high one. The total accumulation locus in the upper quadrant represents (9) with $\dot{k} = 0$.

Figure 11.2 shows a stable Pasinetti equilibrium at P_1. A lower value of g_0/α than the one corresponding to I_1 would cause a bifurcation to a stable Samuelson-Modigliani equilibrium corresponding to a point T_0 (not shown) lying to the left of S. This case corresponds to a *high* value of α: A profit-sensitive investment function produces a more neoclassical macro equilibrium.

Lower values of α increase steady state levels of k and k_π, but k_π goes up faster. With a small enough α, rentiers in steady state hold all the capital at point P_2 where, despite their saving, workers' capital per head is

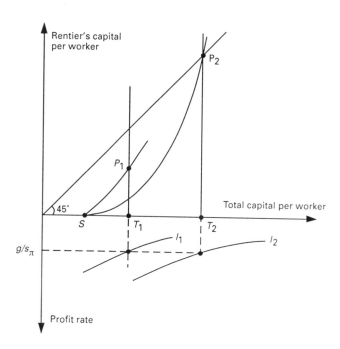

Figure 11.2
Steady states in an investment-driven Pasinetti model

negligible. With an independent investment function, the model thus permits an equilibrium "antidual" to Samuelson and Modigliani's: at point P_2,
workers' accumulation ceases to matter. Indeed, at P_2, where $\dot{k} = \dot{k}_\pi$ and
$\dot{k} = \dot{k}_\pi = 0$, (9) and (5) show that

$$s_w(u - r) = g - s_\pi r = 0.$$

Not only are their capital holdings trifling, but workers' per capita income
$(u - r)k$ falls to zero! The antidual equilibrium is clearly not socially feasible, but the economy would show rapid, investment-driven growth and
increasing inequality until social order breaks down along its trajectory
toward steady state.[2]

The conclusion from the Pasinetti model is that the character of macroeconomic equilibrium depends explicitly on how saving and investment
relationships interact in an economy with well-defined classes. Rentiers are
unimportant in steady state when their saving rate is relatively low and
investers respond robustly to profit opportunities. If they save a lot and
investment is strong and autonomous, rentiers may come to dominate the

scene. Insofar as the model applies to a real economy, specific institutional circumstances will determine its distributional *denouement*.[3]

11.2 A Luxury Commodity and a New Class

We have already seen in chapters 9 and 10 that income redistribution and growth can have interesting interactions in models with more than one sector. Building upon a model originally presented by Taylor and Bacha (1976), a stylized story about class formation and production of a new commodity continues this theme here.

For variety we consider an economy in which the capital stock can be moved instantaneously between sectors—an assumption that makes models easy to manage but is perhaps less realistic than the sectorally fixed capital stocks postulated earlier. Three sectors are presumed to exist— number one produces wage goods, number two a "luxury," and number three investment goods.

There are two types of labor in the model. Unskilled workers have their wage fixed in real terms, do not save, and consume only the wage good. Middle-class or skilled workers have a higher wage, do save, and consume the luxury product. In stylized form they represent people in the top decile or so of the earnings distribution who have enough income to support nonsubsistence spending—think of items like scooters, electrodomestics, and consumer electronics in India today or Italy after World War II. Skilled workers are more productive than unskilled and are assumed to appear on the scene in response to demand for their services—costs of skill upgrading are small enough to be ignored.[4]

The wage of unskilled workers and the price of the wage good can both be normalized at one; the unskilled are assumed to be mobile between jobs in the "modern" sector (the part of the economy to which the model refers) and background subsistence activities. Price formation obeys the rules

$$P_i = b_i + k_i r P_3, \qquad i = 1, 2, 3, \tag{10}$$

where b_i and k_i are each sector's labor/output and capital/output ratios, and r is the rate of profit (uniform across sectors because capital is shiftable). Since $P_1 = 1$, the cost of capital is given by

$$rP_3 = \frac{1 - b_1}{k_1}; \tag{11}$$

that is, there must be a surplus in wage goods production ($b_1 < 1$) for profits to exist. As already observed in chapter 9, such a condition is standard in Ricardian models like the one at hand. In the Ricardian tradition we also assume for simplicity that all profit income rP_3K is automatically saved.

Labor supply (at unitary cost) is

$$N^s = L + wM, \tag{12}$$

where L and M stand, respectively, for employment of the unskilled and skilled. Middle-class workers get a wage $w > 1$, which is equal to their productivity. Equation (12) thus weights workers by productivity to get "effective" labor supply at the fixed unskilled wage.[5]

Labor demand is

$$N^d = b_1 X_1 + b_2 X_2 + b_3 X_3, \tag{13}$$

where the X_i are sectoral output levels, and we conventionally assume that

$$N^d - N^s = 0. \tag{14}$$

With P_1 and the subsistence wage both normalized at 1, excess demand equilibrium for the wage good is

$$L - X_1 = 0. \tag{15}$$

For the luxury good, the analagous condition is

$$\gamma\left(\frac{w}{P_2}\right)M - X_2 = 0, \tag{16}$$

where γ is the skilled workers' marginal propensity to consume. From (15) and (16) it is clear that no consumption demand comes from profit income.

For capital goods the demand-supply balance is

$$(g + \delta)K - X_3 = 0, \tag{17}$$

where g is an investment function described more fully below. The parameter δ can be interpreted either as the rate of depreciation of the capital stock or as a fixed charge associated with production of the luxury good (along the lines of section 10.1). The demand-supply balance for existing capital is

$$k_1 X_1 + k_2 X_2 + k_3 X_3 - K = 0. \tag{18}$$

The seven equations (12) through (18) describe equilibrium in the short run. The first six can be solved to give

$$b_3(g + \delta)K - \left(\frac{1}{\gamma}\right)(P_2 - \gamma b_2)X_2 - (1 - b_1)X_1 = 0. \tag{19}$$

This equation shows that demand for wage goods (and implicitly for unskilled workers) rises with investment demand. But since $P_2 > b_2$ from (10) and $\gamma < 1$, an increase in X_2 (and skilled employment) crowds out demand for X_1.

From (18) written as

$$k_1 X_1 + k_2 X_2 - [1 - k_3(g + \delta)]K = 0,$$

it is clear that supplies of X_1 and X_2 also trade off under the capital constraint. Eliminating X_1 between (18) and (19) gives

$$\lambda(g + \delta - r) - \xi = 0, \tag{20}$$

where $\xi = X_2/K$ and $\lambda = \gamma P_3/(1 - \gamma)P_2$. Equation (20) is a saving-investment balance showing that insofar as the sum of capital stock growth and the rate of the fixed charge (or depreciation) exceeds the profit rate r, demand for the luxury goes up. The mechanism resembles forced saving. If investment rises above the saving supplied by profits, then jobs for skilled workers are generated as a means of raising total savings flows. From (18) or (19), unskilled jobs and demand for wage goods will be crowded out. With plausible parameters, Taylor and Bacha (1976) show that income inequality is likely to worsen overall.

As discussed in section 10.3, the history of a new commodity à la Pasinetti (1981) is likely to involve a period of sales expansion, followed by saturation and finally decline. We can mimic the first phases for the new luxury good with a cubic differential equation for the change in investment demand:

$$\dot{g} = (g - r)(\mu\xi - \xi^2) = (g - r)\xi(\mu - \xi). \tag{21}$$

The rationale goes as follows: The $(g - r)$ term reflects animal spirits in the form of a positive feedback of investment into increased capital formation itself—an idea that also enters into the models of long-term accumulation in industrialized economies discussed in the following section. The profit rate r is a convenient base point for this effect, but investors' animation could be normalized around any reference growth rate exceeding $r - \delta$ just as well. The term $(\mu\xi - \xi^2)$ shows that capital formation is stimulated by output of luxury goods $(\mu\xi)$ but that this effect is dampened by the ξ^2 term as the market saturates when ξ grows large. The logistic relationship $\xi(\mu - \xi)$ is equivalent to the trade-off (along the

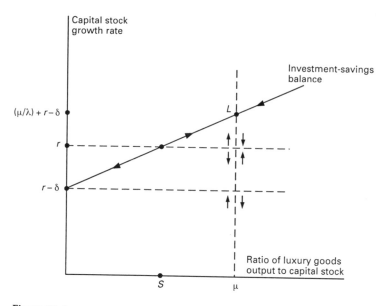

Figure 11.3
Steady state equilibria in the model with luxury goods

mathematicians' "center manifold") that permits bifurcation in the Pasinetti model. It means that $\dot{g}$ vanishes along the vertical axis in figure 11.3 as well as on the vertical line originating at μ. Since $\dot{g} = 0$ along the horizontal line at $g = r$ also, the diagram illustrates multiple possibilities for macroeconomic equilibrium.

Suppose that luxury goods suddenly can be produced. If their technology involves economies of scale or indivisibilities, then the fixed charge and the possibility of skilled workers' saving make the investment-saving balance take the form (20) instead of a simpler $g - r = 0$. Alternatively, (20) may have applied all along if depreciation is important. Either way, short-run equilibrium always satisfies this equation, represented by the schedule labeled "investment-saving balance" in the diagram.

The small arrows illustrate investment dynamics from (21). They show that the nonluxury, low-level equilibrium at $g = r - \delta$ is stably approached by g and ζ along the investment-saving schedule. Any small surge in capital formation and/or production of luxury goods would stimulate further investment because of the positive values of ζ and $(\mu - \zeta)$ in (21), but so long as g falls below the target level r, then $\dot{g} < 0$ and the growth rate would return to $r - \delta$.

The alternative equilibrium position L (standing for "luxury" accompanied by a faster growth rate $g = (\mu/\lambda) + r - \delta$) is stable also but will only be reached if luxury goods production ξ is raised above the threshold level S by the state's or some entrepreneur's Big Push. There is a saddle-point at $\xi = S$ along the $g = r$ schedule which separates the two stable growth attractors; that is, with $g > r, \xi > 0$, and $\xi < \mu$ in (21), then $\dot{g} > 0$. The growth ridge has to be scaled if the economy is to switch between patterns of circular flow. When it is crossed, the equilibrium at L is the relevant attractor. It represents a saturation point, since when $\xi > \mu$, investment damping takes over and $\dot{g}$ turns negative from (21).

Transition to the new equilibrium requires a nonmarginal change at the outset. When and if it occurs, positive feedbacks through investment demand between production of a new good and the class that consumes it alter the character of the macro system. The new circular flow may combine scale economies, increased inequality, and faster growth in the sort of situation described by Furtado (1972) and Tavares (1972) two decades ago.

11.3   Distribution and Accumulation Dynamics in an Industrialized Economy

Although the institutional emphasis in this book has been on the developing world, models like the ones here are frequently used for rich economies as well. In this section, following Weisskopf (1988), we investigate long-term dynamics of distribution and growth along lines recently laid out by Marxist scholars. To ease comparison with our earlier results, a broadly Kaleckian formalism like that in chapters 3 and 10 is employed.

As usual, ω is the real wage and b the labor/output ratio in a one-sector economy. Unit labor cost is $\lambda = \omega b$, and the profit share $\pi = 1 - \lambda$. Capacity utilization $u(= X/K)$ depends on λ via aggregate demand, and the investment function can be written as

$$g = g(\lambda, u, g_0),$$

with the first partial derivative negative and the other two positive. The term g_0 will be used below to capture dynamic factors influencing capital accumulation.

Slightly modifying the treatment in section 10.2, we assume that productivity growth responds to investment,

$$\hat{b} = -\phi(g).$$

Following equation (11) in chapter 10, dynamics of unit labor cost can be written in the form

$$\hat{\lambda} = \xi_\lambda[\bar{\lambda}(g) - \lambda] + \xi_u(u - \bar{u}) - \xi_\phi\phi(g). \tag{22}$$

We assume that $\partial\hat{\lambda}/\partial g > 0$. The meaning is that increased real wage pressure from faster growth via $\bar{\lambda}(g)$ outweighs the cost-reducing effect of more rapid productivity increases $\phi(g)$.

Glyn and Sutcliffe (1972) emphasized the dynamics of profitability and investment demand in an influential interpretation of capitalist growth since World War II. Their line of argument can be illustrated if we assume that autonomous investment evolves according to a relationship such as

$$\hat{g}_0 = f(\lambda, g_0), \tag{23}$$

with the first partial $f_\lambda < 0$ so that higher unit labor costs and reduced profitability dampen investment over time. Dynamics become more interesting if the second partial is positive, so buoyant animal spirits feed back positively into themselves as they did in equation (21).

Figure 11.4 illustrates the dynamics of (22) and (23). The "labor cost" schedule corresponds to $\hat{\lambda} = 0$, with the small arrows signaling stable adjustment. The "investment" curve represents $\hat{g}_0 = 0$, with the positive feedback loop just mentioned. The configuration of slopes means that a stable steady state is possible but not assured.

Suppose that the labor cost schedule shifts downward to the dashed line. Such an improvement in the profitability structure may plausibly have taken place after World War II. The dynamic response involves a long period of high accumulation followed by a slump after the trajectory crosses the investment schedule. Labor costs rise before accumulation sharply declines but then begin to fall as investment remains depressed. If the model is stable (there may also be a limit cycle), there is an endogenous basis for recovery from economic crisis. Slow accumulation and low capacity use will ultimately "unsqueeze" profits, which in turn will raise the rate of investment itself.

An alternative view, espoused by Bowles, Gordon, and Weisskopf (1986) and Bowles and Boyer (1990), emphasizes class power. This "social structure of accumulation" (or SSA) school puts dynamics on $\bar{\lambda}$ in (22) according to a rule such as

$$\frac{d\bar{\lambda}}{dt} = h(\lambda, \bar{\lambda}), \tag{24}$$

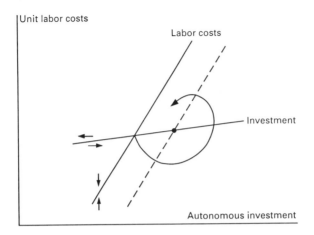

Figure 11.4
Dynamics of accumulation in the medium run

with $\partial h/\partial \lambda < 0$ and $\partial h/\partial \bar{\lambda} > 0$. The former partial derivative shows that higher labor costs dampen the growth of labor militancy (as measured by the target unit labor cost $\bar{\lambda}$) in the short run, but the latter derivative shows a positive feedback of militancy into itself over time.

The dynamics are the same as in figure 11.4, with $\bar{\lambda}$ replacing g_0 as the variable measured along the horizontal axis. Paraphrasing Weisskopf (1988), the story is that the postwar SSA initially provided the institutional foundation for high rates of profit and accumulation from the late 1940s through the mid-1960s. However, by that time rising labor power as measured by $\bar{\lambda}$ posed "challenges to capitalist control" with consequently reduced rates of profit and growth during the following two decades. Ultimate recovery would depend on how rapidly $\bar{\lambda}$ might fall, and its lags into accumulation and aggregate demand more generally in a (possibly) profit-led macroeconomic system. Alternatively, a renewed boom might require construction of a novel social structure of accumulation on a world scale—a political and institutional achievement that does not seem to be immediately in sight.

Notes

Chapter 1

1. The Kuwait example draws upon personal consulting experience, and for that reason cannot be backed up by citations. *Added in proof*: The text was written before the invasion of Kuwait in August 1990. But this unfortunate event does illustrate the basic point being made. No economic plans made in Kuwait even contemplated the possibility of war—in a highly unstable corner of the world where "rationality" would presumably take this contingency into account.

2. The following discussion is based on Lustig (1990) and Taylor (1990).

3. Pandas were optimized by natural selection to consume bamboo with inherited carnivorous digestive tracts. Their strategy is precarious at best; Gould (1987) reports that they have to eat 15 hours a day. Only their cuddly looks—a non-optimized, chance adaptation—keep the pandas alive as their bamboo forests dwindle steadily in the China of today.

4. Schumpeter (1954) is the classic reference on the history of economic analysis, and Kindleberger (1984 and 1985) is very good on different ideas regarding money and finance. Dobb (1973) emphasizes differences between neoclassical and dissident views about the relative importance of marginal productivity rules and class relationships in determining economic equilibrium. Blaug (1985) is the standard mainstream compendium—comprehensive, written with panache, and only mildly reactionary. Unfortunately, these standard references are not very good on the theory of growth. With an emphasis on the economic development literature, Taylor and Arida's (1988) survey complements the material here.

5. The term is due to Amadeo (1989), and post-Wicksellian macroeconomics is discussed in chapters 3 and 4.

6. This terminology is due to Hicks (1965).

7. The key resides in the balance of "financial surpluses" $(I_1 - S_1) + (I_2 - S_2) = 0$, where the subscripts denote sectors, regions, etc. Clearly only three of the four investment and saving functions can be independent; the sector with the residual adjusting variable in some sense bears the burden of growth.

8. Dornbusch and Frenkel (1984) present a model of the 1847 bank run along (unacknowledged) Minskyian lines.

9. The flight from money may of course take some time, as our discussion of Nicaragua in section 1.1 suggests.

Chapter 2

1. It is impossible to do algebraic economics without invoking some such mathematical concept of equilibrium. More metaphorical usages of the word, such as in describing the (excessively?) harmonious nature of many neoclassical models, should be distinguished from its application in describing the solution to a set of equations.

2. The word "causality" is used here to describe the selection of variables which are exogenous (or "predetermined") and endogenous in a set of equations or a model, combined with analysis of how the endogenous ones are influenced by the exogenous ones and themselves. Statistical notions of causality according to which one variable "causes" another if it leads it in time are ignored as irrelevant or misleading. Local earthquakes below the slopes do not "cause" a subsequent volcanic eruption, and money creation can either lead or lag output and/or prices depending on the stance of the central bank, as Davidson and Weintraub (1973) point out.

3. By convention, equations in the text of each chapter are numbered sequentially, while the first figure of an equation number in a table indicates the order of that table in its chapter.

4. The discussion in chapter 1 of output responses to real wage cuts in a demand-driven model signals a case in which the relative magnitudes of the two savings rates matter (also see note 7 below). Besides output, nonzero saving from wages can affect dynamic income flows. If they save, then presumably worker households have accumulated assets in the past, the returns from which should enter their income statements. We ignore this complication as being empirically unimportant, although it can in principle influence dynamic behavior of the macro system. In models with diverse asset/liability specifications, chapters 6 and 11 show that assets held by wage-earners do not substantially alter the nature of long-run macroeconomic equilibrium, so long as "significant" cross-class differentials in saving propensities and/or preferred portfolio compositions exist.

5. We omit tax terms to keep the algebra as simple as possible.

6. In the short run the capital stock K is fixed, so it serves only as a scaling factor. Dividing nominal flows by the value of potential output or full capacity (e.g., $P\kappa K$, where κ is a technical parameter giving the maximum output that can be produced by a given capital stock) would be an alternative normalization. We don't adopt it to avoid carrying along the extra term κ.

7. All these results illustrate a case where the relative magnitudes of saving rates

from nonwage and wage income have a significant influence on the characteristics of macroeconomic equilibrium.

8. Tax shortfalls can be important in practice. According to an "effect" pointed out by Olivera (1967) and Tanzi (1977), there may be reduced real tax when inflation runs faster due to lags in collection. When a history of inflation has not taught the fiscal authorities to invent tax indexation rules, escalating fiscal deficits after price increases accelerate can be a policy headache, as discussed in chapters 4 and 8.

9. If $g > \hat{L}$, a vibrant capitalism will have to absorb petty modes of production outside its own geopolitical domain to make up for the slow natural rate of growth: Imperialism à la Rosa Luxemburg (1951) or massive importation of foreign labor could be the practical solutions. If $\hat{L} > g$, capitalism may collapse, or else the ever-expanding reserve army will force the real wage down until the warranted rate g rises to $\hat{L}$.

10. When linearized, both the Solow growth equation (7) and the Kaldor equation (11) take the form $\dot{x} = dx/dt = x(B - Ax)$, where A and B are constants. Such an equation is stable around a steady state $x = B/A$ in continuous time, but it can easily generate chaotic dynamics in discrete time. The logistic equation $x_{t+1} = Ax_t(1 - x_t)$, where the subscripts denote time periods is a paradigm case (e.g., Baumol and Benhabib 1989). Continuous dynamics of the form $\dot{x} = x(B - Ax)$ can produce bifurcations between distinct growth equilibria in low-dimensional systems, as chapter 11 points out. The Poincaré-Bendixson theorem essentially rules out chaotic dynamics in one- and two-dimensional sets of differential equations (cf. Thompson and Stewart 1986).

11. As already pointed out in chapter 1, the word "stagnationist" is used in this book to describe both a class of growth models and a wage- or consumption-led macro system in which an increase in the real wage leads aggregate demand to rise. The usage should be clear in context.

12. It is helpful if $h(0) = 0$, $d^2h/dg^2 > 0$, and $h'(g) = dh/dg < 0$ when g is negative and $h'(g) > 0$ when g is positive. That is, $h(g)$ should have the same general shape as a parabola centered at the origin.

13. It is easy to see that instability can also arise in savings-driven models where workers and capitalists have different saving propensities and an increase in the labor-capital ratio shifts the income distribution strongly toward labor, for instance, when it has low elasticities of supply and demand. In discrete time, both overlapping generations and worker/capitalist models can generate chaotic dynamics from their single nonlinear difference equations for capital accumulation. Woodford (1989) works out the details of chaos for a worker versus capitalist logistic system of this sort.

14. Marglin (1984, ch. 2) gives stability analysis for discrete time.

15. A succinct presentation of the CES specification appears in Taylor (1979, app. D).

Chapter 3

1. Neoclassical-style determination of b, τ, and other variables by marginal productivity rules is taken up in section 3.3.

2. As argued in chapter 1, it makes sense to attach differential savings rates to income flows, in line with econometric and institutional evidence in the developing world (Taylor 1988a). Formally speaking, we follow Kaldor (1966) in tying saving behavior to type of income rather than to class as in Pasinetti's (1962) growth model, discussed in chapter 11.

3. That is, capacity use is assumed to adjust out of (temporary) equilibrium according to the rule $\dot{u} = \chi(g^i - g^s)$ with $\chi' > 0$, and $\Delta > 0$ is the stability condition.

4. Short-run profit share adjustment follows the rule $\dot{\pi} = \chi[g^i(\pi, \bar{u}) - s(\pi)\bar{u}]$, which will be stable in a stagnationist economy.

5. Recall in passing that the factor-price frontier imposes an inverse trade-off between the real wage and profit rate. Since ω and r can both rise in the Rowthorn-Dutt model of section 3.1, we return to our chapter 2 observation that a neoclassical macro specification is more internally constrained in distributional terms than is a markup formulation.

6. The point is stated clearly in Keynes's introductory chapter 2 on "The Postulates of the Classical Economics." He says that the "theoretically fundamental" difficulty with the classics' model is that "...if money-wages change, one would have expected the classical school to argue that prices would change in almost the same proportion, leaving the real wage and the level of unemployment practically the same as before, any small gain or loss to labour being at the expense or profit of other elements of marginal cost which have been left unaltered" (p. 12). The aggregate demand effects of the "small gains and losses" as well as monetary responses to changing wages and prices are discussed in detail in chapter 19 of *The General Theory*. The aim is to show that money wage cuts may raise output by reducing interest rates and stimulating investment (p. 265) but that similar results can be achieved far less painfully by increasing the money supply.

7. They don't show up, for example, in Solow's (1986) lucid presentation of the mainstream model. He says that using the quantity theory to describe aggregate demand is "childishly simple" but goes ahead and does it anyway.

8. In the text discussion we don't consider capital stock growth explicitly, but mainstream economists would include it along the lines of the Solow growth model presented in chapter 2. They would characteristically define $\bar{\lambda}$ in (1.12) as the steady state solution to (7) in chapter 2, that is, $\hat{L} = g(\bar{\lambda})$. In this setup the steady state growth rate is independent of income distribution, while, as we have seen, distribution itself follows from marginal productivity conditions at full employment. There is not much room for class structure and social conflict in the neoclassical vision of the world!

Chapter 4

1. Alternatively, one could capture lagged indexation effects in continuous time by using integral equations as in Foley's (1986a) circuit of capital models; Laplace transform techniques make discussion of steady states in such a setup fairly straightforward. The interested reader is encouraged to try her hand.

2. The name was coined by Lopes (1984).

3. Terminology is not standardized in inflation models, so what we call the inflation tax is sometimes called "seigniorage," or else seigniorage is the part of its deficit that the government monetizes (to be "financed" by the inflation tax and ongoing growth), etc. Let the reader beware of usages in alternative texts.

4. Attempts at forward-looking indexation tend to break down. The government is usually in charge of the "look," and has strong reasons to bias its inflation forecast downward. See Taylor (1988a) for Brazilian and Mexican examples.

5. If V depends on $\hat{P}$, then a term in $\hat{V} = \hat{V}(d\hat{P}/dt)$ enters (14), and we get a second-order system in $d\hat{P}/dt$ and $\hat{\omega}$. Unsurprisingly, it demonstrates rational expectations saddlepoint (in)stability, as discussed in appendix 4.A. Note also that a differential equation like (15) for the interest rate i instead of ω would go some way toward capturing Wicksell's argument that lagged interest rate increases by the banks will cut off a cumulative process inflation when saving and investment depend on i or the real interest rate $i - \hat{P}$. The analytics are sketched in appendix 4.B.

6. Since we are not carrying taxation terms in the algebra, the Olivera-Tanzi effect would be represented in the model by a positive dependence of γ (interpreted as government dissaving) on $\hat{P}$. Fiscal populism could be captured by making γ an increasing function of $\hat{P}$ or a decreasing function of ω.

7. In a full IS/LM specification augmented with equations like (2.7)–(2.9) for inflation, the interest rate will vary to equilibrate money supply and demand—the ratio $V = PX/M$ comes out of the short-run equilibrium. In such a model extended to deal with economic growth, a natural state variable is the ratio of the value of the capital stock (or full capacity output) to the money supply, say, $V^* = PK/M$. V^* follows its own laws, depending on differential equations for P, K, and M. It usually behaves in stable fashion, another explanation for the modest variation of both V and V^* over time. For a formal treatment, see chapters 5 and 6. Finally, note that in the model of table 4.2, flight from money as inflation accelerates could be modeled by making μ in (2.5) respond to $\hat{P}$ with a coefficient less than u/V. With $\hat{M} = \mu$ by market clearing, velocity would tend to rise from (2.4)

8. If some flex-price commodities are in fixed supply, the demand increase will spill over directly into higher prices. As these accumulate over time, the real wage falls and pressures for money wage increases and (ultimately) reindexation become intense. As Amadeo and Camargo (1989b) show, such developments unrolled over periods measured in months in Argentina and Brazil and were important in

upsetting the heterodox shocks. They can be brought formally into the analysis along the lines discussed in chapter 9. Flex-price increases were of course central to the "old" Latin American structuralist theory of inflation, discussed in chapter 1.

9. Perfect foresight or rational expectations enters this specification, since wealth-holders have to know the change in the price level (a future-dependent variable) in order to adjust velocity correctly to stick with the equation of exchange. Because of the coefficient V/v in (18), both V and $d\hat{P}/dt$ rise more in response to faster money growth when inflation is well underway, or V itself is high.

Chapter 5

1. Only a few developing economies have managed to develop active markets for equity and/or government securities (Taylor 1988a). Except in odd cases such as Zimbabwe where pension funds and insurance companies can be tapped for funds, the consequence is that the state basically finances its deficits by borrowing from the banking system or abroad. Implications of foreign borrowing are taken up in chapters 7 and 8. A stock market could easily be added to the present model along the lines suggested by Taylor and O'Connell (1985); the effects they stress are built into the deposit demand function discussed in the text.

2. Despite the allure of Irving Fisher's (1930) arbitrage condition between the profit rate and real interest rate ($r = i - \hat{P}$) for mainstream economists, there is scant evidence that the nominal rate and inflation move closely—until (as in many highly inflationary economies) the government intervenes to bring them together. For a review of experience in the United States, see Summers (1983). Also note that we assume in this chapter that saving rises as a function of the inflation rate. In the IS/LM system with financial crowding-out (the standard assumption), the implication is an anti-Fisherian inverse response of i to $\hat{P}$, as aggregate demand declines and the IS curve shifts to the left.

3. Crowding-in can also take place through the stock market, as in Taylor and O'Connell (1985).

4. In the North American literature, interest rate cost-push leading to inflation is called the "Wright Patman effect," after a late but once famous (or to bankers, notorious) easy-money congressman from Texas. Latins tend to ascribe the effect to Cavallo (1977), although it was pointed out two decades earlier by Galbraith (1957) and Streeten and Balogh (1957). Morley (1971) gives an early empirical verification for Brazil.

5. Specifically, we assume that (1) a higher u raises $\hat{P}$ and cuts aggregate demand, complementing the standard stability condition for the IS curve; (2) similarly a higher i increases $\hat{P}$ and also cuts demand, strengthening the usual effect via the investment function; (3) if a higher $\hat{P}$ from a higher i raises deposit demand because there is a lower real rate of interest on loans, this effect does not offset the direct reduction in demand due to the interest rate increase; (4) the direct-plus-indirect

effect of a higher u on deposit demand can be either positive or negative, combining both inflation and crowding linkages.

6. In fact any financial crowding-out of private by public investment appears to be offset by complementarity relationships or direct crowding-in. The implications are explored in chapter 8.

7. For a constant inflation rate, the slope of a $\hat{P}\hat{P}$ contour line is $di/dh = -(\partial\psi/\partial u)/(\partial\psi/\partial i)$ from (8).

8. As pointed out in chapter 2, we follow custom in separately analyzing stability of temporary equilibria involving variables like u and i, and steady state growth equilibria involving ω and V. Besides having smoother dynamics than period formulations, continuous time models lend themselves to this distinction between the short and long runs, and we exploit it unconscionably.

9. Indeed, one might argue that the typical monetarist regression equation for velocity (used for example in appendix 4.A), $V = V_0 + v\hat{P}$, is no more than an approximation to the steady state expression $V = (g^i/\gamma) + (1/\gamma)\hat{P}$, appropriately extended to deal with sources of base money emission besides government dissaving.

10. Thompson and Stewart (1986) and Lorenz (1989) are good introductions to ordinary and bizarre outcomes of nonlinear dynamic systems, including the Rössler band and other chaotic attractors. The books have interesting illustrations, respectively, from engineering and economic applications. Guckenheimer and Holmes (1983) is more advanced—a useful compendium of (in)stability theorems to invoke.

11. The discussion in the text describes how the real wage and velocity interact in mutually stabilizing fashion in a wage-led economy. Such negative feedbacks don't necessarily occur in a profit-led system—a further dynamic complication. After a heterodox shock, for example, higher capacity utilization means that the real wage rises and therefore the growth rate (and possibly the inflation rate) declines. Velocity begins to fall, increasing intermediation and reducing the interest rate so that output rises further, and so on. This cross-dynamic instability between ω and V need not necessarily overwhelm their own stable responses, but it could also lead to overall instability or chaos.

Chapter 6

1. An example is the late 1970s expansion of bank reserves and loans due to capital inflows in Argentina, as discussed in the text. This phenomenon is modeled in chapter 7.

2. Or at least, easy asset substitution is the key to Taylor and O'Connell's (1985) formalization of Minsky's discussion of the political economy of financial fragility and crisis.

3. We concentrate on "gold"—a domestic asset—in this section. Speculation in foreign assets as discussed by Frenkel (1983) is the topic of section 7.3.

4. If foreign exchange is the object of speculation, then prolonged orthodoxy may finally lead to repatriation of wealth gained via capital flight. Will this be the story in Mexico in the 1990s?

Chapter 7

1. Since they usually have nonconvertible currencies, developing countries have to peg their exchange rates. A fixed official rate (or rates) under exchange controls creates an environment in which a parallel market will flourish. We do not examine this possibility formally, implicitly assuming that "most" foreign exchange transactions take place in the official market. Even if they do not, parallel rate movements can cause price inflation or output contraction parallel to the impacts of a change in the official rate as discussed in the text. Kamin (1987) works through illuminating models.

2. As condition (1) shows, devaluation can be contractionary through several channels. The one involving a preexisting trade deficit was pointed out by Hirschman (1949) and Cooper (1971); Díaz-Alejandro (1963) emphasized real wage reductions. Krugman and Taylor (1978) pulled these ideas together with a fiscal effect in a model like the one in the text. Since then the literature has exploded: Lizondo and Montiel (1989) give a full-dress review of the theory with fifty-odd citations, originating from the International Monetary Fund of all places. In addition to the WIDER studies noted in the text, two authors associated with the World Bank—Edwards and van Wijnbergen (1989)—review the practice, and conclude that devaluation often proves to be contractionary, especially in the short run where most policy makers focus their attention. With a different country sample Morley (1990) comes to the same empirical conclusion, stressing the importance of reduced investment (from poor expectations and the accelerator in a stagnationist system?) in making output growth fall off.

3. Like all exchange rate maneuvers, adoption of a crawling peg has potent economywide effects. A degree of indexation is added to the system, worsening dynamics of cost-push inflation. Domestic interest rates can rise if Fisherian arbitrage exists between national assets which pay a nominal rate i and assets abroad with an effective return of $j + \hat{e}$, where j is the foreign real interest rate. On the positive side a crawl rules out big fluctuations in $j + \hat{e}$, reducing the risk of destabilizing capital movements as discussed in section 7.3. And as discussed in chapter 4, a crawl is likely to push up cost inflation less than an equivalent maxi-devaluation because it provokes less intense expectations of price jumps.

4. A formal model of Kaldor-Amsden export-led growth appears in section 10.2 where productivity growth can be export driven. Also note that some degree of export "maturity" (certainly including diversification in various dimensions) may be required for a viable crawling peg. Colombia jumped out of a stop-go export cycle when its then-in-power economic team invented the crawl in the late 1960s,

but it had built up several viable export lines previously. Mexico fell into a stop-go cycle in the 1980s as it became an oil mono-exporter with precious little price responsiveness in its J-curve. Some multisectoral implications of export growth are taken up in section 10.4.

5. In increasing order of abstractness, Williamson (1983) and Dornbusch (1980) are solid mainstream presentations. No good structuralist trade–open economy macro textbook exists as yet, although Carlin and Soskice (1990) provide useful material for industrialized economies.

6. That is, in most countries the government offered collaterals for or cosigned loans taken by the private sector during the 1970s. After the debt crisis hit in 1982, most governments were driven to nationalize these obligations, in part responding to pressure from foreign bankers anxious to maintain the formal legitimacy of their claims.

7. The exchange rate was simply frozen in Chile, while *tablitas* ("little tables") of preannounced reductions in the crawl rate were issued by the authorities in Argentina and Uruguay.

Chapter 8

1. In sections 8.7 and 8.8 we also introduce government nonmonetized debt as another asset that the public can hold. The role of asset markets in permitting Chenery's original two gaps to be independent constraints is taken up in appendix 9.A.

2. We omit new credit advanced to households or for working capital. Both uses would presumably depend on the *change* in output, or (after the application of stock-flow conversions in a planning context) the rate of capacity growth g. This extension is left out for simplicity, although noninvestment credit flows are important in practice.

3. Equation (6) shows that private asset accumulation abroad reduces resources available for the banking system to intermediate toward productive investment. In practice, capital flight is often transmitted by underinvoiced exports, overinvoiced imports, and so on, which bleed enterprise cash flows and directly reduce investment through that channel.

4. We assume that running down foreign balances is difficult, as well as unlikely with rapid domestic inflation. Deposits could also be converted to transactions balances, but this possibility will be limited if (as is often the case in developing economies) the ratio of quasi-money to money is low. The authorities may also sustain deposits by raising nominal interest rates along with inflation, along the lines discussed in sections 8.7 and 8.8.

5. In developing economies, the importance of crowding-in was emphasized in the WIDER country studies of recent stabilization programs summarized in Taylor (1988a). A neoclassical rationale is that public and private capital enter in comple-

mentary fashion in the aggregate production function (Arrow and Kurz 1970). The relevance of the phenomenon has been supported by recent econometrics. Chakravarty's (1987) regressions give a coefficient β between one and two for Indian agriculture; Ortiz and Noriega (1988) estimate that it takes a value of unity economywide for Mexico; Barro (1989) comes up with a β of one based on a large cross-country sample; and Aschauer (1989) argues that for the United States, public investment raises the profitability of private capital formation enough to offset direct crowding-out so that the overall level of national investment is raised. A new round of WIDER country studies summarized in Taylor (1990c) gives a range of β coefficients from -0.4 to 1.6 for a sample of 18 developing economies, with the median estimate being 0.5.

6. We omit a possible increase in investment demand as faster inflation reduces the real interest rate, along the lines sketched in section 2.2. A potential decrease in g as the variance of price changes rises with inflation is ignored as well.

7. The model of this chapter omits the interest rate, but it is clear that excess money supply growth should also lead the domestic rate structure to shift downward, making capital flight that much more attractive. Easy credit conditions were observed in the wake of the Brazilian cruzado plan of 1987, for example.

8. Ros (1989) uses a similar trick in presenting his gap model for Mexico.

9. We effectively set the injection to zero by assuming that all interest income iZ is saved.

10. In practice, as any reader of the newspapers can testify, countries receive negotiated levels of capital transfers, with the amounts depending at least as much on political as on economic factors. Which of the polar models of sections 8.7 and 8.8—or a hybrid—applies better in any given country depends on a wide range of circumstances.

Chapter 9

1. Landlords and peasants with a rule determining their shares in agricultural income $P_a X_a$ could be added as in the North–South model of sections 9.5 and 9.6. Econometrically estimated savings rates such as s_a and s_n might run in the range of 0.25 or so, while the saving share of wage income is far less.

2. In practice almost all governments intervene in agricultural markets, carefully separating producer, consumer, and import or export prices via tax/subsidy or marketing board schemes. In the present specification we implicitly assume that (net) exports E are regulated by quotas, so we don't have to deal explicitly with foreign prices. The model can be extended to include wedges among prices, at the cost of more algebra. Some implications of consumer food price subsidies are discussed informally below.

3. The derivative of $\phi(\delta k, z)\delta$ with respect to u is $\gamma_n \phi \eta > 0$. After a bit of manipulation, the derivative of all of (6) with respect to z can be expressed as

$\kappa\lambda(\gamma_a\phi\eta - v) < 0$. For stability we assume that this expression is negative. However, if consumption spending from agricultural income γ_a and the income elasticity η are high while the price elasticity v is low, the inequality might not be satisfied. One interpretation is that the marketed surplus from agriculture is a "perverse" function of the sector's price. Such a response is not unknown in practice and makes the economy tricky to control. For an illustration in terms of agricultural trade, see Chichilnisky (1981) and a subsequent *Journal of Development Economics* debate. In a model with class structure, Lele and Mellor (1981) show that biased technical change in agriculture that increases the sector's labor share can make marketed surplus problems worse.

4. The derivative of industrial excess demand (7) with respect to u is $\gamma_n(1 - \phi\eta) - 1 < 0$. The derivative with respect to z is $\kappa\lambda[v + \gamma_a(1 - \phi\eta) - 1]$, which can be positive if the price elasticity of food demand v and the propensity to consume from agricultural income γ_a are both high.

5. If $T = \kappa z(1 - \gamma_a) - g_a$, then the sign of $dz/d\lambda$ is determined by $-[\gamma_n\phi\eta T + \kappa z(1 - \alpha_n - \gamma_n)(1 - \phi\eta\gamma_a)]$ and the sign of $du/d\lambda$ by $(1 - v)T + (1 - \phi\eta\gamma_a)g_a$.

6. One of the incentives might be higher public investment in agriculture, aimed at stimulating private capital growth in the sector by crowding-in along the lines discussed in chapter 8. Rao (1988) develops the relevant linkages in an interesting growth model.

7. This last result may reverse for a "large" α_n, and is certain to do so if α_n is big enough (or β small enough) to make $\partial\hat{k}/\partial k > 0$. Recall that a relatively big value of α_n (e.g., 0.05 or so) makes the upper diagram's case in which $d(z\lambda)/d\lambda > 0$ more likely.

8. Between the mid-1970s and mid-1980s, there was a big neoclassical discussion of bonanzas under the rubric of Dutch disease, or combined inflation, exchange rate appreciation, and deindustrialization as consequences of sudden access to foreign exchange (e.g., the profits from new natural gas discoveries in The Netherlands in the 1960s). The story is an old one in the primary product exporting economies of the Third World. Indeed, the basic model—neoclassically presented but with obvious structural content—is due to economists from Australia, a slightly richer primary exporter subject to booms and crashes from fluctuating prices of its products. See Salter (1959) and Swan (1960) for the original formulations and Corden (1984) for a useful review paper that does not quite catch the drama of developing economy experience. Besides Barbone, Ocampo (1987) and Rattsø (1990a) give nice extensions of the traded/nontraded story to import quotas.

9. There is also a recent neoclassical literature about macroeconomically visible efficiency losses that supposedly result from firms and individuals directing resources to seek such rents, for example, Krueger (1974). A not completely convincing critique of state intervention follows, propounded in great volume during the 1980s. We do not take up these issues here, but see Shapiro and Taylor (1990) for a critical overview.

10. We skip lightly over a number of interesting issues with this formulation. For example, if the state controls the enclave (think of Mexico's PEMEX and oil), its fiscal position will depend strongly on both external vicissitudes and exchange rate policy. Alternatively, if a large share of the population depends on the export as a main income source (e.g., coffee in many Latin and African countries), distributional implications of changes in export prices can be profound. If producers are shielded from external fluctuations by a state-controlled (and financed) marketing board, fiscal imbalance in response to external price or local exchange rate shocks again rears its ugly head. Finally, note that extra foreign exchange could take the form of external aid. Radical development economists such as Griffin (1970) and Weisskopf (1972) long ago observed that aid is not automatically transformed into extra investment but leads to higher domestic final goods demand of the sort analyzed in the text. In the 1980s the Philippines and Egypt suffered from Dutch disease of the foreign aid variety, as the relevant WIDER country studies point out.

11. Imported and nationally produced intermediates are treated as perfect substitutes in (16). See section 10.4 for a slightly more complicated specification in which such goods substitute imperfectly in satisfying intermediate demands.

12. In deriving (17), it is helpful to note that in $\gamma_n = \alpha(1 - \pi) + (1 - s)\pi$, the term α (or the share of wages in final goods' variable cost) depends on v with a derivative $d\alpha/dv = -\alpha/(1 - \pi)$ so that $\partial(\gamma_n u)/\partial v = -au = -(m + \bar{m})$. The terms in (17) involving the real exchange rate incorporate the differential $dq = q[de/e - (1/\bar{x})dv/v]$.

13. The constants g_0 and γ determine the intercept of the "investment" schedule while z acts as a negative intercept for the "saving" function (making it hit the r_n-axis to the right of the origin).

14. Appendix B in Taylor (1979) presents a succinct description of this particular complete set of demand functions.

15. This assumption is chosen for simplicity and is an extreme version of the two-gap specification in chapter 8. The reader may want to work through a more realistic exercise in which only a fraction of the South's capital is imported, or consult Rattsø (1990b) for a description of the South in gap model terms.

16. As noted in note 10, extra capital inflows are typically not fully directed into extra investment, a point first noted by radicals in the early 1970s but by now widely accepted. Econometric estimates of parameters such as s_z typically range in the vicinity of 0.5 and are clearly less than one.

17. In (25) as K_s grows, the demand intercept θ becomes insignificant; in other words, the Engel elasticity of Northern demand for Southern goods tends toward one. Setting $\theta = \bar{\theta}K_s$ is a manipulative trick to avoid this problem, but in the discussion that follows we save notation by simply setting $\theta = 0$. See section 10.3 for more elaborate treatment of demand shift terms in multisectoral models.

18. The state variables λ and q describe a stable two-dimensional real/financial world growth model, as the reader may wish to verify.

19. Comparison with (25) shows that we continue to assume that $\theta = 0$ for simplicity.

20. This outcome may look implausible, but it shows up in at least one applied global macroeconomic model (McKibbin and Sachs 1989). The joker is that that McKibbin-Sachs specification is a multicountry version of the loanable funds/Ramsey model sketched in appendix 2.A, and it may well exaggerate macroeconomic responses to changes in the interest rate.

21. The same observation applies to a "disequilibrium" interpretation of gap models along the lines of appendix 3.A, where for low or depreciated values of ρ the nontraded supply curve determines output while the demand curve rules for high ρ according to the "short-side rule." The mainstream argument that devaluation is contractionary when the exchange rate is already undervalued in the supply-determined situation is not entirely convincing. As discussed in the text, supply-side determination of nontraded output may be a reasonable hypothesis in some circumstances, but it is not caused exclusively by misalignment of relative prices.

Chapter 10

1. Indeed, Young was following a very old analytical tradition emphasizing increasing returns, to which both Adam Smith and Alfred Marshall made substantial contributions.

2. This feature of scale economies is emphasized by Arthur (1989), who argues that "... increasing returns can cause the economy gradually to lock itself into an outcome not necessarily superior to alternatives, and not entirely predictable in advance." Early development economists thought they could finesse Arthur's problem through planning, setting up complex integer and dynamic programming models to try to optimize investment over time. The first strand of work used a fixed charge cost function like equation (1). It is exemplified by Chenery (1959) and reviewed by Westphal and Cramer (1984) and Pack and Westphal (1986). Manne (1967) and collaborators used a factor rule for costs in dynamic programming to analyze benefits of building plant capacity in advance of expected demand to take advantage of economies of scale. Much later, more neoclassical growth models (Murphy, Schleifer, and Vishny 1989a, 1989b) also emphasize the possibility of multiple equilibria, redraping contributions like Rosenstein-Rodan's in a new generation's analytical *haute couture*. The latest stitching emphasizes decentralized market as opposed to planning equilibria. *Pace* appendix 2.A, the two need not coincide under increasing returns.

3. In a fully dynamic specification fixed capital would be wedded to a technology, and we would have to deal with a CRS-to-IRS dynamic transition (or the other way 'round). Also, for ease in exposition, the fixed charge function will be written hereafter as Cost $= P\phi K + wbX$, where K is the capital stock. This trope lets us set up a model in terms of $u = X/K$ in place of X.

4. The relevant derivative is

$$\frac{d\pi}{d\omega} = \frac{-bu}{\xi(u-\phi)^2}(\xi u + \phi\beta) < 0.$$

5. Rosenstein-Rodan and Nurkse (1953) were the main advocates of balanced growth. Among their antagonists were Hirschman (1958) and Streeten (1959), who wanted unbalanced change to shock the economy from low-level circular flow. They saw development as characterized by uneven sectoral advances, disproportions, and disequilibria, with inflationary and balance of payments tensions arising for different industries at different times. Both figure 10.4 and Arthur's (1989) observations about irreversibility suggest that in many ways, the unbalanced team was closer to getting the story right.

6. In our setup the natural way to capture the effect of productivity growth on investment is to make g_0 a function of λ in (5), with $dg_0/d\lambda < 0$. Animal spirits responses of this sort are discussed in section 11.3.

7. In the 1960s and 1970s many input-output calculations of possible impacts of redistribution on output patterns, foreign exchange use, employment, and so forth, were made using blown-up versions of the present model (with a social accounting matrix linking tens of sectors, several classes of income recipients, etc.). Short-run changes in production composition were typically small, although the consumption basket of the well-to-do usually proved to be import intensive. Progressive redistribution could either raise or reduce employment, depending on differences between classes in marginal propensities to consume labor-intensive services. Morawetz (1974) partially summarizes these investigations.

8. A variant specification in which output composition does affect distribution is sketched later in this chapter.

9. As discussed in chapter 9, a policy aimed at import substitution will expand the domain of nontraded goods. In what follows, we implicitly assume that the traded/nontraded frontier does not change, despite the importance of the buy/make/sell decision discussed in section 10.1.

10. See Taylor (1979 app. D) for the algebra of the CES production specification. How easily the imported and national intermediate replace one another would naturally be measured by their elasticity of substitution.

11. See chapter 9 for analogous results in a fix-price/flex-price framework.

Chapter 11

1. A question of interest for later discussion is whether rentiers will hold some, most, or all of the capital stock? It is easy to see that they will not hold all of it. Combining (6) and (7) shows that $k_\pi < k$ is equivalent to the inequality $(s_\pi - s_w)x_k > g - s_w u$. But at the Pasinetti equilibrium $s_n x_k = g$. Therefore the

inequality simplifies to $u > x_k$, which holds automatically for a CRS neoclassical production function.

2. A value of g_0/α bigger than the one corresponding to the curve I_2 produces an impossible solution with $k_\pi > k$, corresponding to the relationships $g/s_\pi = (g_0/\alpha) + x_k > u$. Even though u exceeds x_k because there are decreasing returns to capital, the inequality can be satisfied for big enough values of g_0/α. An investment function with low responsiveness to profits may simply preclude macro equilibrium, along Harrodian lines.

3. As stated in the text, the model relies on forced saving as its macro adjustment mechanism. An alternative version in which the short-run profit rate is fixed and employment can vary is easy to work out. Distributional changes are naturally determined over time from conflicting income claims according to a rule such as $\dot{r} = \varepsilon(\bar{r} - r) + \delta(k - k_\pi)$. Dual, Pasinetti, and antidual equilibria can easily be shown to be possible in such a formulation.

4. This sort of painless labor promotion is characteristic of models which implicitly include new class formation, ranging from Rosenstein-Rodan's (1943) initial, elegant statement of the requirements for industrial growth to Murphy, Shleifer, and Vishny (1989b), Rodan's most recent avatars.

5. In neoclassical terms the two sorts of workers interchange with an infinite elasticity of substitution. With the standard marginal productivity conditions built in, the text's analysis goes through if the elasticity is finite but "high" (e.g., five or ten), a common econometric result.

References

Abel, Andrew B., and Olivier Jean Blanchard. 1983. "An Intertemporal Model of Saving and Investment." *Econometrica* 51: 675−669.

Amadeo, Edward J. 1989. *Keynes's Principle of Effective Demand*. Aldershot, Hants: Edward Elgar.

Amadeo, Edward J., and Jose Marcio Camargo. 1989a. "A Structuralist Analysis of Inflation and Stabilization." Helsinki: WIDER.

Amadeo, Edward J., and Jose Marcio Camargo. 1989b. "Market Structure, Relative Prices, and Income Distribution: An Analysis of Heterodox Stabilization Experiments." Helsinki: WIDER.

Amsden, Alice. 1989. *Asia's Next Giant: South Korea and Late Industrialization*. Oxford: Oxford University Press.

Arellano, Jose-Pablo. 1985. "De la liberación a la intervención: El mercado de capitales in Chile: 1974−1983." *El Trimestre Economico*. 52: 721−772.

Arida, Persio. 1986. "Macroeconomic Issues for Latin America." *Journal of Development Economics* 22: 171−208.

Arrow, Kenneth J., and Mordecai Kurz. 1970. *Public Investment, the Rate of Return, and Optimal Fiscal Policy*. Baltimore: Johns Hopkins University Press.

Arthur, W. Brian. 1989. "Competing Technologies, Increasing Returns, and Lock-in by Historical Events." *Economic Journal* 99: 116−131.

Aschauer, David. 1989. "Does Public Capital Crowd out Private Capital?" *Journal of Monetary Economics*, 24: 171−188.

Bacha, Edmar L. 1984. "Growth with Limited Supplies of Foreign Exchange: A Reappraisal of the Two-Gap Model." In Moshe Syrquin, Lance Taylor, and Larry Westphal (eds.), *Economic Structure and Performance: Essays in Honor of Hollis B. Chenery*. San Diego: Academic Press.

Bacha, Edmar L. 1990. "A Three-Gap Model of Foreign Transfers and the GDP

Growth Rate in Developing Countries." *Journal of Development Economics* 32: 279–296.

Bagehot, Walter. [1873] 1962. *Lombard Street.* Homewood, IL: Irwin.

Baran, Paul, and Paul Sweezy. 1966. *Monopoly Capital: An Essay on the American Economic and Social Order.* New York: Monthly Review Press.

Barbone, Luca. 1985. "Essays on Trade and Macro Policy in Developing Countries." Ph.D. dissertation. Department of Economics, Massachusetts Institute of Technology, Cambridge.

Barro, Robert. 1989. "A Cross-Country Study of Growth, Saving, and Government." Working Paper No. 2885. National Bureau of Economic Research, Cambridge, MA.

Barro, Robert, and Herschel Grossman. 1976. *Money, Employment, and Inflation.* Cambridge: Cambridge University Press.

Baumol, William J., and Jess Benhabib. 1989. "Chaos: Significance, Mechanism, and Economic Applications." *Journal of Economic Perspectives* 3: 77–105.

Benassy, Jean-Pascal. 1986. *Macroeconomics: An Introduction to the Non-Walrasian Approach.* San Diego: Academic Press.

Birdsall, Nancy. 1988. "Economic Approaches to Population Growth." In Hollis B. Chenery and T. N. Srinivasan (eds.), *Handbook of Development Economics*, vol. 1. Amsterdam: North-Holland.

Blanchard, Olivier Jean, and Stanley Fischer. 1989. *Lectures on Macroeconomics.* Cambridge: MIT Press.

Blaug, Mark. 1985. *Economic Theory in Retrospect.* 4th ed. Cambridge: Cambridge University Press.

Blecker, Robert A. 1989. "International Competition, Income Distribution, and Economic Growth." *Cambridge Journal of Economics.* 13: 395–412.

Boutros-Ghali, Youssef R. 1981. "Essays on Structuralism and Development." Ph.D. dissertation. Department of Economics, Massachusetts Institute of Technology, Cambridge.

Bowles, Samuel, and Robert Boyer. 1990. "A Wage-Led Employment Regime: Income Distribution, Labor Discipline, and Aggregate Demand in Welfare Capitalism." In Stephen Marglin and Juliet Schor (eds.), *The Golden Age of Capitalism: Reinterpreting the Postwar Experience.* Oxford: Clarendon.

Bowles, Samuel, David M. Gordon, and Thomas E. Weisskopf. 1986. "Power and Profits: The Social Structure of Accumulation and Profitability of the Postwar U.S. Economy." *Review of Radical Political Economics* 18: 132–167.

Brandt, Willy (Chair) 1980. *North-South: A Program for Survival.* Cambridge: MIT Press.

Caballero, Jose Maria, and J. Mohan Rao. 1990. "Agricultural Performance and Development Strategy: Retrospect and Prospect." *World Development* 18: 899–913.

Cardoso, Eliana A. 1979. "Inflation, Growth, and the Real Exchange Rate: Essays on Economic History in Brazil. Ph.D. dissertation. Department of Economics, Massachusetts Institute of Technology, Cambridge.

Cauas, Jorge. 1973. "Short-Term Economic Policy." In Jagdish N. Bhagwati and Richard S. Eckaus (eds.), *Development and Planning: Essays in Honor of Paul Rosenstein-Rodan.* Cambridge, MA: MIT Press.

Cavallo, Domingo. 1977. "Stagflationary Effects of Monetarist Stabilization Policies." Ph.D. dissertation. Department of Economics, Harvard University, Cambridge.

Chakravarty, Sukhamoy. 1980. *Alternative Approaches to a Theory of Economic Growth: Marx, Marshall, and Schumpeter.* R. C. Dutt Lecture on Political Economy. Delhi: Orient Longman.

Chakravarty, Sukhamoy. 1987. *Development Planning: The Indian Experience.* Oxford: Clarendon.

Chenery, Hollis B. 1959. "The Interdependence of Investment Decisions." In Moses Abramovitz (ed.), *The Allocation of Economic Resources.* Stanford: Stanford University Press.

Chenery, Hollis B., and Michael Bruno. 1962. "Development Alternatives in an Open Economy: The Case of Israel." *Economic Journal* 72: 79–103.

Chichilnisky, Graciela. 1981. "Terms of Trade and Domestic Distribution: Export-Led Growth with Abundant Labor." *Journal of Development Economics* 8: 163–192.

Coase, Ronald. 1937. "The Nature of the Firm." *Econometrica* 4: 386–405.

Cooper, Richard N. 1971. "Currency Devaluation in Developing Countries." Princeton: *Essays in International Finance.* No. 86.

Corden, W. M. 1984. "Booming Sector and Dutch Disease Economics: Survey and Consolidation." *Oxford Economic Papers* 36: 359–380.

Darity, William A., Jr. 1981. "The Simple Analytics of Neo-Ricardian Growth and Distribution." *American Economic Review* 71: 978—993.

Darity, William A., Jr., and Bobbie L. Horn. 1988. *The Loan Pushers: The Role of Commercial Banks in the International Debt Crisis.* Cambridge, MA: Ballinger.

Davidson, Paul, and Sidney Weintraub. 1973. "Money as Cause and Effect." *Economic Journal* 83: 1117–1132.

Dennett, Daniel C. 1987. *The Intentional Stance.* Cambridge: MIT Press.

Diamond, Peter A. 1965. "National Debt in a Neoclassical Growth Model." *American Economic Review* 55: 1126–1150.

Díaz-Alejandro, Carlos F. 1963 "A Note on the Impact of Devaluation and the Redistributive Effect." *Journal of Political Economy* 71: 577–580.

Díaz-Alejandro, Carlos F. 1981. "Southern Cone Stabilization Plans." In William Cline and Sidney Weintraub (eds.), *Economic Stabilization in Developing Countries.* Washington, DC: Brookings Institution.

Dobb, Maurice. 1973. *Theories of Value and Distribution since Adam Smith.* Cambridge: Cambridge University Press.

Domar, Evsey. 1944. "The 'Burden of Debt' and National Income." *American Economic Review* 34: 798–827.

Domar, Evsey. 1950. "The Effect of Investment on the Balance of Payments." *American Economic Review* 40: 805–826.

Dornbusch, Rudiger. 1980. *Open Economy Macroeconomics.* New York: Basic Books.

Dornbusch, Rudiger, and Jacob A. Frenkel. 1984. "The Gold Standard Crisis of 1847." *Journal of International Economics* 16: 1–27.

Duesenberry, James. 1958. *Business Cycles and Economic Growth.* New York: McGraw-Hill.

Dutt, Amitava K. 1984. "Stagnation, Income Distribution, and Monopoly Power." *Cambridge Journal of Economics* 8: 25–40.

Dutt, Amitava K. 1986. "Growth, Distribution, and Technological Change." *Metroeconomica* 38: 113–134.

Dutt, Amitava K. 1990. *Growth, Distribution, and Uneven Development.* Cambridge: Cambridge University Press.

Edwards, Sebastian, and Sweder van Wijnbergen. 1989. "Disequilibrium and Structural Adjustment." In Hollis B. Chenery and T. N. Srinivasan (eds.), *Handbook of Development Economics,* vol. 2. Amsterdam: North-Holland.

Eichner, Alfred S. 1980. "A General Model of Investment and Pricing." In Edward Nell (ed.), *Growth, Profits, and Property.* Cambridge: Cambridge University Press.

Eisner, Robert, and Robert H. Strotz. 1963. "Determinants of Business Investment." In Commission on Money and Credit, *Impacts of Monetary Policy.* Englewood Cliffs, NJ: Prentice Hall.

Eldredge, Niles. 1985. *Time Frames: The Evolution of Punctuated Equilibria.* Princeton: Princeton University Press.

Ellman, Michael. 1975. "Did the Agricultural Surplus Provide the Resources for the Increase in Investment during the First Five Year Plan?" *Economic Journal* 85: 844–864.

Eyzaguirre, Nicolas. 1989. "El Ahorro y la Inversión bajo Restricción Externa y Fiscal." *Revista de la CEPAL* 38: 31–48.

Fanelli, Jose Maria, Roberto Frenkel, and Carolos Winograd. 1987. "Argentina." Stabilization and Adjustment Policies and Programmes Country Study No. 12. Helsinki: WIDER.

Farrell, Michael J. 1959. "The Convexity Assumption in the Theory of Competitive Markets." *Journal of Political Economy* 67: 377–391.

Findlay, Ronald. 1973. *International Trade and Development Theory*. New York: Columbia University Press.

Fischer, Stanley. 1977. "Long-Term Contracts, Rational Expectations, and the Money Supply Rule." *Journal of Political Economy* 85: 191–205.

Fisher, Irving. [1930] 1967. *The Theory of Interest: As Determined by the Impatience to Spend Income and the Opportunity to Invest It*. New York: Augustus M. Kelley.

Fitzgerald, E. V. K. 1989. "The Analytics of Stabilization Policy in the Small, Semi-industrialized Economy." In E. V. K. Fitzgerald and Rob Vos (eds.), *Financing Economic Development: A Structural Approach to Monetary Policy*. London: Gower.

Foley, Duncan K. 1986a. *Money, Accumulation, and Crisis*. London: Harwood Academic Publishers.

Foley, Duncan K. 1986b. "Stabilization Policy in a Nonlinear Business Cycle Model." In Willi Semmler (ed.), *Competition, Instability, and Nonlinear Cycles*. New York: Springer Verlag Lecture Notes in Economics and Mathematical Systems.

Foley, Duncan K. 1987. "Liquidity-Profit Rate Cycles in a Capitalist Economy." *Journal of Economic Behavior and Organization* 8: 363–376.

Franco, Gustavo. 1986. "Aspects of the Economics of Hyperinflations: Theoretical Issues and Historical Studies of Four European Hyperinflations in the 1920's." Ph.D. dissertation. Department of Economics, Harvard University, Cambridge.

Franke, Reiner, and Willi Semmler. 1989. "Debt Financing of Firms, Stability, and Cycles in a Dynamical Macroeconomic Growth Model." In Willi Semmler (ed.), *Financial Dynamics and Business Cycles: New Perspectives*. Armonk, NY: M. E. Sharpe.

Frenkel, Roberto. 1983. "Mercado Financiero, Expectativas Cambiales, y Movimientos de Capital." *El Trimestre Economico* 50: 2041–2076.

Friedman, Milton. 1968. "The Role of Monetary Policy." *American Economic Review* 58: 1–17.

Furtado, Celso. 1971. *The Economic Growth of Brazil*. Berkeley: University of California Press.

Furtado, Celso. 1972. *Análise do "Modelo" Brasileiro*. Rio de Janeiro: Civilização Brasileira.

Galbraith, John Kenneth. 1957. "Market Structure and Stabilization Policy." *Review of Economics and Statistics* 31: 50–53.

Galbraith, John Kenneth. 1961. *The Great Crash, 1929*. Boston: Houghton Mifflin.

Geertz, Clifford. 1963. *Agricultural Involution: The Process of Ecological Change in Indonesia*. Berkeley: University of California Press.

Gerschenkron, Alexander. 1962. *Economic Backwardness in Historical Perspective*. Cambridge: Harvard University Press.

Gibson, Bill. 1985. "A Structuralist Macromodel for Post-revolutionary Nicaragua." *Cambridge Journal of Economics* 9: 347–369.

Giovannini, Alberto. 1985. "Saving and the Real Interest Rate in LDC's." *Journal of Development Economics* 18: 197–217.

Glyn, Andrew, and Bob Sutcliffe. 1972. *Capitalism in Crisis*. New York: Pantheon.

Gould, Stephen Jay. 1987. *An Urchin in the Storm*. New York: Norton.

Green, Reginald, and Xavier Kadhani. 1986. "Zimbabwe: Transition to Economic Crisis, 1981–83: Retrospect and Prospect." *World Development* 14: 1059–1083.

Griffin, Keith B. 1970. "Foreign Capital, Domestic Savings, and Economic Development." *Bulletin of the Oxford University Institute of Statistics* 32: 99–112.

Guckenheimer, John, and Philip Holmes. 1983. *Nonlinear Oscillations, Dynamical Systems, and Bifurcations of Vector Fields*. New York: Springer-Verlag.

Harcourt, Geoffrey. 1972. *Some Cambridge Controversies in the Theory of Capital*. Cambridge: Cambridge University Press.

Harrod, Roy. 1939. "An Essay in Dynamic Theory." *Economic Journal* 49: 14–33.

Hart, Gillian. 1986. "Interlocking Transactions: Obstacles, Precursors, or Instruments of Agrarian Capitalism?" *Journal of Development Economics* 23: 177–203.

Hicks, John R. 1965. *Capital and Growth*. Oxford: Clarendon.

Hirschman, Albert O. 1949. "Devaluation and the Trade Balance: A Note." *Review of Economics and Statistics* 31: 50–53.

Hirschman, Albert O. 1958. *The Strategy of Economic Development*. New Haven: Yale University Press.

Houthakker, Hendrik S. 1976. "Disproportional Growth and the Intersectoral Distribution of Income." In J. S. Cramer, A. Heertje, and P. Venekamp (eds.), *Relevance and Precision: Essays in Honor of Pieter de Wolff*. Amsterdam: North-Holland.

Hume, David. [1752] 1969. "Of the Balance of Trade." In Richard N. Cooper (ed.), *International Finance*. Harmondsworth: Penguin.

Johansen, Leif. 1960. *A Multi-Sectoral Study of Economic Growth*. Amsterdam: North-Holland.

Kaldor, Nicholas. 1940. "A Model of the Trade Cycle," *Economic Journal* 50: 78–92.

Kaldor, Nicholas. 1956. "Alternative Theories of Distribution." *Review of Economic Studies* 23: 83–100.

Kaldor, Nicholas. 1957. "A Model of Economic Growth." *Economic Journal* 67: 591–624.

Kaldor, Nicholas. 1961. "Capital Accumulation and Economic Growth." In F. A. Lutz and D. C. Hague (eds.), *The Theory of Capital*. New York: St Martin's.

Kaldor, Nicholas. 1966. "Marginal Productivity and the Macro-Economic Theory of Distribution." *Review of Economic Studies* 33: 309–319.

Kaldor, Nicholas. 1982. *The Scourge of Monetarism*. Oxford: Oxford University Press.

Kalecki, Michal. 1971. *Selected Essays on the Dynamics of the Capitalist Economy*. Cambridge: Cambridge University Press.

Kalecki, Michal. 1976. *Essays on Developing Economies*. London: Harvester Press.

Kamin, Stephen. 1987. "Devaluation, External Balance, and Macroeconomic Performance in Developing Countries." Ph.D. dissertation. Department of Economics, Massachusetts Institute of Technology, Cambridge.

Keynes, John Maynard. 1930. *A Treatise on Money*. London: Macmillan.

Keynes, John Maynard. 1936. *The General Theory of Employment, Interest, and Money*. London: Macmillan.

Keynes, John Maynard. 1939. "Relative Movements of Real Wages and Output." *Economic Journal* 49: 34–51.

Kim, Youngsoo. 1987. "Three Essays on Economic Growth and Financial Liberalization." Ph. D. dissertation. Department of Economics, Massachusetts Institute of Technology, Cambridge.

Kindleberger, Charles P. 1978. *Manias, Panics, and Crashes*. New York: Basic Books.

Kindleberger, Charles P. 1984. *A Financial History of Western Europe*. London: Allen and Unwin.

Kindleberger, Charles P. 1985. *Keynesianism vs. Monetarism and Other Essays in Financial History*. London: Allen and Unwin.

Krueger, Anne O. 1974. "The Political Economy of the Rent-Seeking Society." *American Economic Review* 64: 291–303.

Krugman, Paul. 1987. "The Narrow Moving Band, the Dutch Disease, and the Competitive Consequences of Mrs. Thatcher: Notes on Trade in the Presence of Dynamic Scale Economies." *Journal of Development Economics* 27: 41–55.

Krugman, Paul, and Lance Taylor. 1978. "Contractionary Effects of Devaluation." *Journal of International Economics* 8: 445–456.

Kuznets, Simon S. 1971. *Economic Growth of Nations: Total Output and Production Structure.* Cambridge: Harvard University Press.

Lal, Deepak, and Sweder van Wijnbergen. 1985. "Government Deficits, the Real Interest Rate, and LDC Debt: On Global Crowding-out." *European Economic Review* 29: 157–191.

Landes, David. 1969. *The Unbound Prometheus.* Cambridge: Cambridge University Press.

Larrain, Felipe, and Jeffrey Sachs. 1986. "Contractionary Devaluation, and Dynamic Adjustment of Exports and Wages." National Bureau of Economic Research, Cambridge, MA.

Lele, Uma, and John W. Mellor. 1981. "Technical Change, Distributive Bias, and Labor Transfer in a Two-Sector Economy." *Oxford Economic Papers* 33: 426–441.

Lewis, W. Arthur. 1954. "Economic Development with Unlimited Supplies of Labor." *Manchester School of Economics and Social Studies* 22: 139–191.

Lizondo, J. Saul, and Peter J. Montiel. 1989. "Contractionary Devaluation in Developing Countries: An Analytical Overview." *International Monetary Fund Staff Papers* 36: 182–227.

Lopes, Francisco L. 1984. "Inflação Inercial, Hiperinflação, e Disinflação: Notas e Conjecturas." Departamento de Economia, Pontificia Universidade Catolica, Rio de Janeiro.

Lopes, Francisco L., and Edmar L. Bacha. 1983. "Inflation, Growth, and Wage Policy: A Brazilian Perspective." *Journal of Development Economics* 13: 1–20.

Lorenz, Hans-Walter. 1989. *Nonlinear Dynamical Economics and Chaotic Motion.* Berlin: Springer-Verlag.

Lubell, Howard. 1947. "Effects of Redistribution of Income on Consumers' Expenditure." *American Economic Review* 37: 157–170.

Lucas, Robert E., Jr. 1988. "On the Mechanics of Economic Development." *Journal of Monetary Economics* 22: 3–42.

Lustig, Nora. 1980. "Underconsumption in Latin American Economic Thought: Some Considerations." *Review of Radical Political Economics* 12: 35–43.

Lustig, Nora. 1990. "From Structuralism to Neo-structuralism: The Search for a

Heterodox Paradigm." In Patricio Meller (ed.), *Neo-structuralism, Neo-monetarism, and Adjustment in Latin America.* Boulder, CO: Westview.

Luxemburg, Rosa. 1951. *The Accumulation of Capital.* London: Routledge and Kegan Paul.

Malinvaud, Edmond. 1977. *The Theory of Unemployment Reconsidered.* New York: Halstead Press.

Manne, Alan S. (ed.). 1967. *Investments for Capacity Expansion: Size, Location, and Time-Phasing.* Cambridge: MIT Press.

Marglin, Stephen A. 1974. "What Do Bosses Do: The Origins and Functions of Hierarchy in Capitalist Production." *Review of Radical Political Economics* 6: 60–112.

Marglin, Stephen A. 1984. *Growth, Distribution, and Prices.* Cambridge: Harvard University Press

Marglin, Stephen A., and Amit Bhaduri. 1990. "Profit Squeeze and Keynesian Theory." In Stephen Marglin and Juliet Schor (eds.), *The Golden Age of Capitalism: Reinterpreting the Postwar Experience.* Oxford: Clarendon.

McKibbin, Warwick J., and Jeffrey D. Sachs. 1989. "The McKibbin-Sachs Global (MSG2) Model." Washington, DC: Brookings Institution.

Meade, James. 1961. *A Neo-classical Theory of Economic Growth.* London: Allen and Unwin.

Minsky, Hyman P. 1975. *John Maynard Keynes.* New York: Columbia University Press.

Minsky, Hyman P. 1986. *Stabilizing an Unstable Economy.* New Haven: Yale University Press.

Modigliani, Franco, and Tommaso Padoa-Schioppa. 1978. "The Economy with '100% Plus' Wage Indexation." Department of Economics, Massachusetts Institute of Technology, Cambridge.

Morawetz, David. 1974. "Employment Implications of Industrialization in Developing Countries." *Economic Journal* 84: 411–452.

Morley, Samuel A. 1971. "Inflation and Stagnation in Brazil." *Economic Development and Cultural Change* 19: 184–203.

Morley, Samuel A. 1990. "On the Effect of Devaluation in LDC's." Department of Economics, Vanderbilt University, Nashville.

Murphy, Kevin M., Andrei Shleifer, and Robert Vishny. 1989a. "Income Distribution, Market Size, and Industrialization." *Quarterly Journal of Economics* 104: 537–564.

Murphy, Kevin M., Andrei Shleifer, and Robert Vishny. 1989b. "Industrialization and the Big Push." *Journal of Political Economy.* 97: 1003–1026.

Myrdal, Gunnar [1939] 1967. *Monetary Equilibrium*. New York: Augustus M. Kelley.

Ndulu, Benno. 1986. "Investment, Output Growth, and Capacity Utilization in an African Economy: The Case of the Manufacturing Sector in Tanzania." *Eastern Africa Economic Review* 2: 14–30.

Noyola Vasquez, Juan F. 1956. "El Desarollo Economico y la Inflación en México y Otros Paises Latinoamericanos." *Investigacion Economica* 16: 603–648.

Nurkse, Ragnar. 1953. *Problems of Capital Formation in Underdeveloped Countries.* Oxford: Basil Blackwell.

Ocampo, Jose Antonio. 1987. "The Macroeconomic Effect of Import Controls: A Keynesian Analysis." *Journal of Development Economics* 27: 285–306.

Olivera, Julio H. G. 1967. "Money, Prices, and Fiscal Lags: A Note on the Dynamics of Inflation." *Banco Nazionale del Lavoro Quarterly Review* 20: 258–267.

Olivera, Julio H. G. 1970. "On Passive Money." *Journal of Political Economy* 78: 805–814.

Ortiz, Guillermo, and Carlos Noriega. 1988. "Investment and Growth in Latin America." Washington, DC: International Monetary Fund.

Pack, Howard, and Larry E. Westphal. 1986. "Industrial Strategy and Technological Change: Theory vs. Reality." *Journal of Development Economics* 22: 87–128.

Pasinetti, Luigi L. 1962. "Rate of Profit and Income Distribution in Relation to the Rate of Economic Growth." *Review of Economic Studies* 29: 267–279.

Pasinetti, Luigi L. 1981. *Structural Change and Economic Growth*. Cambridge: Cambridge University Press.

Patinkin, Don. 1965. *Money, Interest, and Prices*. New York: Harper and Row.

Preobrazhenski, Evgeny. 1965. *The New Economics*. Oxford: Clarendon.

Quisumbing, Ma. Agnes R., and Lance Taylor. 1989. "Resource Transfers from Agriculture." In Sukhamoy Chakravarty (ed.), *The Balance between Industry and Agriculture III: Manpower and Transfers*. London: Macmillan.

Ramsey, Frank P. 1928. "A Mathematical Theory of Saving." *Economic Journal* 38: 543–559.

Rao, J. Mohan. 1988. "Distribution and Growth with an Infrastructure Constraint." Department of Economics, University of Massachusetts, Amherst.

Rattsø, Jørn. 1990a. "Medium Run Adjustment under Import Compression: Macroeconomic Analysis Relevant for Sub-Saharan Africa." Department of Economics, University of Trondheim, Norway.

Rattsø, Jørn. 1990b. "The Asymmetric Relation between Sub-Saharan Africa and the Rest of the World: A Theoretical Analysis of the Role of Import Compression." Department of Economics, University of Trondheim, Norway.

Robertson, D. H. 1926. *Banking Policy and the Price Level.* London: Macmillan.

Robertson, D. H. 1933. "Saving and Hoarding." *Economic Journal* 43: 399–413.

Robinson, Joan. 1953–54. "The Production Function and the Theory of Capital." *Review of Economic Studies* 21: 81–106.

Robinson, Joan. 1962. *Essays in the Theory of Economic Growth.* London: Macmillan.

Robinson, Joan. 1974. "History vs. Equilibrium." Thames Papers on Political Economy. Thames Polytechnic, London.

Romer, Paul M. 1986. "Increasing Returns and Long-Run Growth." *Journal of Political Economy* 94: 1002–1037.

Ros, Jaime. 1987. "On the Macroeconomics of Heterodox Shocks." Helsinki: WIDER.

Ros, Jaime. 1988. "On Inertia, Social Conflict, and the Structuralist Analysis of Inflation," Helsinki: WIDER.

Ros, Jaime. 1989. "Medium Term Perspectives on the Mexican Economy." Helsinki: WIDER.

Rosenstein-Rodan, Paul N. 1943. "Problems of Industrialization of Eastern and South-Eastern Europe." *Economic Journal* 53: 202–211.

Rosenstein-Rodan, Paul N. 1961. "Notes on the Theory of the Big Push." In H. S. Ellis and H. C. Wallich (eds.), *Economic Development for Latin America.* New York: St. Martin's.

Rowthorn, Bob. 1982. "Demand, Real Wages, and Economic Growth." *Studi Economici* 18: 2–53.

Rybczynski, T. M. 1955. "Factor Endowment and Relative Commodity Prices." *Economica* 22: 336–341.

Salter, W. E. G. 1959. "Internal and External Balance: The Role of Price and Expenditure Effects." *Economic Record* 35: 226–238.

Samuelson, Paul A. 1947. *Foundations of Economic Analysis.* Cambridge: Harvard University Press.

Samuelson, Paul A., and Franco Modigliani. 1966. "The Pasinetti Paradox in Neoclassical and More General Models." *Review of Economic Studies* 33: 269–301.

Schor, Juliet B. 1985. "Changes in the Cyclical Pattern of Real Wages: Evidence from Nine Countries, 1955–80." *Economic Journal* 95: 452–468.

Schumpeter, Josef A. 1934. *The Theory of Economic Development.* Cambridge: Harvard University Press.

Schumpeter, Josef A. 1954. *History of Economic Analysis.* Oxford: Oxford University Press.

Semmler, Willi. 1984. *Competition, Monopoly, and Differential Profit Rates.* New York: Columbia University Press.

Sen, Amartya K. 1963. "Neo-classical and Neo-Keynesian Theories of Distribution." *Economic Record* 39: 54–64.

Shapiro, Helen, and Lance Taylor. 1990. "The State and Industrial Strategy." *World Development* 18: 861–878.

Sismonde de Sismondi, J. C. L. 1815. "Political Economy." *Sir J. D. Brewster's Edinburgh Encyclopedia.* Edinburgh.

Solow, Robert M. 1956. "A Contribution to the Theory of Economic Growth." *Quarterly Journal of Economics* 70: 65–94.

Solow, Robert M. 1986. "Unemployment: Getting the Questions Right." *Economica* 53 (suppl.): s23–s34.

Sraffa, Piero. 1960. *Production of Commodities by Means of Commodities.* Cambridge: Cambridge University Press.

Steindl, Josef. 1952. *Maturity and Stagnation in American Capitalism.* Oxford: Basil Blackwell.

Stiglitz, Joseph E. 1988. "Economic Organization, Information, and Development." In Hollis B. Chenery and T. N. Srinivasan (eds.), *Handbook of Development Economics,* vol. 1., Amsterdam: North-Holland.

Streeten, Paul. 1959. "Unbalanced Growth." *Oxford Economic Papers* 11: 167–190.

Streeten, Paul, and Thomas Balogh. 1957. "A Reconsideration of Monetary Policy." *Bulletin of the Oxford University Institute of Statistics* 19: 331–339.

Summers, Lawrence H. 1983. "The Nonadjustment of Nominal Interest Rates: A Study of the Fisher Effect." In James Tobin (ed.), *Macroeconomics, Prices, and Quantities: Essays in Memory of Arthur M. Okun.* Washington, DC: Brookings Institution.

Sunkel, Osvaldo. 1960. "Inflation in Chile: An Unorthodox Approach." *International Economic Papers* 10: 107–131.

Swan, Trevor W. 1960. "Economic Control in a Dependent Economy." *Economic Record* 36: 51–66.

Sylos-Labini, Paolo. 1984. *The Forces of Economic Growth and Decline.* Cambridge: MIT Press.

Tanzi, Vito. 1977. "Inflation, Lags in Collection, and the Real Value of Tax Revenue." *International Monetary Fund Staff Papers* 24: 154–167.

Tavares, Maria da Conceição. 1972. *Da Substituição de Importaçoes ao Capitalismo Financeiro*. Rio de Janeiro: Zahar.

Taylor, John B. 1980. "Aggregate Dynamics and Staggered Contracts." *Journal of Political Economy* 88: 1–23.

Taylor, Lance. 1979. *Macro Models for Developing Countries*. New York: McGraw-Hill.

Taylor, Lance. 1983. *Structuralist Macroeconomics*. New York: Basic Books.

Taylor, Lance. 1985. "A Stagnationist Model of Economic Growth." *Cambridge Journal of Economics* 9: 383–403.

Taylor, Lance. 1988a. *Varieties of Stabilization Experience*. Oxford: Clarendon.

Taylor, Lance. 1988b. "Macro Constraints on India's Economic Growth." *Indian Economic Review* 23: 145–165.

Taylor, Lance. 1989a. *Stabilization and Growth in Developing Countries: A Structuralist Approach*. London: Harwood Academic Publishers.

Taylor, Lance. 1989b. "Demand Composition, Income Distribution, and Growth." In George R. Feiwel (ed.), *Joan Robinson and Modern Economic Theory*. New York: New York University Press.

Taylor, Lance. 1990a. "Economic Openness: Problems to Century's End." Helsinki: WIDER.

Taylor, Lance. 1990b. "Structuralist CGE Models." In Lance Taylor (ed.), *Structuralist Computable General Equilibrium Models: Socially Relevant Policy Analysis for the Developing World*. Cambridge: MIT Press.

Taylor, Lance. 1990c. "Foreign Resource Flows and Developing Country Growth." Helsinki: WIDER.

Taylor, Lance, and Persio Arida. 1988. "Long-Run Income Distribution and Growth." In Hollis B. Chenery and T. N. Srinivasan (eds.), *Handbook of Development Economics*, vol. 1. Amsterdam: North-Holland.

Taylor, Lance, and Edmar L. Bacha. 1976. "The Unequalizing Spiral: A First Growth Model for Belindia." *Quarterly Journal of Economics* 90: 197–218.

Taylor, Lance, and Frank J. Lysy. 1979. "Vanishing Income Redistributions: Keynesian Clues about Model Surprises in the Short Run." *Journal of Development Economics* 6: 11–29.

Taylor, Lance, Jose Antonio Ocampo, Renato Aguilar, Stefan deVylder, and Teresa Hellgren. 1989. *Nicaragua: The Transition from Economic Chaos toward Sustainable Growth*. Stockholm: Swedish International Development Authority.

Taylor, Lance, and Stephen O'Connell. 1985. "A Minsky Crisis." *Quarterly Journal of Economics* 100: 871–885.

Thompson, J. M. T., and H. B. Stewart. 1986. *Nonlinear Dynamics and Chaos.* New York: Wiley.

Tobin, James. 1969. "A General Equilibrium Approach to Monetary Theory." *Journal of Money, Credit, and Banking* 1: 15–29.

van Wijnbergen, Sweder. 1986. "Macroeconomic Aspects of the Effectiveness of Foreign Aid: On the Two-Gap Model, Home Goods Disequilibrium, and Real Exchange Rate Misalignment." *Journal of International Economics* 21: 123–136.

Varian, Hal R. 1984. *Microeconomic Analysis.* 2nd ed. New York: Norton.

Vos, Rob. 1989. "International Finance, Global Adjustment, and North–South Relations." In E. V. K. Fitzgerald and Rob Vos (eds.), *Financing Economic Development: A Structural Approach to Monetary Policy.* London: Gower.

Weisskopf, Thomas E. 1972. "The Impact of Foreign Capital Inflow on Domestic Saving in Underdeveloped Countries." *Journal of International Economics* 2: 341–378.

Weisskopf, Thomas E. 1988. "The Analytics of Neo-Marxian Crisis Theory." *Keizai Kenkyu* (The Economic Review) 39: 193–208.

Westphal, Larry E., and Jacques Cramer. 1984. "'The Interdependence of Investment Decisions' Revisited." In Moshe Syrquin, Lance Taylor, and Larry Westphal (eds.), *Economic Structure and Performance: Essays in Honor of Hollis B. Chenery.* New York: Academic Press.

Whitaker, John K. 1975. *The Early Writings of Alfred Marshall.* London: Macmillan.

Wicksell, Knut. 1935. *Lectures on Poltical Economy,* vol. 2. London: Routledge and Kegan Paul.

Williamson, John. 1983. *The Open Economy and the World Economy.* New York: Basic Books.

Winograd, Carlos. 1987. "Active Crawling Peg, Disinflation, and Macroeconomic Stability." Paris: École Normale Supérieure.

Woodford, Michael. 1989. "Finance, Instability, and Cycles." In Willi Semmler (ed.), *Financial Dynamics and Business Cycles: New Perspectives.* Armonk, NY: M. E. Sharpe.

Young, Allyn. 1928. "Increasing Returns and Economic Progress." *Economic Journal* 38: 527–542.

Index